мыс. толстой

WZW¼W

мыс. Чиниатикій

Острова Кадьяна

ıрской Савани

караб. нва

MATERIALS FOR THE STUDY OF ALASKA HISTORY, NO. 14

RUSSIAN ROUND-THE-WORLD VOYAGES, 1803-1849

WITH A SUMMARY OF LATER VOYAGES TO 1867.

By
N. A. IVASHINTSOV

Translated by Glynn R. Barratt
Edited by Richard A. Pierce

THE LIMESTONE PRESS
P.O. Box 1604
Kingston, Ontario, Canada   K7L 5C8

International Standard Book Number 0-919642-76-4

Printed and bound in Canada by:
Brown & Martin Ltd., Kingston, Ontario

CONTENTS

 * Maps

ILLUSTRATIONS

I. F. Krusenshtern, Iu. F. Lisianskii, L. V. Hagemeister,
V. M. Golovnin.

M. P. Lazarev, O. E. Kotzebue, F. F. Bellingshausen,
M. N. Vasil'ev.

G. S. Shishmarev, F. P. Wrangell, F. P. Lütke,
I. I. von Schants

Men of Vostok and Mirnyi at Queen Charlotte Sound, southern
New Zealand, May 30, 1820. Artist, P. Mikhailov.

Endpapers: The Neva at Kadiak, 1804. The ship Sitka, 1855.

INTRODUCTION

One of the keys to the early history of countries
bordering the Pacific Ocean is shipping. In isolated
Russian America or Kamchatka, Australia, Spanish California
or the Sandwich (Hawaiian) Islands the movement of ships
was history itself. Ships brought supplies and took away
colonial products, transported new personnel or those who
were departing, provided communication with the motherland
and other establishments, and made possible the exploration,
settlement or exploitation of new areas. Thus, their
comings and goings provide firm dates, and a frame
of reference for various facts. If this or that official
came on a certain ship, the date can usually be ascer-
tained, or vice versa; information about the voyage may
indicate from whence he came, and when. Other passengers
or ship personnel may be seen as contacts, or may have
written about the voyage. Such details can also indicate
just when certain instructions reached the colony, or when
reports or complaints reached the homeland. Thus can be
avoided the error of some writers who treat exchanges of
information in the light of modern instant communications,
whereas there was always a lag of many months.

For reconstruction of the history of the Russian
colonies in North America this historical auxiliary can
be particularly useful in the absence of other information.
Compilations of shipping data therefore prove their worth,
and this volume, the earliest and in many ways still the
best guide to the remarkable series of circumnavigations
undertaken by Russia in the first half of the last
century deserves to be brought from obscurity.

Russkie krugosvetnyia puteshestviia, s 1803 po 1849
god (Russian round-the-world voyages, from 1803 to 1849)
first appeared in Zapiski gidrograficheskago departamenta
(Notes of the Hydrographic Department), St. Petersburg,
books 7 and 8, in 1848 and 1849. The author, Captain
(later Rear Admiral) Nikolai Alekseevich Ivashintsov
(1819-1871), although not yet thirty, had already dis-
tinguished himself as a hydrographer and naval historian.
The book was intended for the guidance of Russian naval
officers. By the 1870's, the day of coal and iron, part
of the work had only academic interest, but much of the
data on currents, routes, winds and tides, local resources
and natural phenomena, were still of value. In 1872,
when the Zapiski had become rare, the account was
reprinted separately. The new edition was virtually
unchanged except for a fuller account of the voyage of
the transport Baikal (1848-49), added by the naval
historian Sgibnev.

The concept of voyages to the Pacific was not new in
Russia. It had appeared as early as the 16th century,
when Russians as well as western Europeans were thinking
about reaching China by a northern sea route. Peter the
Great contemplated the feasibility of both a northern and
southern route. In the summer of 1724, Peter proposed
sending an expedition around Africa to India in order to
persuade the Great Mogul to conclude a trade treaty.
In the following year he ordered the famous expedition
to clear up geographical mysteries in the northern Pacific.

In 1732, during preparation for the Bering expedition,
N. F. Golovin, the head of the Admiralty College, proposed
sending two frigates and a transport around South America
to Kamchatka. Golovin had in mind aid to Bering, development of trade, especially with the Japanese, investigation
of mineral resources of North America, and the training of
Russian seamen. The Golovin proposals were not taken up,
but their merit was shown by the vast effort needed for
the Bering expedition. There was no industry in Siberia,
so everything required had to be carried by riverboat and
on packhorses. Anchors and cannon had to be sent in pieces,
to be rejoined at their destination. It took a year for
any given item to reach its destination, and eight years
to accumulate supplies and to build ships for the expedition.

After Bering came the discovery, group by group, of
the Aleutian islands, by private expeditions seeking furs.
In 1783, G.I. Shelikhov founded the first permanent Russian
settlement in North America, on Kodiak Island. Shelikhov
had plans for commerce and colonization along the Pacific
coast as far south as California, so urged that Russia
get established in those regions before other powers
moved in. He was also concerned about the perennial
problem of supply, and in 1785 proposed sending goods to
Russian settlements by sea from Arkhangel'sk or St.
Petersburg.

Shelikhov's proposals found support in government
circles, and in 1786, plans were laid for a squadron to be
sent from Kronshtadt to the Far East. Graf A.A. Vorontsov
and the Vice-President of the College of Foreign Affairs,
A.A. Bezborodko, urged the project in order to supply
Russian ports on the Pacific, to exclude private traders
of other nations, to force the Chinese to resume trade,
then broken off, and to seek new lands. Captain of 1st
Rank G.I. Mulovskii was chosen to head a flotilla of five
ships. However, outbreak of the Russo-Swedish war forced
abandonment of the plan, and Mulovskii himself was killed
in a naval battle.

The idea of round-the-world voyages as an aid to
Russian operations in the Pacific remained alive in the
minds of young naval officers such as I.F. Krusenstern and
I.F. Lisianskii, both of whom had served under Mulovskii.

In 1793, when Russia and England were drawn together by
the common danger of revolutionary France, they and other
Russian naval officers were assigned to the British fleet
for training. During several years of this service, in
the Caribbean, the Mediterranean, and in the Far East,
these officers had ample opportunity to observe the
benefits which Britain derived from her far-flung trade,
and to absorb British methods of seamanship and navigation.

When Krusenstern returned from his service under the
British flag in 1799, he submitted to the Emperor Paul I
a proposal for a round-the-world expedition. Such voyages,
he urged, could supply Russian Pacific holdings faster and
more cheaply than transport across Siberia, would help
prepare seamen for merchant fleet duty, and would make
naval personnel hardy and experienced. Some vessels could
remain in the Pacific to aid operations there.

Krusenstern's plan was supported by Admiral N.S.
Mordvinov, head of the Naval Ministry, by N.P. Rumiantsov,
chief of the College of Commerce, and by N.P. Rezanov, a
leading figure in the newly-formed Russian-American Company.
As a result, the Emperor Alexander I in 1802 gave permis-
sion to send two ships on such a voyage, the renowned
expedition headed by Krusenstern, in the Nadezhda, and
Lisianskii, in the Neva.

This first Russian round-the-world expedition
showed the flag, impressed foreign competitors in the
Pacific, brought needed supplies to Russian America, and,
through the Neva, gave immediate practical aid in
re-establishing the settlement at Sitka. The expedition
also gained deserved glory for scientific achievements.
Locations of many known points on the maps were corrected,
and new discoveries were made. The outermost island of
the Hawaiian chain still bears Lisianskii's name. Ocean
currents were studied, and biological and ethnographic
materials were collected. Krusenstern, Lisianskii, the
Company employee Shemelin, the naturalist Langsdorf, and
even one of the shipwrecked Japanese taken home on the
Nadezhda wrote accounts of the voyage. Krusenstern's charts,
published in an atlas, served for years as aids to
navigation.

Later voyages followed a similar pattern. Most took
nearly a year, in either direction. Most went by way of
Cape Horn, some by the Cape of Good Hope. On several
occasions, ships tried to round Cape Horn and failed, then
had to head eastward and go the other way instead. At
first all took the round-the-world route, but later more
returned by the same route taken. Sometimes vessels were
left in the colonies, as was the Neva when sent out again
in 1806. Frequently, two ships made the voyage together.
Thus the Suvorov, an American vessel purchased in Kronshtadt,
was sent in 1816 in company with the Kutuzov, purchased in
Le Havre.

Besides supply vessels, naval vessels were also sent
to the Pacific, to show the flag and to perform scientific
missions. Thus, the naval sloops Otkrytie and Blagonamerennyi were sent out in 1819 to explore the Bering Strait
area and seek either a northeast or northwest passage.
Both performed valuable hydrographic and other investigations, supplementing explorations made in 1816 by the brig
Riurik, under Lieutenant O.E. Kotzebue, a private expedition fitted out at the personal expense of the wealthy
Count Rumiantsev.

But although these voyages helped to solve the supply
problem and to fortify Russian territorial claims by their
explorations, they did little to protect the Russian-American
coasts against contraband trade. Foreign skippers, chiefly
New Englanders, continued to trade ammunition, guns and
liquor to the Indians for furs, at once building up the
native offensive power and depriving the Company of profits.
Lieutenant V.M. Golovnin, who visited Russian-America on
the naval sloop Kamchatka in 1818, in particular urged
preventive action. As a result, Russia banned all foreign
trade in Russian-America in 1821, barring approach of
foreign vessels within 100 miles of the coast. This
decree, to be backed up by sending armed cruisers at one-
year intervals, in effect closed the entire North Pacific.

However long-awaited by the Company, this resort to
vigorous measures did more harm than good. After the first
cruiser, the sloop Apollon, warned off an American ship
from Sitka, other law-abiding traders stayed away, while
contraband traders continued to operate as before. A food
shortage arose in Sitka and in the winter of 1823-24 the
frigate Kreiser had to go to San Francisco to get supplies
for the colony. In St. Petersburg, protests by British
and American ambassadors caused Russia to back down.
Fearing that he had gone too far, the Emperor Alexander I
ordered his cruisers to take no action except within a
cannon shot of the coast, virtually nullifying his decree.
Finally, the decree was set aside entirely by the
conventions with the United States in 1824 and with Great
Britain in 1825. The former permitted American vessels
to trade on the Russian-American coasts for a period of
ten years; the latter set the boundaries between Russian
and British America--the present Alaska boundary. The
two agreements secured international recognition of
Russian territorial claims, but were a bitter disappoint-
ment to empire-builders who still cherished the earlier
dreams of Shelikhov and Rezanov of a more vigorous Russian
policy in North America.

The food shortage caused in the colonies by this naval
interlude coincided with failure of Company supply ships
to appear. The ship Elisaveta, built in Hamburg and sent
out in 1821 with the brig Riurik, developed a leak and
had to be sold at a heavy loss at Simonstown, Cape Colony.
The Riurik continued to the colonies, but because of her

small size could bring little cargo. There was so little
food at Sitka that Governor Murav'ev was unable even to
fit out the Riurik for her return voyage, and had to hold
her in the colonies. The hardships were compounded by
failure to send another supply ship, the Elena, purchased
in 1823 in New Bedford. Plans for the voyage were cancelled because the stockholders in St. Petersburg wrongly
judged on the basis of statistics that there were already
sufficient supplies in Sitka. There were not, and it took
voyages by the Elena, in 1824, and the naval transport
Krotkii, in 1824, to restore the situation.

During the 1830's the Company supplemented cargoes
carried in its own vessels by hiring foreign vessels to
carry freight to the colonies. Thus, the British ship
Caernarvon was sent in 1831, and vessels belonging to the
Boston firm of Boardman & Co. were sent in 1837 and 1838.
The Company then concluded an agreement with the Hudson's
Bay Company for supply of the colonies on that company's
ships. Although regarded as advantageous at first, this
was eventually found expensive by the Russians and
unprofitable by the British, so that in 1846 the agreement
was cancelled and the Russian-American Company again began
to send freight in its own ships or in hired vessels.

During the early 1850's, in what was to be a final
effort to combat financial decline, the Company began to
build up its own fleet with large modern sailing vessels
capable of making a rapid turnover of goods. The Imperator
Nikolai I was built in Hamburg for the Company in 1850,
the Tsesarevich in 1851, the Sitkha, at 1,200 tons the
largest of the Company vessels, in 1852, and the Kamchatka
in 1853. These vessels took cargoes to Sitka, there took
on furs which were taken to China, newly opened to trade,
where the furs were sold and tea purchased for transport
to Russia. Several voyages of that type proved profitable,
until the Crimean War forced all company vessels to take
refuge in Russian or neutral ports. The Sitkha, on her
maiden voyage, was taken by the enemy off Petropavlovsk.

The personnel of these vessels of the later phase of
the Russian-American Company's history were mainly hired
merchant seamen rather than naval personnel. Most of the
commanders were Finlanders, for example Conradi, Krogius,
Iuselius,Ridell and Ior'ian (Jurgen?). A majority of the
crew members were from Finland or other nations. Because
of their non-Russian, purely commercial character, and
because they usually went to Russian-America and back via
Cape Horn instead of making complete voyages around the
world, these later voyages have been virtually ignored by
Russian maritime historians. They should not be, for they
were generally profitable, they indicate creditable
organizing talent on the part of the Company leadership, and
they were a vital sustaining force for the Russian-American
colonies. If there was at any time a chance for Russian
colonization in North America to succeed it was in the

1850's, when diversification of products - ice for
California, timber and salted fish for the Sandwich
Islands, and tea for European Russia, along with the
abortive coal-mining venture on the Kenai Peninsula -
promised means of supplementing the income from the
declining fur trade.

The diverse origins of Russian-American Company commanders, seamen and vessels illustrates the fairly weak
capability of Russia as a sea power at that time. Most
of the merchant vessels used by the Company were built
abroad. On the other hand, most of the naval vessels
sent to the Pacific at this time were built in Russia, and
the long voyages were excellent means for training personnel.
The voyages may be said to have had their grounding in the
experience which Krusenstern, Lisianskii, Golovnin and
other early commanders gained at the end of the 18th
century while in service with the British navy. Their
experience, developed and improved on in practice, was
passed on to subordinates. Kotzebue, who sailed under
Krusenstern on the Nadezhda, later commanded the round-the
-world voyages of the Riurik (1815-1818) and the Predpriiatie
(1823-1826). Khromchenko, who sailed under Kotzebue on
the Riurik, later commanded the Elena (1828-1830) and the
Amerika (1831-1833). Golovnin, on the Kamchatka (1817-1819)
had under him Lütke, commander of the Seniavin (1826-1829)
and three future governors of Russian-America - Murav'ev,
Wrangell, who was later commander of the Krotkii (1825-1827),
and Etholen, who commanded several Company ships in the
Pacific. Many others rose to high positions elsewhere in
the navy, so that besides their significance for the colonies,
the voyages may be regarded as having been a school for
Russian admirals.

Conditions on the voyages, as revealed in various
accounts, were standard for sailing voyages of that day.
Storms, especially in rounding Cape Horn, periods of calm
in the horse latitudes, and long periods without fresh
food were predictable. Disease took its toll. Scurvy,
tuberculosis, and venereal disease appeared frequently.
The most unlucky voyage was that of the ship Borodino in
1819-1821, on which one man drowned and 40 passengers and
crewmen died of what was believed to be cholera. Yet,
places on these vessels were coveted by young officers,
and some made several such voyages. Most of the vessels
carried passengers, though Company officials and their
families usually took the land route, by way of Siberia.
That too offered hardship, but less privation.

The cost of the voyages is unclear, as is the relation
between Company and State finances in fitting them out.
More on this can probably be revealed in specific aspects
of the Company economic history. The question is of some
importance because of its relation to the picture of the
Company held by its opponents, and use in engineering the
sale of Russian America.

The limited extent of the shipping between Russia and her American colonies by standards of that day, when compared with the British East India Company, or the Hudson's Bay Company, belies its effect. Even though the total tonnage of all the ships involved would not equal that of one modern freighter, the goods they bore were vital to the maintenance of the Russian colonies.

The major items shipped were foodstuffs, ammunition and weapons, tools, equipment and raw materials for ship-building, copper smelting, blacksmithing and other industries. Thus the first steam engine in Russian America, for a small harbor craft to be built at Sitka, was shipped in 1837. Others followed, including a large unit for use in the coal mines opened on the Kenai Peninsula in 1856. Trade goods, essential for the fur trade, were another important item, but as Company officials in St. Petersburg frequently sent goods which were too high priced or not in demand, over the years great quantities of useless material accumulated in the warehouses in Sitka, tying up Company funds in frozen assets. After the cession of Alaska, American merchants bought whole cargoes of these goods for shipment to San Francisco and resale at discount prices. Luxury items, which helped to ease the stay of Company employees, constituted another important element in cargoes. They included an extensive library brought by Rezanov, at least one piano, a billiard table for the club for Company employees established in Sitka by Governor Etholen in 1840, an organ for the Lutheran church, household furniture, and, on every voyage, alcoholic beverages. In Governor Kupreianov's time, stones were sent from St. Petersburg to Sitka to be engraved for an atlas of the North Pacific regions, and later were sent back to Russia for printing. Rich ethnographic collections, and materials for zoological and botanical study were frequently sent. The skeleton of a sea cow, obtained from the Komandorskie Islands and shipped to Russia in the 1850's, now to be seen in a Moscow museum, is the only complete one of this extinct species.

Some scholars who have written on this subject, beginning with Ivashintsov himself, overstress the mere feat of global navigation, and and pay little or no attention to voyages which did not actually circle the earth. Yet the latter were equally useful and important and based on good seamanship. We must remember that during the early 19th century voyages around the world were not unusual. Some New England skippers in the Northwest Coast and China trade made two and three such voyages, and one made seven. The Russian voyages between European Russia and points in the Pacific - usually involving Russian-America - whether complete circumnavigations or not, merit study because they were mostly for one purpose - supply - followed over a long period in a fairly consistent manner, generally achieved their aim, and also were often of scientific importance. As a major factor in the development and maintenance of the Russian colonies, these voyages are an essential part of the history of European colonization of North America and the growth and change which followed.

Ivashintsov's lists of personnel on each voyage are given as they appear in the original work, except for a few obvious errors, which have been corrected (Appendix I). I have omitted tables showing the longitudes where each vessel crossed the equator, and where they met and lost the trade winds when they rounded Cape Horn or the Cape of Good Hope (pp. 151-219 of the 1972 edition).

Added is a section on later voyages (Appendix 2). Ivashintsov's list goes only to 1849, but other voyages were made almost annually, until 1867. Some of these are derived from N.N. Zubov's lists in Russkie moreplavateli (Russian seafarers), Moscow, 1953, and Otechestvennye moreplavateli - issledovateli morei i okeanov (Our country's seafarers - students of the seas and oceans), Moscow, 1954. However, Zubov omits a number of routine voyages of supply, some originating in Hamburg, skippered by foreigners, or incomplete circumnavigations. Others were found in the Company correspondence, and in the Company otchety (annual reports), St. Petersburg, 1841-1865. The list is incomplete with regard to hired foreign vessels, the voyages of the Russia-Finland Whaling Company vessels, and the movements of naval vessels such as those of Admiral Popov's squadron.

Also added are maps of many of the voyages; most of them were adapted from ones in N.N. Zubov, Otechestvennye moreplavateli.

Ivashintsov gives place names as he found them in his sources. Here, Russian names no longer on the map (e.g., Moller, Greig, Volkonskii and Arakcheev), translations into Russian of foreign names (e.g., Sviatoi Krutskii and Sviatoi Paskhi, for Santa Cruz and Easter Island), and Russian renderings of native names (e.g., Mediuro, Eregup, Nuku Giva, for Majuro, Erikub, and Nuku Hiva) are given as they appear on modern English charts. Exception: the Russian name Zund, for the Danish Oresund. Other exceptions: where the original native - or what was thought to be the native name - was adapted by the Russians in territories occupied by them, as Aliaska (the Alaska Peninsula), Unalashka, Kad'iak, Sitkha, and Atkha, and are close to present day spelling. However, strict textual correctness is sacrificed to utility when there exists a standard anglicized equivalent. Thus, St. Matthew Island, not Sv. Matvei. Alternative forms are indicated in parentheses.

Dates are given as they appear in the text. Ivashintsev used the Julian (old style) calendar, which in the 19th century was 12 days behind the Gregorian (new style) calendar. To convert Ivashintsev's dates, add 12. Thus the Nadezhda and Neva left Kronshtadt on 26 July/8 August 1803.

Ivashintsov expresses wind velocity in the old way, by the type of sail which could be used. A very light wind, not 1-6 balls on the Beaufort scale, or up to 11 meters per second, was a topsail (bramsel'nyi) wind, because the full amount of canvas, including the topsail, could be used. Others ranged along the scale to an underseil' (lower sail) wind, 10-11 balls, or up to 33 meters per second, which permitted carrying only the lower sails, reefed.

Footnotes, where possible, have been merged with the text. Translation follows the Library of Congress system.

This translation of the Russian edition of 1872 was made by Professor Glynn R. Barratt, of Carleton University, Ottawa, Canada, and Waikato University, Hamilton, New Zealand. A specialist in Russian language and literature, and in Russian maritime history, he has brought an unusual range of talents to this task. His forthcoming Russia in Pacific Waters, now pending publication, will be a major contribution to the history of Russian maritime activity in the Pacific. His The Russian Navy and Australia to 1825, Melbourne, 1979, and Bellingshausen, a visit to New Zealand: 1820, Palmerston North, 1979, add interesting sidelights to the history of Russian voyages south of the Equator.

For further reading, see the works of N.N. Zubov, mentioned agove; P.A. Tikhmenev, History of the Russian-American Company, University of Washington Press, Seattle and London, 1978 (a translation of the Russian work of 1861-1863); James R. Gibson, Feeding the Russian Fur Trade. Provisionment of the Okhotsk Seaboard and the Kamchatka Peninsula, 1639-1856, University of Wisconsin Press, Madison, Milwaukee and London, 1969, and Imperial Russia in Frontier America. The Changing Geography of Supply of Russian America, 1784-1867, Oxford University Press, New York, 1976; and the many works of actual participants in the round-the-world voyages, beginning with Krusenstern and Lisianskii. Ella Lurie Wiswell's recent translation of V.M. Golovnin, Around the World on the Kamchatka, 1817-1819, University of Hawaii Press, Honolulu, 1979, makes this important maritime chronicle available in English for the first time.

Richard A. Pierce

Queen's University

Kingston, Canada

The Russian-American Company Vessel <u>Nadezhda</u>
(Kruzenshtern)
1803-06

Gaining new rights and privileges during the reign of the Emperor Alexander I, the Russian-American Company decided to establish direct contact by sea with its American colonies. With this object in view, early in 1803 the Main Office of the Company resolved, in accordance with a project drafted by Captain-Lieutenant Kruzenshtern, to equip two vessels and, having laden them with objects and materials of which the settlements had need, to send them thither that same summer. Hitherto all these supplies had reached America via Okhotsk with major difficulty and with heavy loss - besides which, they had often taken no less than two full years to reach their destination and arrived in such a condition as to be quite useless.[1] On their voyage back to Russia, the two ships in question were to carry peltry from the colonial storehouses of the Company, and to exchange this cargo in Canton for Chinese products.

To this original object of the expedition there was soon added another; the despatching of an embassy to Japan to establish trade relations with that country. The rank of Envoy was bestowed by the Russian Government on one of the Company's principal shareholders, Chamberlain [<u>Kammerger</u>] Rezanov. Command of the squadron and the captaincy of one of the vessels, the <u>Nadezhda</u>, was given to the prime mover of the expedition, Captain-Lieutenant Kruzenshtern, an officer already well acquainted with distant seas. Captain-Lieutenant Lisianskii commanded the <u>Neva</u>. Both these officers had only recently returned to Russia from England, having served as volunteers in that country's navy.

The ships had been expressly bought in England for the coming voyage, and then sailed to Russia. As a mark of His Majesty the Emperor's especial interest in the undertaking, they were permitted to fly the naval ensign. The selection of officers and crews, as well as the provisioning of both ships with their victuals and stores, was left to the experience and skill of the commanders. The results completely justified this trust; and even now, when much has been improved in navigation and naval hygiene, the voyages of Captains Kruzenshtern and Lisianskii may be viewed, in numerous respects, as exemplary ones.

---

[1] See the <u>Voyage</u> of Captain Kruzenshtern, pt. 1 (intro.) and <u>Two Voyages</u> to America by the Naval Officers Khvostov and Davydov.

The plan of the expedition was as follows: having entered the Great Ocean round Cape Horn or the Cape of Good Hope, the Nadezhda and the Neva were to proceed in company as far as the Sandwich Islands. From there, Captain Kruzenshtern had orders to proceed to Avacha Bay in Kamchatka and, having unloaded the supplies that he had brought into the Company's storehouses, to sail on to the shores of Japan and Nagasaki. On the voyage back to Russia from Japan, he was to undertake investigations of the Sea of Japan and of the west coasts of Nippon, Matsmai, and Sakhalin; also to examine the mouth of the Amur, the Shantar Islands from the nearer side, and the Kurile chain. Returning to Kamchatka, Captain Kruzen-shtern was to take on a Company cargo, sail to Canton, and thence, when all commercial transactions were completed, together with the Neva to return to Russia by way of the Cape of Good Hope. On his proceeding from the Sandwich Islands, Captain Lisianskii was to make for the island of Kadiak, where the Company's main factory then stood, and to winter in the harbor of St. Paul. While wintering, he was to survey Kadiak and its environs and, having laden the Neva with furs, to arrive in Canton in the spring.

With scientific work in mind, there were invited to join the expedition an astronomer and naturalists well-known for their learning and experience in their respective spheres. Together with the Envoy and his suite, these men were in Captain Kruzenshtern's vessel.

On July 16, 1803, the Nadezhda and the Neva set out from Kronshtadt Roads. On August 5 they came to Copen-hagen, there to take on the remainder of the Company freight and part of their sea-going provisions. The ships were reloaded here, and on August 27 they departed. However, they failed to pass beyond the Zund (Oresund) until September 3, having spent a whole week at Elsinore because of the contrary winds. In the Kattegat, a storm separated them. Captain Kruzenshtern, once having crossed the North Sea, met the British frigate Virginia near the English coast; and the Envoy and the astronomer, Horner, proceeded in the Virginia straight to London, while the Nadezhda, pushing on into the Channel, dropped anchor in Falmouth Roads on September 16. There, she joined the Neva, which had arrived two days before.

At length, the Envoy and the astronomer, Horner, returned from London bringing instruments. Having taken on an extra six-month supply of Irish saltbeef, both vessels put to sea again on September 23, and that same day lost sight of European shores.

On September 28, in lat. 37° 30' N, long. 14° W, the hitherto following SE wind fell off. For the remainder of the passage to Teneriffe, variable south-westerlies prevailed. On October 8, the Nadezhda and the Neva reached

2

Santa Cruz roadstead, where they stayed until the 15th
while wines and fresh provisions were purchased. Moving
on from here to the Equator, they passed on October 25
within sight of São Antonio (one of the Cape Verde
Islands), and shortly thereafter met with the NE trade
winds, in which they sailed until November 3. For the
next ten days, until at last they reached the SE trade
winds, both ships were in the zone of calms. On
November 14 the Russian ensign for the first time ever
crossed into the Southern Hemisphere. Of all the
officers and seamen, only the commanders of the vessel
had crossed the Equator before.

Losing the SE trade wind (around lat. 14°S), the
Nadezhda and the Neva proceeded down the coast of South
America. On November 25 they reached lat. 19°S, and the
following two days were occupied in a search for the island of Ascension, which was supposed to lie in about
20°S and between long. 30° and 38°W. Not finding the
island, Captain Kruzenshtern grew convinced that it could
not exist in the area between lat. 20° 10' and 20° 30'S
stretching as far as long. 37°W. On December 1, the ships
drew close to the eminence of Cabo Frio, the longitude
of which was reckoned from the Nadezhda, by lunar
observations, at 41° 31' 30"W. On December 9, both
vessels dropped anchor by the island of Santa Catharina,
in Santa Cruz Roads, where Captain Kruzenshtern proposed
to let his people rest and to prepare for the hard
passage around Cape Horn.

Examination of the vessels' masts and spars revealed
that the Neva's mainmast was unsound and ought to be
changed. The felling and preparing of trees suitable
for this and, in particular, the task of bringing the
timber to the ship delayed the squadron in this place
for longer than Captain Kruzenshtern had expected. They
at length put out to sea on January 3, 1804, and headed
for Cape Horn, fixing Easter Island and Nuku Hiva as
rendezvous locations.

The voyage as far as Cape Horn went tolerably well.
And, having withstood only a few high winds, the Nadezhda
and the Neva entered the South Sea on February 20. On
March 2 (from long. 82° 56'W), they began to press north.
On the 12th, in lat. 47°S and long. 97°W, they were
separated in a period of mists and storms. Accompanied
by a persistent NW wind, Captain Kruzenshtern decided,
wasting no time, to sail directly to Kamchatka, touching
only briefly at the island of Nuku Hiva for the rendezvous with the Neva. Given this plan, he was obliged to
abandon his previous intention of devoting several summer
months to geographical exploration in Oceania. But such
a sacrifice was in the Company's best interest: any
delay in the delivering of goods to their destination
would have caused losses.

On April 5, the Nadezhda crossed the Tropic of
Capricorn in long. 104 1/4°W. On the 24th, Hatutu, one
of the Marquesan Islands, showed itself; and the
following day, they dropped anchor in Port Anna-Maria
on the coast of Nuku Hiva (in the Washington Island
group). Two days later, the Neva also arrived. She had
called at Easter Island, and there passed a few days
waiting for the Nadezhda.

Water supplies and provisions were now replenished
insofar as this was possible. That done, the Nadezhda
and the Neva left Nuku Hiva, proceeding towards the
Sandwich Islands where their orders were to separate.
Becalmed by the entrance to the bay, the Nadezhda was
nearly wrecked on being drawn by both current and swell
towards a nearby cliff. With great difficulty, the crew
managed to tow her off into the middle of the entrance:
in the process, a stream-anchor cable was lost, and there
was not time to raise it. During his ten day sojourn
in the Washington Islands, Captain Kruzenshtern had
surveyed the southern part of Nuku Hiva, and had moreover
discovered, near Port Anna-Maria, a new and most convenient bay, which he had named after Admiral Chichagov.
Besides this, various points on the islands, Hatutu
[Fetugu], Chinoa, and Nuku Hiva had been fixed by
astronomical observations.

Having spent a day vainly seeking an island supposedly
sighted by Marchand, to the west of Nuku Hiva, Captain
Kruzenshtern was not minded to proceed in that direction
for fear of a strong easterly current, which was running
powerfully (some 20 miles in 24 hours). On May 13, in
long. 146°W, both ships crossed the Equator for the
second time, and thereupon, up to lat. 8°N, came into the
zone of calms. The fresh NE trade wind which they then
encountered, bore them swiftly towards Hawaii (Sandwich
Islands). From here, not pausing, Captain Kruzenshtern
continued on his way towards Kamchatka, while Captain
Lisianskii, after a four-day rest on the island, proceeded
to Kadiak.

From the Sandwich Islands, Captain Kruzenshtern set
a course between the 17th and 18th degrees of northern
latitude, that was, between the routes taken by Captains
Cook and Clerke, on the one hand, and, on the other, by
merchantmen sailing from the Islands to Canton. On June
3, in lat. 17°N and long. 169° 30'W, a great many birds
were spotted in flight from the Nadezhda. No land was
observed, however. Captain Kruzenshtern imagined that
there must near this spot lie some as yet unknown island
or rock. His supposition was fully justified later: in
1807, islands were discovered in lat. 16° 53'N, long.
169° 32'W by Captain Smeaton of the English frigate
Cornwallis, and were named after him.[1]

_____

[1] See Precise Atlas of the South Sea, comp. Captain
Kruzenshtern, pt. II, appendix: published in 1836.

On June 6, from long. 176° 46', the Nadezhda followed
a north-westerly course: Captain Kruzenshtern had her so
steered that she did not approach the routes once taken by
Captains Cook and Clerke by less than one hundred miles.
On the 10th, she crossed the Tropic of Cancer in long.
181° 56'W. The NE trade wind, fresh until now, began to
blow irregularly and soon gave way completely to variable
winds.

Captain Kruzenshtern had been meaning to sail to the
westward for some time, when he reached the 36th parallel
of northern latitude, in order to check the existence of
land shown as lying to the east of Japan on old Spanish
and certain other charts. Strong west winds and fogs
forced him, however, to abandon this intention. Over the
next two days, though signs of land were indeed observed
(between lats. 38° and 42°N), the prevailing gloom made
it impossible to be sure of it. On July 2, the Nadezhda
arrived in Petropavlovsk harbor - almost one year since
her sailing from Kronshtadt. Once the cargo had been
discharged into storehouses ashore (except for 6,000 puds
of iron, which were left for want of the time to unload
them), the ship was recaulked, since a significant leak
had appeared during the voyage from Cape Horn. Sails and
rigging were also set to rights. When this work was
finished, and when the ship had been provisioned to the
maximum possible extent, Captain Kruzenshtern again put
out to sea, on August 27, to fulfil the second object of
his mission - the delivering of the embassy to Japan.

Though the lateness of the season did not allow him
to contemplate geographical explorations on his way to
Nagasaki, nonetheless, wishing to perform whatever useful
service he might for science, Captain Kruzenshtern set a
course between the former routes of Captains Clerke and
Gore, with the intention of examining that area of water
in long. 214°W and between 33° and 37° of northern latitude.
For in these waters, on the maps of Laperouse and some
others, various doubtful islands were indicated.

The stormy weather which had accompanied the
Nadezhda from Kamchatka fell off on September 3, when she
was near lat. 39°N and in long. 208°W. Over the following
days, Captain Kruzenshtern traversed that region in which
he expected to find land. But the search was fruitless,
although there were signs of land. By the 9th he had
reached the parallel of Van Diemen's Strait, and one
week later (in lat. 32°N, long. 226° 22'W) the voyagers
sighted the shores of Japan, near which, on September 20,
they survived a typhoon. When this hurricane struck,
the mercury in the Nadezhda's barometer fell beneath the
lowest gradation, to reappear only three hours later.
Captain Kruzenshtern believed that at its lowest the
barometer had stood at 27". The ship herself had been in
great danger, moreover, there being land to leeward
towards which she had been steadily driven. But an abrupt
change of wind, from ESE to WNW, saved her from destruction.

5

The damage inflicted by this typhoon was disproportionately slight: for nothing was lost but two ship's boats, smashed by a wave, and a quantity of parted ropes.

During the succeeding days, Captain Kruzenshtern sailed along the southern shore of Kyushu, passing through Van Diemen's Strait and astronomically fixing the positions of all conspicuous points and islands. On September 26 he arrived at Nagasaki.

As is well known, the embassy to Japan had no success. The Japanese received it with various inconveniencing precautions, and some five months elapsed in the wait for the arrival of a commissioned Imperial representative with whom negotiations might begin. In the end, the Japanese not only refused to establish any relations whatsoever with Russia, but actually declined gifts brought in our Sovereign's name.

On April 5, 1805, Captain Kruzenshtern left inhospitable Nagasaki and, by way of the Korean Strait, entered the Sea of Japan, intending to survey that basin, which was then almost unknown to European navigators. On April 28 he stood at anchor in a newly discovered bay of the north shore of the island of Matsumae, which he named in honor of the Chancellor, Count Rumiantsev. On the passage from Nagasaki to this bay, they determined the positions of Tsushima, Kol'net, Goto and other islands belonging to Kyushu and Nippon. They also surveyed the NW coast of Nippon itself, the entry to the Gulf of Sangar, and the whole W and NW coast of Matsumae. The total number of points fixed astronomically, in the Seas of Japan and Okhotsk was more than a hundred.[1]

From the natives of Rumiantsev Bay, Captain Kruzenshtern gathered a little information about Matsumae and Sakhalin: whereupon, on May 1, he passed through Laperouse Strait into Aniva Bay on the southern shore of Sakhalin. Thence he set sail, on May 4, and made a survey of the eastern shore as far as Cape Patience. Meeting large quantities of ice near this cape on May 15, he was obliged to abandon the work and to return to Kamchatka. Passing through the Kurile chain, he discovered (May 18) a group of little islands, The Stone Snares,[2] near which the ship was almost wrecked on meeting such a powerful current that at 8 knots she was drawn back towards a hidden reef. Only with great difficulty did Captain Kruzenshtern make his way from here and back into the Sea of Okhotsk, where an unforeseen storm had to be

---

[1] See Voyage of Captain Kruzenshtern, pt. III, pp. 398-402; also his Atlas of the South Sea, pt. II - Northern Hemisphere.

[2] The natives call these islets Mussir', or sea lion, and "The Rock".

suffered. The very next day, the Nadezhda passed out into
the ocean by way of a strait between Onekotan and
Kharamukotan Islands. Four days later she reached
Petropavlovsk harbor.

Here Chamberlain Rezanov, the Envoy, left the
Nadezhda and set out for Kadiak in the Company brig
Mariia. Returning thence to Okhotsk, he set out for St.
Petersburg by land but died at Krasnoiarsk on the way.
Captain Kruzenshtern returned to Sakhalin, there to continue his hydrography. On June 23 he left Avacha Bay,
and on the 30th, passing through Nadezhda Strait - between the islands of Mataua and Rashaua - into the Sea
of Okhotsk. On July 7, he was approaching Cape Patience.
From here, Captain Kruzenshtern continued his investigation of the eastern shore of Sakhalin. Rounding its
northern extremity (July 28), he then sailed south
towards the River Amur's mouth. On August 1, in lat.
53° 30' 50"N, he sighted a northern channel, separating
Sakhalin from the mainland. Encountering a strong
current which flowed from the south, as well as completely
fresh water, he concluded that the mouth itself was near
and imagined, with Laperouse, that Sakhalin was joined
to the mainland south of the River Amur's mouth by an
isthmus - or was separated from it by a very shallow
channel. The constant, northward-flowing current (which
Laperouse had not observed), still further persuaded
Captain Kruzenshtern that this was the correct supposition.[1]

As it was, the lack of water in the channel hindered
the Nadezhda from moving southwards down it, while the
absence of a safe harbor where they might have waited
in security while rowed boats made a survey of the
river-mouth, rendered it impractical to send off a longboat which had been prepared in Nagasaki for the purpose.

The following day, a SE wind and the strong current
running from the gulf hampered Captain Kruzenshtern in
his attempt to examine the nearby shore of Tartary. Having
stood two days at anchor in Nadezhda Bay, which was open
to the sea (on the west coast of Sakhalin), he set off
back to Kamchatka. On this passage, the position of the
island of St. Iona was fixed (lat. 56° 25' 30"N, long.
143° 51' 45"W). On August 19, the Nadezhda reached
Petropavlovsk harbor, crossing the better part of the
Sea of Okhotsk in fog and with a strong wind. The lateness of the season and the need to reach Canton in time
kept Captain Kruzenshtern from examining the Shantar Islands
and the adjacent mainland. The islands remained almost
unknown until 1829, when they were surveyed by Lt. Koz'min

---

[1] The explorations of Captain Nevel'skoi demonstrated the
inaccuracy of these suppositions (see sect. 34). A. Sgibnev.

of the Corps of Naval Pilots.[1]

The readying of the ship for the return voyage to
Russia, the reloading of her holds, and the augmenting of
provisions, which were furnished on instructions by
Okhotsk and by Iakutsk, held Captain Kruzenshtern in
Petropavlovsk more than one month. But at last, on
September 23, he left the shores of Kamchatka for a final
time, and sailed for Canton where he was to rejoin the
Neva. On this passage, he vainly sought the islands
Rico-de-Plata, Guadalupe, Malibragos, San Sebastian de
Lobos, and San Juan, all of which were shown on ancient
maps. Stormy weather, especially between lats. 38⁰ and
31⁰N, greatly hampered these investigations. On October
14, in lat. 31⁰N and long. 208⁰ 30', the ship encountered
a storm not unlike the earlier typhoon off the shore of
Japan. There were many indications of the proximity of
land in the following days, near lat. 27⁰N and long.
215⁰W. Near this place, the Bonin-Jima Islands were
sought and found, in 1827, by Captains Beechey and Lütke.
On October 25, when lying in sight of the Vulcanos Islands
(by the Tropic of Cancer), the Nadezhda at last met the
NE monsoon winds and pressed west. On the stormy night
of November 6, and by way of the strait between the
islands of Batan (Bashi) and Formosa, Captain Kruzenshtern
entered the China Sea, reaching Macao two days later.
On November 21, when Captain Kruzenshtern (who had
completed all his business), was already making ready to
leave, the Neva arrived at Macao with a cargo of furs.
Both ships then moved up to Whampoa.

By the beginning of January 1806, all necessary
business on the Company's behalf had been transacted and
the ships stood laden with goods to the value of 263,000
silver rubles. The Chinese authorities, however, continued
to delay them under various empty pretexts for another
month: so that the Nadezhda and the Neva did not go on
their way until January 29.

However, with the assistance of the NE monsoon, their
voyage through the China Sea was swift. On February 12
both vessels crossed the Equator for the third time.
Having made the risky passage through the Sunda Strait,
where the Nadezhda was all but thrown on rocks, they
entered the Indian Ocean on the 21st.

Emerging from the Sunda Strait, the ships met a
westerly monsoon which forced them to bear south to lat.
12⁰ 31'S. At this latitude, the wind gave way to the SE
trade wind. Pressing on towards the Cape of Good Hope,
they crossed the southern tropic on March 15, in long.
296⁰ 55'W. But on April 3, when already in the meridian

---

[1] See Zapiski, (Transactions) of the Hydrographic Department, Part IV.

8

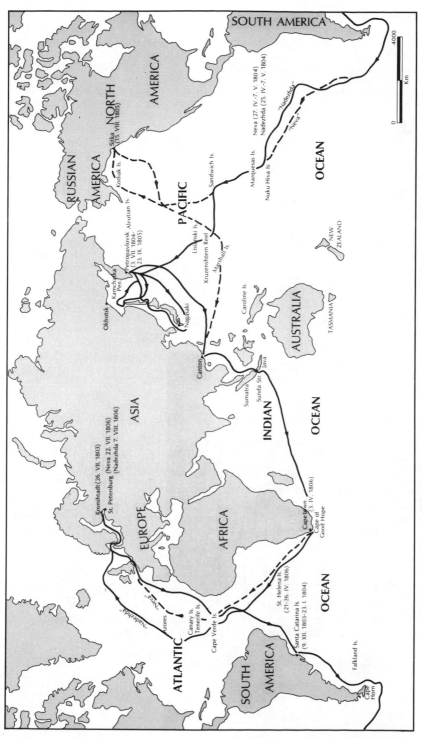

VOYAGE OF KRUZENSHTERN AND LISIANSKI ON THE "NADEZHDA" AND "NEVA" (1803-1806)

of St. Petersburg, the two vessels lost sight of each other in conditions of poor visibility. On rounding the Cape of Good Hope soon afterwards, Captain Kruzenshtern set a course for the appointed rendezvous, the island of St. Helena, and arrived there on the 21st. Not finding Captain Lisianskii there, and having taken on no fresh provisions, which were then in short supply on the island itself, Captain Kruzenshtern set out once more and, on May 10, crossed the Equator for the fourth time.

On May 28, the Nadezhda left the tropics, and the trade wind was replaced, soon afterwards, by a calm that lasted ten days; moderate variable winds then blew.

Having heard the news of a rupture between Russia and France while at St. Helena, Captain Kruzenshtern decided to avoid the English Channel and a possible encounter with unfriendly vessels. He set a course around the coasts of Ireland and Great Britain. Going around the Orkney Islands (July 6), he paused four days at Copenhagen and at Elsinore; after a two-week crossing of the Baltic Sea, he reached Kronshtadt on August 7, 1806 after an absence of 3 years and 12 days.

Besides its geographical work and the specimens of natural history collected, Captain Kruzenshtern's voyage offered a further noteworthy feature: the excellent state of the crew's health. During this three-year expedition, not a single crew member perished from disease, and even the number of the sick was insignificant.

Details of this first circumnavigation by our mariners may be found in the following publications:

1. A Voyage Round the World in 1803-1806, Performed in the Ships Nadezhda and Neva, Under the Command of Captain Lieutenant Kruzenshtern, By Command of His Imperial Majesty, Alexander I: St. Petersburg, 1809-12, in 4 pts., xxv, 388, 471, and 449 pp. The first two parts contain an historical account of the expedition, the last two - tables of reckonings, astronomical readings, observations on currents, gulfs, etc., and several essays relating to the natural sciences.

2. A Journal of the First Voyage by Russians Round the Globe, Written, Under H.I.M. the Emperor's Protection, by Chief Factor O. Shemelin of the Russian-American Company: St. Petersburg, 1816-18, in 4 pts. In this book are to be found many interesting observations on trade with China and Japan and certain other topics.

3. A Voyage Round the World by Captain-Lieutenant Lisianskii.

The Russian-American Company Vessel <u>Neva</u>
(Lisianskii)
1803-06

Having parted company with the <u>Nadezhda</u> at the
Sandwich Islands, Captain Lisianskii rested four days in
Kealakekua Bay. He then proceeded on his way to the
island of Kadiak, and on July 1, 1804, arrived in the
harbor of St. Paul after a passage from Kronshtadt of 10
months and 22 days. Here, Captain Lisianskii received
information to the effect that Collegiate Assessor Baranov
was at Sitkha Island with all the colonial forces, to
wrest back from the Kolosh [Tlingit] the settlement of
Arkhangel'sk which they had destroyed, and that Baranov
requested his, Lisianskii's, assistance. In consequence
of this news, Captain Lisianskii put the ship in the best
possible repair and, on August 3, set out for Sitkha
Island. He reached the Arkhangel'sk fort on the 10th.

Early in October the fort was regained, with the
loss of six Russians and several Aleuts during a repulsed
attack. Having brought this affair to a conclusion and
taken hostages from among the savages, Captain Lisianskii
returned to Kadiak on November 16.

In the winter season, he occupied himself with a
survey of the island's coasts and various ethnographic
enquiries. Details of these matters are set forth in
his <u>Voyage</u>. The ship, meanwhile, was being readied for
her voyage to Canton and was taking on a Company cargo.

Captain Lisianskii left St. Paul harbor on June 2,
1805 and on the 10th called into Sitkha Bay where he
remained on Company business until the 20th of August.
During this time, a survey was made of adjacent shores
and inlets.

It was Captain Lisianskii's intention, on the passage
to Canton, not to call at the Sandwich Islands but to
proceed directly to lat. 45° 30'N, long. 145°W; to sail
thence to the west as far as long. 165°W; then to move
south to the latitude 36° 30'N and sail west along it as
far as 180 degrees of longitude; and, finally, to proceed
from there to the Marianas. In this fashion, he would
cross an expanse of water then practically unknown, and
would inevitably pass through the spot where Captain
Portlock had observed signs of land in 1786 - and where
Captain Lisianskii himself, on his passage from the
Sandwich Islands to Kadiak, had seen a sea-otter.

On August 27, in lat. 48° 17'N and long. 139° 30'W,
several signs of the proximity of land were spotted (and
sea bears (fur seals) showed themselves. Neither on
that nor on the following three days, however, was a shore
observed. On September 4, they passed near the spot where

11

Captain Portlock had seen seals (lat. 44° 10'N, long. 151°
4'W), but here too no land was found. On September 14,
and lying already in long. 165°W without finding the
expected islands, Captain Lisianskii turned south, then
sailed along lat. 36° 30'N as far as long. 167° 45'.
Meeting with strong westerly winds here, he set a course
for the Mariana Islands.

On October 3, in lat. 26° 40'N and long. 173° 23'W,
a multitude of birds surrounded the ship. Imagining that
land must exist, Captain Lisianskii took proper precaution;
nevertheless, by 10 p.m. his ship sat on a coral reef.
When dawn broke, it transpired that the Neva was near a
low and uninhabited island, which a reef surrounded. The
ship was pulled off into deep water; but a squall soon
drove her back onto coral, where she remained right until
evening, having, however, sustained no significant damage.
The recovering of guns and other objects that had been
thrown overboard in order to lighten the Neva while she
was pulled off the reef delayed Captain Lisianskii
until October 7. The island which had very nearly been
the grave of the Neva's crew was named in honor of her
commander. It lies in lat. 26° 2' 48"N, long. 173° 42'
30"W.

Captain Lisianskii now so laid his course as to
arrive in long. 180° at lat. 17°N. On October 11, in
lat. 22° 15'N and long. 175° 32'W, breakers were observed
not far from the ship. Although the gloom made it
impossible, both that day and the next, to examine the
breakers more closely, still Captain Lisianskii estimated
the position of the reef - which he named after Captain
Kruzenshtern - as being lat. 22° 15'N, long. 175° 37'W.

The NE trade wind sprang up in lat. 15°N; until then
and right from Lisianskii Island, light variable winds
prevailed, mostly from the west. Taking advantage of the
trade wind, Captain Lisianskii passed through the Marianas
archipelago on November 4. He sailed between Tinian and
Aguam, determining the position of the south-eastern
extremity of the former as lat. 14° 56' 52"N and long. 213°
40' 20"W. On the passage from Sitkha to the Marianas
Islands the sea current had mostly flowed to the NE or SW.
The latter tendency was the stronger, and carried the ship
some 150 miles south and as much as 200 west.

On November 10, on the passage from Tinian to Formosa,
the ship met a typhoon: though sailing under only a reefed
storm mizzensail, she so heeled over that 'her leeward side
was in water up to the masts.'[1] As it had on the Nadezhda,
the barometer sank, during this storm, to a point below
the lowest mark. In its fury, the yawl was smashed,
gangways were torn off, and numerous objects were swept
overboard from the quarterdeck. A significant amount of

---

[1] Voyage of Captain Lisianskii, part II, p. 236.

peltry was soaked, and later jettisoned. The sorting out and restowing of the holds continued for several days.

On November 16, passing to the south of Formosa, Captain Lisianskii entered the China Sea, and on the 26th rejoined the Nadezhda at Canton. The voyage thence to the Cape of Good Hope was performed by both ships together. But on April 3, 1806, near the meridian of St. Petersburg, they were separated in gloomy weather, and Captain Lisianskii set a course between lats. 36° and 37°S to the southern limit of Agulhas Bank. Rounding the Cape of Good Hope on April 20, and shortly thereafter encountering the NE trade wind, he resolved to take full advantage of the favorable conditions in order - not calling at the arranged rendezvous spot, the island of St. Helena - to sail straight to Europe.

Although supplies of water and provisions on board were adequate, and no great need of replenishing them was to be foreseen on a successful passage, still Captain Lisianskii took the precaution of making for the Equator on a course that would take him across it at about 17°W. The frequent rains to be met in those waters would allow him to replenish his store of fresh water in case of need, while provisions could be had at the Cape Verde Islands, near which his route would pass.

Continuing his voyage with a steady trade wind, Captain Lisianskii sailed into the Northern Hemisphere in long. 16° 48'W. One month later, accompanied by variable winds, he passed the Azores, and on the 14th he dropped anchor in Portsmouth Roads, 142 days out from Canton. He had successfully completed one of the longest and boldest of passages.

After a two-week rest at Portsmouth, Captain Lisianskii put out to sea and, having paused briefly in the Downs and at Elsinore because of unfavorable winds, came into Kronshtadt on July 24. The voyage was described by Captain Lisianskii in the work: A Voyage Round the World in 1803, 1804, and 1805, By Command of the Emperor Alexander 1, in the Ship Neva Commanded by Captain-Lieutenant Iurii Lisianskii: St. Petersburg, 1812: ix, 246, and 335 pp.

3

The Russian-American Company Vessel Neva
(Hagemeister)
1806-07

But lately returned to Kronshtadt, the Neva was once again, that very year, selected for a voyage out to Sitka with a cargo of various supplies of which the colonies had need. She set out from Kronshtadt on October 20, 1806, under the command of Lt. Hagemeister. Having supple-

mented his cargo at Copenhagen with various equipment for
the colonial shipping, he went on.   But on passing through
the Zund on November 19 he met a fresh contrary wind,
which held the ship ten days at Elsinore.

     Crossing the Kattegat and Skagerrak with following
winds, Lieutenant Hagemeister set a course around Great
Britain, in order to avoid encounters with French
cruisers. Between December 4 and 10, the Neva fought
with a SW storm; on the 16th, from lat. 63° 30'N,
Hagemeister moved south into the Atlantic.

     Moderate easterly winds soon brought the ship to the
limits of the NE trade wind, which in turn gave way, in
lat. 4° 30'N to the calms that are usual in that part of
the ocean. Picking up the SE trade wind at the Equator,
Lt. Hagemeister set his course towards the Brazilian
shore. On this passage, he determined the position of
the island of São Paulo as being 28° 43'W, and on
January 13 dropped anchor in All Saints' Bay (Bahia).

     Here, inspection revealed damage in the sheathing
and rigging. These matters were attended to, and the
cracked bowsprit was replaced by a new one. Thereupon,
Lt. Hagemeister sailed from Bahia on February 26, 1807,
and held a course for the Cape of Good Hope. On March 13,
he crossed the southern tropic in long. 35°W; the meridian
of Greenwich was crossed in lat. 39° 30'S. Lt. Hagemeister continued along this parallel of latitude, eastward as far as long. 68° 30'E, then proceeded SE. On
May 21, in lat. 45° 37'S and long. 137°E, he began to
move north. The south-eastern tip of Van Diemen's Land
came into sight on May 26. On June 4, the Neva arrived
in Port Jackson, probably the first Russian ship to reach
the mainland of Australia. On their passage from the
Cape of Good Hope to Australia, they had had mostly W and
NW winds, at times very strong (e.g., between April 5-17
and in lat. 40°S, by the meridian of Madagascar).

     Having rested his people and replenished his supplies
of water and victuals, Lieutenant Hagemeister proceeded
northward, entering the torrid zone on July 9 and in
long. 183°E. But here, against all expectations, the
easterly wind that had followed him from Australia's
shores gave way to prolonged near-calms. The Neva reached
long. 167°W and lat. 21°S in ten days, nevertheless; and
here at last there sprang up a SE wind, albeit a rather
inconstant one. With it, Lt. Hagemeister proceeded up
the 167th meridian (W), crossed the Equator for the second
time on August 1, and, having encountered the NE trade
wind, passed out of the tropic zone on the 15th of that
month, in long. 168° 30'W. From here, he laid a course
for Sitkha Island. Accompanied now by moderate SE and SW
winds, he sighted the coast of America on September 7, on
the 13th, he entered the port of Novo-Arkhangel'sk, (so
named since its recapture from the Kolosh). The cargo

14

destined for this place was unloaded. Lt. Hagemeister then
set out for Kadiak Island, which he reached on October 9.
He had been 11 months and 9 days on the voyage from
Kronshtadt.

The following year (1808), Lt. Hagemeister again sailed
to Sitkha and then to the Sandwich Islands and to Petropavlovsk. After this, he himself returned to St. Petersburg
by way of Okhotsk and Irkutsk, while the Neva remained for
service in the colonies. In 1813, being then commanded
by Lt. Podushkin, she was wrecked on the Northwest Coast
of America in lat. 57°N.

4

The Navy Sloop Diana

(Golovnin)

1807-09

When it was decided to send the Neva on a second
voyage to the colonies, Imperial instructions followed
to the effect that she should be sent, not alone, but
with a warship that could give her protection on the
voyage. The principal object of sending a warship,
however, was to have her undertake exploration of those
parts of the Pacific Ocean which went with the Russian
possessions in Asia and America. The 16-gun sloop Diana
was chosen for the purpose. A 90' vessel of 300 tons,
she had only just been built on the River Svir'. She
was brought to St. Petersburg. Lieutenant Golovnin, who
for several years had served as a volunteer in the English
fleet, was posted her commander.

After significant alterations had been made to her
in view of her coming voyage, the sloop was brought to
Kronshtadt, at the end of March 1807, to be armed and
laden. In place of ballast, as much as 6,000 puds of
various supplies (rigging, iron, etc.) for Kamchatka
and Okhotsk, were stowed in her hold. In all other
respects, however, she was fitted out on the models of
the Nadezhda and the Neva, although armed with 14 six-
pounders, 4 eight-pound carronades, and the same number
of falconets.

The Neva had set out to sea, meanwhile (already in
the autumn of 1806); the sloop Diana had, therefore, to
sail alone.

Lieutenant Golovnin left Kronshtadt on July 25, 1807.
Between August 4 and 7 he passed through the Zund - at
that very moment when the English were besieging Copenhagen
from the landward and blockading it by sea. Having passed
two days at Elsinore, he entered the Kattegat on the 10th
and, encountering several SW and W storms in the Skagerrak
and the North Sea, came to Portsmouth after a voyage of
43 days from Kronshtadt.

15

The delivery of items ordered for the sloop in London delayed Lt. Golovnin in Portsmouth for about two months. When at last he had secured all that he needed for the Diana, he weighed anchor. On November 1 he entered the Atlantic Ocean, where a following storm assisted his passage until the 4th, when he reached lat. 48°N, causing no significant damage. (Only two of the ship's boats were broken by the constant agitation.) In general, the sloop proved to have sound qualities save where speed was concerned: even in the most favorable of conditions, she made no more than eight knots.

Continuing under variable winds and weather, the Diana approached the island of Porto-Santo on November 15. Not wishing to lose the helpful northerly wind, Lt. Golovnin decided not to call at the Canary Islands, as he had earlier planned to do, but to take on supplies of wine and other items in Brazil. With this in view, he set a course for the island of São Antonio in order, having there checked his chronometer, to proceed directly down to the Equator, which he now planned to cross in long. 26° or 27°W. Losing the trade wind in lat. 7°N, he entered the zone of equatorial calms, and proceeded only with great difficulty: there followed almost incessant squalls and downpours, and currents were erratic. The crew were worn out with their labor and by the intolerable heat. However, the passage through this zone, which lasted almost two weeks, had no real effect on their health. Lt. Golovnin crossed the Equator on December 20 in long. 27° 11'W, having two days earlier reached the SE trade wind. On January 1, 1808, in lat. 20° 45'S and long. 35° 13'W, he passed extremely close to the supposed location of the island of Ascension; but he observed no indications of land,[1] and went on his way towards the island of Santa Catharina, which he reached nine days later.

Once his business here was finished, Lt. Golovnin set out towards Cape Horn (January 19). Passing between the mainland and the Falkland Islands, he thought of sailing straight to the Marquesas Islands, once having rounded the cape. On the 26th he passed the mouth of the River La Plata; on February 9, under moderate but variable winds, he reached the latitude of Cape Horn; and on the 12th he actually crossed its meridian, in lat. 58° 12'S. But here, the successful voyage of the Diana came to an end. Throughout the two following weeks she encountered storms from the W and NW, and Lt. Golovnin, knowing from the experiences of other mariners that in that stormy time of the year one could hardly expect the weather to change for the better, and not wishing to exhaust his crew and lose time in a battle with the wind, decided to proceed towards Kamchatka by the longer but surer route

_____

[1] It has now been shown that Ascension Island does not exist.

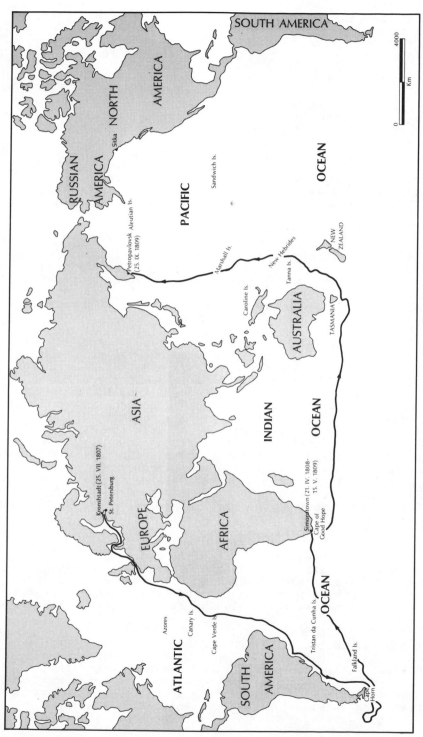

VOYAGE OF GOLOVNIN ON THE "DIANA" (1807–1809)

around the Cape of Good Hope and Australia. In keeping with this plan, he moved south, on February 29, from lat. 56° 30'S and long. 70°W, and made for the Cape of Good Hope, where he proposed to call and to rest.

As far as Tristan da Cunha (March 27), the _Diana_ was accompanied by the earlier W and NW storms. Afterwards, however, and right to the cape itself, moderate winds and changeable weather prevailed. On April 1, the sloop crossed the meridian of Greenwich (in lat. 35°S). Two weeks later the shores of Africa came into view, and on April 21 they dropped anchor in Simon's Bay.

But here, Lt. Golovnin found not a respite, but captivity. By reason of the Russian break with England, the sloop was held despite the fact that her commander had papers from the English Government granting her free passage even in the event of a war with Russia.

After a fruitless wait of 13 months for a reply from England to the protest that he had lodged, Lt. Golovnin considered himself within his rights to break an undertaking extracted from him by force - not to leave the roadstead; and all the more so since the English were proving unwilling even to provision his people.

To appreciate all the daring of such an act, of which indeed there are few examples to be found in other navies, it suffices to know that the _Diana_ stood, double-anchored, in the innermost corner of the bay and among English warships. Her sails were unbent, exit from the bay was possible only with a NW wind, and her company was seriously short of provisions. Such obstacles, however, did not shake Lt. Golovnin's resolution. At dusk on May 15, 1809 and in a NW squall, he hoisted storm staysails, cut his ropes and, turning into the wind on a spring, went out of the bay. It was immediately noticed from the nearest English frigate that the sloop was moving, and the flagship was informed of the fact by loud-hailer; but whether or not steps were taken to begin chase is unknown. By 9 p.m. that evening, the _Diana_ was in the open sea and flying under all sails.

Avoiding a meeting with English cruisers, Lt. Golovnin went south to lat. 40°S. He then swung east, planning to pass by Australia and New Zealand up to the archipelago of the New Hebrides and then, traversing the eastern part of the Caroline chain of islands, to sail on to Kamchatka.

On May 23 the sloop crossed the meridian of St. Petersburg, in lat. 42° 30'S. On June 17 she passed by the southern tip of Van Diemen's Land at a distance of 120 miles. Lt. Golovnin ascribed the success of this passage by the _Diana_ (of some 6,000 miles), which was achieved despite her poor sailing speed, to the following current and to winds which blew constantly from the W or NW. After meeting a two- or three-day easterly storm

between latitudes 33° and 31°S, he approached the New
Hebrides group on June 25. The next day he dropped anchor
in Resolution Harbor, on the coast of Tana Island. Even
as she entered, the sloop had very nearly met destruction
- she was becalmed **near a reef**. But **a north wind** had sprung
up and drawn her out of this perilous position.

On July 31, Lt. Golovnin left the New Hebrides. Insofar as the circumstances allowed, he had replenished
his stores of victuals and water. On August 4, the
island of Tikopia came in sight; on the 7th, in lat. 7°S,
the Diana lost the trade wind from the SE. Crossing the
Equator in long. 191° 30'W, Lt. Golovnin proceeded to
lat. 10°N under variable winds and in rainy weather.
Meeting the NE trade wind, he left the tropics on
September 2, cutting across the Caroline Archipelago
through the Marshall group. He had been 36 days crossing
the torrid zone.

For the remainder of the voyage to Kamchatka, or at
least until September 13, wind and weather favored the
sloop. The shores of the peninsula showed themselves ten
days after this date, and on the 25th the Diana reached
her destination, Petropavlovsk harbor. Two years and two
months had elapsed since her departure from Russia.

That same autumn, Lt. Golovnin proceeded to Novo-
Arkhangel'sk on Sitkha Island. Returning thence to
Kamchatka, he remained there for the whole of 1810. On
April 20, 1811, he received directions from the Naval
Minister to make a survey of the southern Kurile and the
Shantar Islands, together with their shorelines. Setting
out without delay to execute this work, he completed a
description of the Kurile chain by early July; but having
stopped at Kunashiri Island to water, he was taken
captive by the Japanese, together with Navigator Khlebnikov,
Midshipman Mur (Moore), and four sailors.

The following works have been published about the
Diana's voyage out to Kamchatka and the adventures that
followed there:

1. The Voyage of the Russian Imperial Sloop Diana
from Kronstadt to Kamchatka, in 1807-1809, Under the
Command of Navy Lieutenant V. Golovnin: St. Petersburg,
241 and 243 pp.

2. Abridged Memoirs of Captain-Lieutenant Golovnin
Regarding his Voyage in the Sloop Diana, To Survey the
Kurile Islands in 1811: St. Petersburg, 1819: 146 pp.

3. Memoirs of Navy Captain Golovnin Regarding His
Adventures During Captivity by the Japanese in 1811-1813:
St. Petersburg, 1816: 285, 206 & 169 pp.

4. <u>Memoirs of Navy Captain Rikord Regarding his</u>
<u>Voyage to the Shores of Japan in 1812-1813, Undertaken</u>
<u>to Liberate Captain Golovnin and his Companions</u>: St.
Petersburg, 1816: 137 pp.

5. The <u>Works and Translations of V. M. Golovnin</u>:
5 pts., with portrait of the author, maps, and plans:
St. Petersburg, 1864. The <u>Voyage of Diana</u> of 1807-11 is
included in vol. 1.

5

The Russian-American Company Vessel <u>Suvorov</u>

(M. P. Lazarev)

1813-16

Wars with neighboring maritime Powers, which had
continued for a number of years, did not allow the
Russian-American Company to send further vessels to their
colonies until 1813. In that year, the ship <u>Suvorov</u>
(100' in length), was appointed to deliver a cargo to
Novo-Arkhangel'sk under the command of Lieutenant M. P.
Lazarev.

Lt. Lazarev sailed from Kronshtadt on October 9,
1813, and on the 19th reached Karlskrona, where he attached
himself to a merchant convoy. Following this convoy,
which had the protection of armed vessels, he called at
both Malmö and Göteborg for a few days. From this last
port, he set sail alone and, having successfully crossed
the North Sea, he dropped anchor in Portsmouth Roads on
November 27.

At Portsmouth, he took on a final part of the Company's
cargo, which had been ordered in London. Once certain
alterations to the ship's internal arrangements and to her
rigging had been completed, he joined a convoy of West
Indies-bound vessels sailing under the cover of three
warships of the line and two brigs. With these, he proceeded as far as the island of Porto-Santo. From here,
the convoy turned to the west; but Lt. Lazarev continued
on his way with the NE trade wind to lat. 6°N. They were
eleven days in the equatorial zone of calms and rain, and
endured extreme heat (as much as 25 1/2° Reaumur in the
shade). But on April 22 they reached Rio de Janeiro,
after a 52-day voyage from the English Channel.

When the Company's business was completed, Lt. Lazarev
left Brazil (May 23), intending to enter the South Sea
around the Cape of Good Hope and Australia. Meeting with
a strong westerly wind in lat. 32°S and long. 36°W, on
June 12 he passed within sight of the island of Diego-
Alvarez, the geographical position of which he reckoned
at lat. 40° 19'S and long. 9° 11'W. Proceeding along this
parallel of latitude, with following storms, he reached

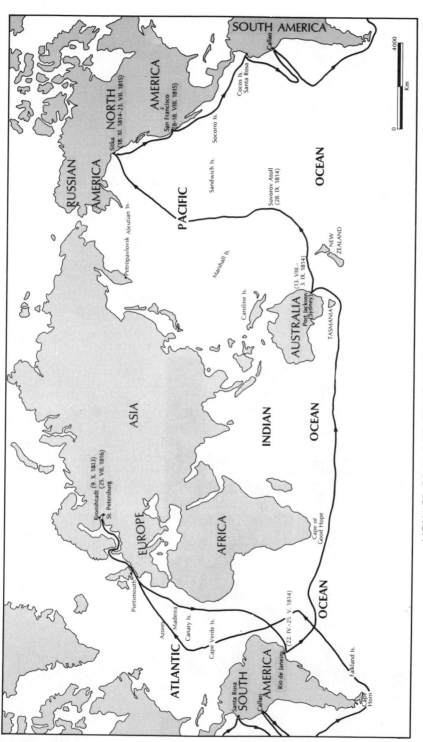

VOYAGE OF M. LAZAREV ON THE "SUVOROV" 1813-1816

the meridian of the Cape of Good Hope by the 20th. In
the Indian Ocean, he sailed between lats. 40° and 44°S
and, having encountered two violent storms on this
passage, on August 1 passed the SW extremity of Van
Diemen's Land. On the 13th he dropped anchor in Port
Jackson.

Lt. Lazarev employed the time of his sojourn at Port
Jackson in wooding and provisioning, baking ship's biscuit
(a quantity of biscuit had been soaked during the recent
storms), and in seeing to work of various kinds of board.
On September 3 he put to sea again and, passing in sight
of Lord Howe Island, on the 15th reached lat. 30° 12'S
and long. 177° 7'W. On that day, at about 4 p.m., a
slight jolt was felt in the ship, as though from touching
a shoal; however, there were no indications that the
waters were shallow. Lt. Lazarev supposed that his
vessel had run onto a sleeping whale, of which there
swam many within sight of the Suvorov.

On September 28, in lat. 13°S and long. 196° 30'E,
the lieutenant discovered a group of five small, uninhabited coral islands, which he named, in honor of his
ship, the Suvorov Group. On the chart attached to his own
journal, the southernmost of these five islands is shown
in lat. 13° 13'S and long. 163° 31'W; taken at the
longest, the group extends about nine miles from NE to SW.

The SE trade wind ceased by the Suvorov Islands, and
the NE trade wind sprang up two days later. With this,
on October 10, Lt. Lazarev crossed the Equator; and on
the 22nd and in long. 169°W the northern tropic was also
crossed. For several days even after that, the NE wind
continued to blow with great force (as far as lat. 33°N),
accompanied by squalls and poor weather which, together
with westerly storms a little later, followed the Suvorov
right to the American coast, sighted on November 11. On
November 18, Lieutenant Lazarev brought his ship into
Novo-Arkhangel'sk harbor.

The next year (1815) he sailed for furs to the
islands of St. Paul and St. George, then back to Sitkha by
late May, began to prepare for his return voyage to
Kronshtadt. Having taken on a cargo that consisted, for
the most part, of peltry and objects to be sold in Lima,
he left Novo-Arkhangel'sk on July 23, making straight for
San Francisco harbor in order to water and provision.
As a result of unforeseen circumstances, he had been unable
to do either at Sitkha.

Leaving California, Lt. Lazarev sailed southward
along the American coast. On August 31, when passing by
the islands of St. Bertha and Socorro he determined their

position as being lat. 18° 45'N, long. 110° 40' 16''W,[1] then proceeded with variable SE and NE winds in poor weather. On September 24, he stopped to check chronometers at the Cocos Islands (lat. 5° 30'N), then made a four-day call at the Spanish settlement of Santa Rosa, near the Equator on the shore of Columbia. Crossing into the Southern Hemisphere, he encountered a land breeze from the S, on October 9, which forced him to bear to the SW for a whole month. On November 8, when 1,790 miles to the SW of Lima, Lt. Lazarev turned east, and arrived at Callao on the 25th. Company business and work on the ship detained him in Lima until mid-February of the following year. During this time, the longitude of Callao port was reckoned, by many lunar observations, at 77° 5' 15''W.

Having received from the Spanish Viceroy at Lima a collection of local antiquities and certain other articles, to be presented to the Imperial Court at St. Petersburg, and having taken on the goods purchased in Lima, Lt. Lazarev put out to sea. Early in March, strong SW winds began to blow. These accompanied him as far as Cape Horn, near which the ship was several days battling with winds and storms.

Rounding Cape Horn at the end of March, Lieutenant Lazarev proceeded south of the Falkland Islands, then to the NE until April 9 and lat. 29° 30'S, long. 19° 50'W. Here, they were met by a NE wind which obliged Lt. Lazarev to sail NW. The Equator was crossed on April 27, after the Suvorov had put in at the island of Fernando de Noronha, which lies by the coast of Brazil near Cabo de São Roque.

Leaving the trade wind behind, in lat. 26°N, and continuing under variable easterly winds, Lt. Lazarev reached Portsmouth on June 6. Here he stayed, for various necessities, about three weeks, arriving at Kronshtadt on July 25, 1816, 2 years and 9 1/2 months after sailing thence.

6

The Brig Riurik

(Kotzebue)

1815-18

The problem of discovering a passage through the Northern Icy [i.e., Arctic] Ocean had long occupied all the Maritime Powers, and Russia, for her part, had made

---

[1] The readings were taken on the shore of Socorro Island, where Lt. Lazarev stopped for a few hours. The long. was reckoned by lunar distances and chronometers: Capt. Colnett gives it as 110° 4'W.

more than one attempt at solving it both from landward and from seaward; but since the time of Chichagov's unsuccessful expedition (1765-66), we had abandoned such enterprises, for protracted wars by land and sea had not allowed Russia to concern herself with scientific expeditions. But finally, when universal peace reigned over Europe, long neglected academic problems once again provoked a general interest. One of the principal champions of science in Russia, at this time, was Count N. P. Rumiantsev, a man already famed for his services in that field.

At the beginning of 1815, Count Rumiantsev decided to fit out at his own expense an expedition that would seek a passage through the Arctic Ocean from Bering Strait, by the coast of America. With that object in mind, the brig Riurik was built in an Abo yard; she was of 180 tons, and command over her was given to Navy Lieutenant Kotzebue, who had earlier been a cadet in the Nadezhda on her voyage round the world.

Lt. Kotzebue had instructions to occupy himself, not only with the main object of the expedition, but also with geographical and scientific research in Oceania. Invited to join him as companions were persons celebrated for their knowledge of the natural sciences; Lt. Kotzebue himself received both naval and scientific instructions prepared by Captain Kruzenshtern and the astronomer Horner, the better to manage his own work.

On July 30, 1815 Lt. Kotzebue left Kronshtadt Roads. Having called in at Copenhagen to pick up the savants Wormskiöld and Chamisso, he reached Plymouth without trouble a few days later. Here, he was to take on instruments and maps that had been previously ordered in London.

The commander of the Riurik had chosen Plymouth as his port-of-call in England specifically because one could enter the ocean from it in one day; he was mistaken however, in this calculation. It almost seems as though the sea wished to test the voyagers right at the outset of their daring enterprise. Twice south-west storms forced Lt. Kotzebue to put back; and once, at night, the brig was very nearly cast onto rocks. He finally entered the Atlantic Ocean on October 5. Reaching the parallel of the Strait of Gibraltar, in long. 15° 20'W, on the 21st, he dropped anchor in Santa Cruz roadstead, Teneriffe, on the 28th.

Having taken on provisions at Teneriffe, Lt. Kotzebue sailed again on November 1 and, passing within sight of the Cape Verde Islands, crossed the Equator on the 23rd. From here he set a course for Cabo Frio, wishing to fix the cape's longitude; but not succeeding in this, because of gloomy conditions, he turned to the south and on December 12 arrived at the island of Santa Catharina.

24

Having rested his company and readied the brig for the
voyage around Cape Horn, he sailed on from there on
December 28.

Early in January of 1816, the Riurik battled with SW
storms for six consecutive days (in lat. 45°S, long. 57°W).
The commander almost perished at this juncture: a giant
roller came in from the stern and threw him overboard, but
by good fortune he was able to cling on to a coil of
rope. The brig herself sustained no little damage on her
upper part and rudder, while some of the ship's powder
and biscuit was soaked.

Having rounded Cape Horn and met a SW storm to boot,
Lt. Kotzebue laid a course for Conception Bay on the west
coast of South America, meaning there to put his vessel
into a condition to proceed on her way, and, moreover,
to replace the provisions that had been soaked in the
storm. On February 11, the Riurik stood at anchor
opposite the town of Talcahuano.

Lt. Kotzebue put his ship in the best possible order
and put to sea again in early March. He now laid a
course towards the supposed position of 'Davis Land'.
On March 16 he reached lat. 27° 20'S and long. 88°W, and
sailed along that parallel of latitude for five days, as
far as long. 95° 30'W, seeing not the slightest
indication of land. On the 25th, he passed the desolate
little islet of Sala-y-Gomes, and on March 28 dropped
anchor in Cook's Bay, on the coast of Easter Island.

To the great consternation of Lt. Kotzebue, the
natives met him with hostility, with the result that he
was forced immediately to return on board the brig,
accompanied by a hail of stones. Leaving the shore, he
noticed that the huge stone figures of which Cook,
Laperouse, and Lisianskii had written, had been smashed.[1]

Passing through the archipelago in a northerly
direction, he looked over Schouten's 'Dog Island' on
April 16; but in view of the considerable variance in
reckoning of latitude, he called it 'Doubtful Island'
(lat. 14° 50'S, long. 138° 47'W). Over the days that
followed, and in this sequence, were discovered these
uninhabited groups of islands: the Rumiantsevs (lat.
14° 47'S, long. 144° 35' 50"W); the Spiridovs, or
Schoutens ('Hurrah Islands', lat. 14° 41'S, long. 145°
7'W); the long chain of the Riuriks (the Palliser
Islands and Schouten's Fly Island, in lat. 15° 11' 45"S,
long. 146° 39' 35"W - northern extremity); and, finally,

---

[1] The reasons for this reception by the islanders subsequently became clear: in 1805, a certain American ship-
master had robbed them. It was he who also smashed the
statues.

the Kruzenshterns, in lat. 15° 0'S, long. 148° 48'W.[1]

On April 28, the brig neared the supposed position of 'Boumans Eylanden'. Searching for neither these nor the 'Roggeveen Islands', Lt. Kotzebue set a course for the Penrhyn Group, which had been seen by their discoverer, Captain Sever, in 1788, only once, and from a distance. On May 1, he examined these islands, which proved to be like those in the lower archipelago, i.e., they were a chain of coral rock formations of low elevation, although inhabited. The position of the center of this group was reckoned at lat. 9° 1' 35"S, long. 157° 44' 32"W.

Crossing the Equator in long. 175° 27'W, Lt. Kotzebue so steered as to cut across the northern Mulgrave Islands, which were then hardly known at all. On his passage to this archipelago, on May 21 he discovered a chain formed by two separate island-clusters, joined by a coral reef. The position of the channel between the clusters he astronomically determined to lie in lat. 11° 11' 20"N, and long. 190° 1' 43"W. These were named the Kutuzov and the Suvorov Islands. The former had inhabitants (the natives call their islands Udirik and Tagan). The newly discovered groups belonged to the eastern reach of the extensive Caroline Archipelago, familiar on maps under the name of Marshall Islands.

Proposing to examine these localities once more on his return voyage, Lt. Kotzebue now hastened to Kamchatka. On June 3, in lat. 31° 49'N, long. 200° 15'W, he observed indications of the proximity of land, but the mists which accompanied the Riurik right to Kamchatka made it impossible to ascertain whether or not an isle existed. On the 13th (lat. 47°N) the Riurik encountered a most violent storm, after which such a severe frost set in that pieces of ice fell from the rigging and the sails. On June 19, she arrived at Petropavlovsk harbor. Here she was sheathed in copper taken from the sloop Diana.

Preparing for sea with the greatest possible speed, Lt. Kotzebue left Kamchatka on July 15 and headed for Saint Lawrence Island. By reason of illness, one of the two other officers in the brig stayed on at Petropavlovsk, so that Lt. Kotzebue was obliged to complete the remaining part of his voyage with only one officer, fulfilling both his own duties and those of officer-of-the-watch. On the 20th he sighted Bering Island and determined the position of its northern tip as lying in lat. 55° 17' 18"N, long. 194° 6' 37"W. Because of fogs, the position of Saint

---

[1] On his second voyage, Captain Kotzebue found that all longitudes determined by him in 1816 "were 7' 30" too far eastward"; here they were "everywhere corrected". See Admiral Kruzenshtern's Atlas of the South Sea, supplement, 1836, p. 108.

Lawrence Island remained unchecked. On July 30, the
shores of Asia and America were simultaneously visible
from the Riurik. She was then off Cape Prince of Wales
and St. Diomede Islands, from which Ratmanov Island
was soon seen.[1]

Following the coast of America northward, Lt.
Kotzebue found little Shishmarev Bay (lat. 66° 14'N, long.
166° 24'W), with Sarychev Island at its entrance, and on
August 1 entered an extensive gulf, the eastern shore of
which was hidden from his view. Supposing that this
might be a passage to the Arctic Ocean, Lt. Kotzebue
proceeded in the direction of the gulf; but he perceived
that it was bounded, on the east, by lofty shores. Sailing
round this gulf and reaching open sea near its northern
cape (where the gulf itself ended), he named the cape
after Captain Kruzenshtern (lat. 61° 30'N, long. as given
by Cook). The newly discovered gulf received the name
of Kotzebue Sound.

Intending to continue his investigations of these
regions the next year, Lt. Kotzebue next proceeded to the
coasts of Asia. On the 19th he approached the continent's
easternmost tip and, moving down the shore toward the
south, went into St. Lawrence Bay. He determined the
positions of several new points, and sailed out on the
24th. On September 7 he arrived at Illiuliuk harbor,
Unalashka. Thence he proceeded to San Francisco in
California, there to take on all provisions necessary for
a summer cruise in the tropics.

Leaving California on November 1, the Riurik headed
for the Sandwich Islands. On this passage, from
November 11 (lat. 25°N, long. 138° 1'W) until November 16
and the stirring of the NE trade wind (in lat. 22° 30'N),
there blew a strong SW wind - an unusual occurrence in
such latitudes and so far from the mainland. On the 27th,
Lt. Kotzebue arrived at Honolulu.

During a three-week sojourn on the island of Oahu,
much information was gathered about the Sandwich Islands,
and a detailed survey was made of Honolulu harbor itself.
The latitude of the Riurik's anchorage in it was determined
to be 21° 17' 57"N, and the longitude - 157° 52'W. Compass
declination: 10° 57'E; Magnetic va.: 43° 39'.

---

[1] Lt. Kotzebue erred, considering "Ratmanov Island" the
fourth in the Diomede group and therefore claiming it
as a new discovery. In his Atlas of the South Sea,
Admiral Kruzenshtern shows only three St. Diomede islands:
Ratmanov, Kruzenshtern, and the Fairvai Rock. Capt.
Beechey examined this group in 1828. See below, the
Voyage of Capt. Vasil'ev.

From the Sandwich Islands, Lt. Kotzebue sailed on to the locality of the discoveries of the preceding year: the Suvorov and Kutuzov Islands. On this passage, on January 1, 1817 he discovered yet another - New Year Island (lat. 10° 8' 27"N, long. 189° 4' 40"W), which its natives called 'Miadi' - and four days later, yet another, likewise inhabited, group, the Rumiantsev or Otdia Islands (lat. 9° 8' 9"N, long. 189° 43' 45"W). Lt. Kotzebue remained in the lagoon of the Otdia Islands until the beginning of February, occupied in surveying the surrounding shores and in making their inhabitants' acquaintance. Moving to the south after this, he consecutively discovered these groups: the Chichagov or Erikub Group (median lat. 9° 6'N, long. 189° 56'W); the Arakcheev or Kaven (Kwajalein) Group (the largest island lying in lat. 8° 54' 21"N, long. 188° 11'W); the Traversay or Aur Group (lat. 8° 18'N, long. 187° 48'W); and the Kruzenshtern or Ailuk Group (Kapeniuro Island in lat. 10° 27' 25"N, long. 190°W). These five groups, together with 'Miadi' and the new groups discovered subsequently (Likiep, Arno, Majuro, and Mili) form that chain of coral islands now known as the Radak Chain. It is inhabited by a very gentle people, very like the natives of the Caroline Chain or Archipelago, of which Radak forms the eastern part.

Lt. Kotzebue's observations on the Radak islands, and on islands in a parallel chain, the Ralik islands, offer rich material for the future historian and geographer. They are included in his account of his voyage.

On March 12, 1817, the Riurik left the newly-discovered archipelago and moved swiftly north. Passing between the Kutuzov and Suvorov Islands and touching at Cornwallis Island (found to lie in lat. 14° 39' 29"N, long. 191° 0' 25"W)[1] Lt. Kotzebue laid a course for Unalashka, where there awaited him the baidaras that had been prepared for the coming search in the Arctic Ocean.

On April 3, in lat. 34° 27'N and long. 193° 47'W, a heavy westward current was observed, and the following day - various indications of land. The hope of discovering land, however, remained unrealized.

On the 13th, during a storm, a huge roller broke over the brig, rushing across the deck and smashing the bowsprit. One of the four sailors then standing on the deck had a leg broken; the others were wounded, as was also the commander. The loss of the Riurik had seemed inevitable, but the storm suddenly quietened. Five days after this, she was all but wrecked on Unimak Island. She finally

---

[1] In Admiral Kruzenshtern's view, this island is the Gaspar-Rico of the ancient mariners: See Atlas of the South Sea, pt. II, p. 17, and supplement, p. 6.

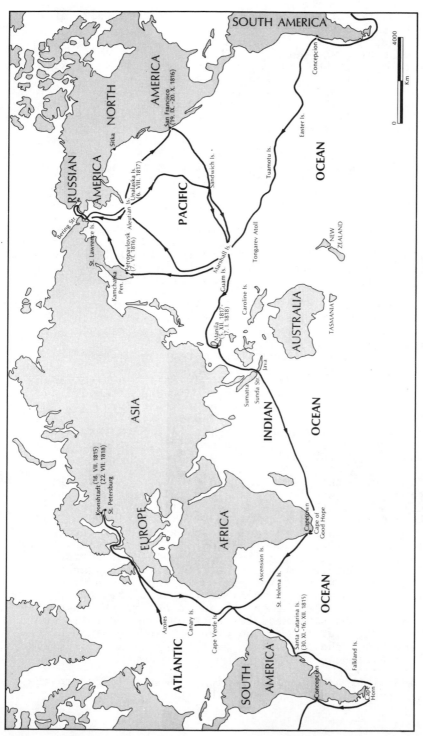

VOYAGE OF KOTZEBUE ON THE "RURIK" (1815–1818)

SOUTH AMERICA

RUSSIAN AMERICA

NORTH AMERICA

San Francisco (19. IX.–20. X. 1816)

Sitka

Easter Is.

Concepción

Bering Str.

St. Lawrence Is.

Unalaska Is. (6. VIII. 1817)

Aleutian Is.

Petropavlovsk (7. VI. 1816)

Kamchatka Pen.

Sandwich Is.

Tuamotu

PACIFIC OCEAN

Marshall Is.

Tongarev Atoll

Guam Is.

Manila 5. XII. 1817–17. I. 1818

Caroline Is.

NEW ZEALAND

Java

Sumatra

Sunda Str.

ASIA

AUSTRALIA

TASMANIA

INDIAN OCEAN

Kronshtadt (18. VII. 1815) (22. VII. 1818)

St. Petersburg

EUROPE

AFRICA

Capetown

Cape of Good Hope

Ascension Is.

Azores

Canary Is.

Cape Verde Is.

St. Helena Is.

ATLANTIC OCEAN

Santa Catarina Is. (30. XI.–16. XII. 1815)

SOUTH AMERICA

Concepción

Falkland Is.

Cape Horn

Concepción

4000

Km

0

arrived at Unalashka on April 24, just as a fresh storm was rising on the sea.

The brig was put to rights, insofar as that was possible, and they put to sea again on June 29, taking along several baidaras and 15 Aleuts for the coastal survey work about the Arctic Ocean. Calling at the islands of St. Paul and St. George again, they stood at anchor on July 10 off the east shore of Saint Lawrence Island. But here Lt. Kotzebue was forced to abandon a further northward voyage: his chest weakness - a result of a bruise received in the April storm - had worsened to such a point that he could not continue his work in that cold dry climate without patent danger to his life.

According to his instructions, he was to take a return route through the Torres Strait. Since his vessel was in poor condition and had long been short of provisions, however, Lt. Kotzebue judged it necessary to call at Manila, where he trusted to find all that he needed. He proposed, on the voyage there, to take certain plants from the Sandwich Islands to Radak.

In keeping with this new plan, he returned to Unalashka and, sailing thence on August 18, reached latitude 40°N three weeks later, after a struggle with strong S winds and a current that bore the Riurik 5° to the east. He entered Honolulu harbor on October 1.

On his passage from the Sandwich Islands to Radak, Lt. Kotzebue sought and determined the position of the Smith Islands, discovered by the frigate Cornwallis in 1807;[1] but he himself was very nearly wrecked on them. Their latitude was found to be 16° 45' 36"N, and their longitude 190° 30' 40"W. The next day, the Riurik stood at anchor by Otdia Island.

Leaving the plants that he had brought here, Lt. Kotzebue went on his way, and the following day discovered yet another island group - the Count Heyden or Likiep Group - in lat. 9° 51' 30"N, long. 190° 46' 30"W. He intended, on the voyage to Manila, to seek out the islands of Ralik, which the Radak islanders said were in a line parallel with their own, lying out further to the west. But the brig was carried so far to the west in the course of a stormy night that not one of the islands in question was visible the next morning. The necessity of hastening on to Manila before the change in the NE monsoon prevented Lt. Kotzebue from devoting more time to the search. In the event, however, discoveries in the Ralik chain did fall to the lot of Russian mariners, as we shall see.

---

[1] In Admiral Kruzenshtern's view, these islands are the Camizares Islands, discovered by the Spanish in 1786.

Proceeding between the 8th and 11th parallels of northern latitude, Lt. Kotzebue found not one of the islands indicated in some charts. After numerous experiments on the salinity, temperature, and color of sea water, he came to the conclusion that the depth of water between the Radak and Mariana islands was appreciably less than the average in the tropics. On November 23, the Riurik dropped anchor in the harbor of Caldera-de-Apra, on the island of Guam.

Having there collected fresh information about the Caroline Archipelago in general, and drawn a plan of Caldera Bay, Lt. Kotzebue put to sea on the 28th and, with the aid of the NE monsoon, reached Manila by December 17.

Repair of the brig and provisioning with all necessities delayed him here until the end of January 1818. Continuing his voyage across the China Sea, he entered the Indian Ocean by way of the Sunda Strait in mid-February, and on March 4 left the tropics. Near the Cape of Good Hope, he was for several days on end held up by great storms. Passing south of the shoal (lat. 35° 18'S), in order to take advantage of a following current (of 3 miles per hour), he dropped anchor in Table Bay on the 30th.

Here, the Riurik encountered the French corvette L'Uranie, in which Captain Freycinet was commencing his celebrated voyage round the world.

Leaving the Cape in mid-April and sailing within sight of the islands of St. Helena and Ascension (long. reckoned at 14° 22' 30"W), Lt. Kotzebue crossed the Equator for the fourth time in long. 20° 26'W. On June 3 he reached the parallel of the Azores, reaching Portsmouth two weeks later. Spending five days at Portsmouth and another at Copenhagen, he returned to his native town of Reval on July 22. On August 3, he dropped anchor in the River Neva opposite the residence of Count Rumiantsev, after a voyage of three years.

The expedition has been described in the following work: A Voyage to the South Sea and to Bering Strait, For the Discovery of a North-East Passage, Undertaken in the Years 1815-1818, and Sponsored by His Excellency the Chancellor, Count N. P. Rumiantsev, in the Riurik, Under the Command of Navy Lieutenant Kotzebue: St. P., 1821-23: xxi, 168, 345, & 538 pp. Included in the first two parts of this work is a full account of the voyage; in the final part are remarks by the scientists who participated in the expedition.

7

The Russian-American Company Vessel <u>Kutuzov</u>
(Hagemeister)
1816-19

Appointed chief manager of the Russian colonies in America in place of Collegiate Assessor Baranov, Captain-Lieutenant Hagemeister was required to proceed to the place of his new duties as commander of two Company vessels, the <u>Kutuzov</u> and the <u>Suvorov</u>, both carrying cargo for the colonial settlements and for trade in certain South American ports. The <u>Suvorov</u> was under the command of Lt. Ponafidin.

On September 8, 1816, both vessels left Kronshtadt, arriving on the 13th at Copenhagen, where they supplemented their cargo. They proceeded on the 24th. They soon traversed the Kattegat and Skagerrak and emerged into the North Sea; but they at once met a westerly storm from which they were obliged to seek shelter in the Norwegian port of Kvalefjörd.

From here Captain Hagemeister continued on his way, around the Shetland Islands, coming in sight of them on October 5, by the meridian of Greenwich. Having battled with a NW storm for the next three days, he entered the Atlantic on the 10th and, from the parallel of St. Petersburg in long. 4°W, turned south towards the Azores, where he proposed to rest. Continuing under SE and NE winds, he approached the island of Graciosa on October 23. Knowing that its roadstead was not altogether secure in a SE wind, Captain Hagemeister thought of sailing straight to Brazil. Fearing, however, that his people might suffer from a water shortage if he did so, he made a one-week call at the island of Santiago, in the Cape Verde Group. Only on November 13 did he sail on thence, making for the Equator.

Meeting with nothing remarkable on his passage through the torrid zone, he was left by the SE trade wind in lat. 15°S, after which, for several days and as far as lat. 20°S, a SE wind prevailed. This in turn gave way to light W, SW and NW winds. In mid-December he reached Rio de Janeiro.

Various matters and pieces of work, including the replacement of the <u>Kutuzov</u>'s rudder, detained Captain Hagemeister more than three weeks at Rio de Janeiro. Putting out to sea on January 7, 1817, he laid a course for Cape Horn, accompanied by a NE coastal wind, and reached lat. 32° 30' by the 12th. But from this time on, the vessels' passage was greatly slowed by contrary winds, so that they did not enter the channel between Patagonia and the Falkland Islands until the 30th; and here they were met by a storm.

On February 12, not far from the Cape Horn meridian, the vessels lost sight of each other on a murky night. Captain Hagemeister pressed on, with W and NW winds. On March 3, in lat. 34°S and long. 79°W, he met the SE coastal trade wind; and with it, he arrived at Callao on the 17th of that same month. Less fortunate in her latter passage, the Suvorov arrived there only on the 29th.

In Lima, Captain Hagemeister sold a part of the goods in his vessel. Equalizing cargoes in the Suvorov and the Kutuzov, he put to sea on May 8 and followed the coast of America to Guayaquil. On May 15, the Suvorov separated and made directly for Sitkha; the Kutuzov briefly stood in Guayaquil Bay by Santa Clara Island, whence she moved across to Bajos-de-Payahos. Having transferred the goods destined for Guayaquil onto Spanish vessels, and taken on other goods, Captain Hagemeister moved on to the southern part of the bay and the mouth of the River Tumbes, there to water. On July 17 he sailed and on the 22nd, near the Galapagos Islands, crossed the Equator. On doing so, he lost the SE coastal breeze.

Strong winds and squalls alternately accompanied him until the end of August. In lat. 20°N, long. 122° 30'W, he met with a steady NE wind, and headed to the north-west. Shortly thereafter, he crossed the Tropic of Cancer (124°W long.), and on September 9, passing beyond the limit of the trade wind (in lat. 40°N, long. 136° 30'), turned towards land. On the 17th he reached Bodega or Rumiantsev Bay, north of the port of San Francisco in California.

Remaining there until October 1 to transmit the cargo destined for the nearby Company settlement of Ross, Captain Hagemeister then proceeded into the port of San Francisco to purchase grain, of which the colonies had need. Completing the purchase, he set out for Sitkha Island on October 31, reaching Novo-Arkhangel'sk on November 21.

Assuming the direction of the colonies, Captain Hagemeister visited Rumiantsev Bay a second time the following year (July 6-18) on his way to Monterey, where he sought grain. At Monterey, he met Captain Golovnin, who had come in the sloop Kamchatka to inspect the colonies; having completed his business with Capt. Golovnin, he headed back for Novo-Arkhangel'sk by September 10.

Captain Hagemeister now readied his vessel for the voyage back to Russia and, with a cargo of sandlewood and peltry, sailed from Sitkha on November 27, 1818. He had with him, as a passenger, the former (Chief) Manager of the colonies, Collegiate Assessor Baranov.

On the passage to the Sandwich Islands, which were passed on December 24, and within sight of Kauai, the Kutuzov was pursued by westerly storms; and between these came calms, with a tremendous swell. Meeting the trade wind in about 16°N, Captain Hagemeister took full advantage of it as far as the China Sea, where it gave way to the NE monsoon.

Halting a week to rest at the island of Guam, Captain Hagemeister then proceeded on his way,[1] entering the China Sea itself, between Richmond and Babuyan Islands, on February 15. On the 28th he crossed the Equator and early in March dropped anchor in Batavia roadstead. His commercial affairs complete, he put to sea again on April 12, and three days later entered the Sunda Strait; (on April 16, Collegiate Assessor Baranov died of a fever with which he had fallen ill in Batavia. His corpse was given a sea burial.) but, delayed by calms, he reached the Indian Ocean only on the 19th. Soon after, he encountered the NE trade wind. On May 3rd he crossed the southern tropic in long. 71°E and thereafter, as far as the Cape of Good Hope, struggled with W and NW storms which, however, resulted in no serious damage to the vessel.

Rounding the Cape of Good Hope on June 6, Captain Hagemeister set a course for the Equator. On the 29th he passed within sight of Ascension Island. Five days later, he entered the northern hemisphere in long. 23°W. The exhausting passage through the zone of calms lasted about two weeks. At last, on July 19 and in lat. 13° 30'N, a NE wind sprang up and followed the _Kutuzov_ to the 32nd parallel.

Taking advantage of fair winds, Captain Hagemeister soon reached the latitude of the English Channel, and on August 22 he arrived at Portsmouth. Here he stayed until the 25th, when he proceeded on his way, passing through the Zund on September 1 and dropping anchor in Kronshtadt Roads on the 7th.

8

The Russian-American Company Vessel _Suvorov_

(Ponafidin)

1816-18

Parting company with the _Kutuzov_ on the passage from Callao to Novo-Arkhangel'sk, on May 27, 1817, Lieutenant Ponafidin crossed the Equator for the second time in long. 103° 30'W, and three days later lost the SE trade wind. Accompanied instead by light westerly winds, he came to Rooz Island, which he reckoned by observations to

---

[1] On January 31, when the anchor was weighed for the passage into Unata Bay, the vessel was almost thrown ashore because of the breaking of a rope attached to a stream-anchor, cast when the mooring was slipped.

lie in lat. 18° 29'N, long. 115° 11'W, on June 20. Pressing
on westward, he encountered the NE trade wind on the 26th,
in lat. 20°N, and proceeded with it as far as the 40th
parallel. He arrived at Novo-Arkhangel'sk on July 20.

Here Lt. Ponafidin remained until the January
following. His vessel was hauled onto a sandbank and was
sheathed in copper. Laden with peltry, cocoa, and other
goods for St. Petersburg, she sailed from Sitkha on January
12, heading for Cape Horn.

On the 27th, in lat. 40°N, long. 144°W, the Suvorov
met a great storm coming from the east. Continuing
under variable moderate winds, on February 18 she entered
the zone of constant north-easterlies in lat. 17°N.
Within a week, however, she lost these winds (in lat. 4°
30'N), and did not encounter south-easterlies until March
9, on crossing the Equator. On March 13, Lieutenant
Ponafidin dropped anchor in Port Chichagov, on the island
of Nuku Hiva.

On the passage thence to Cape Horn, they passed
through the Tuamotu Archipelago, within sight of Trinity,
Charlotte, and Karnefuta. On April 4, as they crossed
the southern tropic, the SE trade wind ceased to accompany
them. Calms or light westerly breezes continued until
35°S. On the 21st, in lat. 39° 30'S, long. 108°W, the
cold so intensified, under a high SW wind, that snow fell.
There now descended damp and cloudy weather which, with
brief gaps, followed them to Cape Horn and beyond. Winds
were variable, mostly westerly and sometimes extremely
strong. However, the ship made good headway. On May 13
she crossed the meridian of Cape Horn (in lat. 57° 47'S)
and she continued under the earlier westerly winds as
far as 40°S, in long. 45° 30'W.

Scurvy having now appeared among the crew - a result
of the protracted dampness - it became necessary to put
in at one of the nearest American ports, and on June 6
the Suvorov dropped anchor at Rio de Janeiro. After one
month, the crew's health was completely restored. Those
sick with the scurvy (nine men) had grown well ashore,
and the Suvorov went on her way, accompanied by the SW
coastal wind, as far as 18°S lat. Here, that wind gave
way to the trade wind. On July 24 the Suvorov entered the
northern hemisphere in long. 29° 43'W.

Lt. Ponafidin lost the SE trade wind in lat. 7°N, and
encountered a NE wind only on August 3, in lat. 15°N and
long. 29°W. Having found it, however, they remained with
this trade wind right to the 35th parallel of northern
latitude. On August 23, the Suvorov passed in sight of the
island of Fayal. A week later, she entered the English
Channel and, crossing the North Sea and Skagerrak under
strong SW winds, came to the Kattegat. But here, there
were calms. Having remained three weeks at Copenhagen, Lt.
Ponafidin came to Kronshtadt Roads on October 19, 1818.

9

The Navy Sloop Kamchatka
(Golovnin)
1817-19

At the close of 1816, an Imperial edict was promulgated: a warship was to be sent to the North Pacific
Ocean. The Government now had in view, 1) the supplying
of various materials and naval stores to the ports of
Okhotsk and Petropavlovsk; 2) an inspection of the
Russian-American Company's colonies; and 3) the determining of the geographical positions and the charting of
those localities within the Russian territories facing
the North Pacific Ocean which, as yet, had not been
examined with care.

For these objects, the sloop Kamchatka was built at
St. Petersburg. She was a vessel of 900 tons, 130' in
length. Command of her was given to Captain of the 2nd
rank Golovnin, an officer well known for his voyage in
the sloop Diana and his sojourn in Japan.

Leaving Kronshtadt on August 26, 1817, the sloop
Kamchatka reached the Kattegat on September 5 and,
crossing the North Sea with a fresh following wind,
dropped anchor in Portsmouth roadstead on the 10th.   In
Portsmouth, Captain Golovnin's instructions were to
water, take on rum and varied stores, also to purchase
astronomical instruments, books, and charts. Having
purchased all these objects, he put to sea again on
September 21, and met the open ocean the next day.

A northerly wind brought him to the Canary Islands
in twelve days. Not wishing to lose the fair weather,
Captain Golovnin did not call at Teneriffe, proceeding
instead directly to Brazil. On October 5 he passed the
island of Ferro. He was accompanied by a fresh northerly
wind which turned into a regular trade wind, and followed
him until October 13.

The Kamchatka remained no more than five days in the
calm zone. Winds remained changeable and conditions
fair, and on the 23rd, in long. 29° 30'W, she crossed the
Equator. On November 1, in lat. 20° 28'S, the SE trade
wind yielded to a northerly coastal wind, with which, on
November 5, the sloop came down to Rio de Janeiro.

Captain Golovnin remained here until November 22 to
take on various stores and see to various pieces of work.
He then laid a course for Cape Horn. On December 1, the
NE winds left him, and variable winds blew until the 19th.
At this juncture, the sloop was in sight of Staten Land
(Cape San Juan). Throughout the passage from Rio de
Janeiro, a constant northward-flowing current was observed.
South of 40°S, its speed was 30 miles per 24 hours, even
more.

Rounding Cape Horn, from December 20, 1817 to January 17, 1818, the sloop often struggled against storms, in damp weather. Starting on December 26 and in lat. 58° 30'S, she moved northward, and on January 5 (in lat. 33° 30'S and long. 74° 30'W) she met with a coastal wind from the SE, with which, on February 8, she came to Callao.

Having transmitted despatches from the Spanish envoy at Rio de Janeiro to the Spanish viceroy of Peru, and taken on fresh stores, Captain Golvonin put out to sea again on February 18. Leaving the shores of South America, he proposed to sail with the trade wind as far as the Galapagos Islands and then to bear north at such a rate as to cross the Equator some three degrees to their west. He would then, following the 13th parallel as far as long. 165°E, have made straight for Kamchatka. Meeting indications of the equatorial calms in lat. 5°S, long. 90°W, however, he was obliged to revise this plan, and he sailed to the 8th parallel of southern latitude, along which he proceeded right to the Marquesas Islands.

On March 3, Captain Golovnin intersected the route taken by Laperouse (in lat. 7° 40'S, long. 110° 54' 58"W), and found himself near the spot where Captain Portlock had believed that he saw land. However, the horizon was perfectly clear, and neither land nor even signs of it were seen. On the 7th, indeed, a flock of land birds was sighted from the sloop. They were flying to the south. The same thing occurred on the following day (in lat. 8° 19'S, long. 120° 30' to 124°W). But poor conditions made it impossible to see far.

On the 13th, passing within sight of Eiao, one of the Marquesas Islands, Captain Golovnin took the opportunity to check his chronometers. Having passed through the Marquesas group, he turned north and soon entered the zone of the NE trade wind. On March 17 (lat. 21° 30'N, long. 146°W), it was observed that the current, flowing westward, was extremely strong - some 30 miles per 24 hours. The sloop crossed the Equator for the second time on the 20th, after a little less than five months in the southern hemisphere.

But the NE trade wind blew very erratically, becoming settled only on the 25th, in lat. 6° 30'N, long. 152°W. On March 28 and from the 13th parallel of northern latitude, Captain Golovnin turned to the west in order, having once reached long. 175°E, to make straight for Kamchatka. On April 4 (lat. 16° 56'N, long. 185° 27'W), he passed close to the spot where Wake Reef is indicated on charts, but did not see it; on the 6th, he passed beyond the limits of the NE trade wind (in lat. 20° 30'N), at the end of a most successful passage through the tropical zone. The highest temperature had been in excess of 26° Reaumur, on March 15.

37

Pressing on northward, the sloop crossed the Tropic
of Cancer on April 8 in long. 192° 30'W. Shortly thereafter, she encountered a tremendous storm (on the 12th),
during the course of which a roller struck her stern and
smashed a boat. From this time until the end of April,
the voyage proceeded under variable winds and weather.
On the 29th, the shores of Kamchatka were seen: poor
visibility detained the sloop in their vicinity for some
days. But at length, on May 3, the Kamchatka entered
Petropavlovsk harbor after a voyage from Russia lasting
eight months with no more than 34 days at anchor.

Among the hydrographic tasks entrusted to Captain
Golovnin was the surveying of the Northwest Coast of
America between 60° and 65°N. He was to survey this
coast, however, only if it had not already been charted
by Lt. Kotzebue in the brig Riurik. From information received at Petropavlovsk, it appeared that Lt. Kotzebue
had already made all necessary preparations for the survey.
However, the survey of that coast was actually undertaken
much later. As we saw above, illness did not allow Lt.
Kotzebue to continue his work in the Bering Sea. Captain
Golovnin therefore addressed himself to other points in
his instructions, specifically, to the determining of
the positions of the Aleutian Islands which had not been
fixed with proper precision, and to the inspection of the
colonial settlements.

Once all the goods brought for Kamchatka and Okhotsk
had been unloaded, Captain Golovnin set out for Bering
and Mednyi Islands. He determined the positions of both
these, then proceeded along the Aleutian chain attempting
to stay inside the routes of former mariners. Though
mists and cloud seldom allowed of any observation on the
passage, still certain points were fixed astronomically.
On July 9, the sloop Kamchatka entered St. Paul harbor on
the island of Kadiak. The nine days spent there were
sufficient for the Company establishments all to be inspected while, meantime, the sloop's officers drew up a
chart of Chiniatsk Bay. From Kadiak, Captain Golovnin
went on to Novo-Arkhangel'sk, arriving on July 28 after a
passage completed amidst almost unbroken mists.

Articles destined for this place and belonging to the
Company (in weight some 2,800 puds) were unloaded. That
done, Captain Golovnin set sail for Monterey on August 19
for a meeting with the governor of the colonies, Captain
Hagemeister, who was there purchasing grain. The sloop
met two great storms on this passage, which lasted till
September 6. From Monterey, Captain Golovnin put in at
Bodega (Rumiantsev) Bay, and thence, on the 27th, began
his return voyage to Russia, intending to take on
necessary provisions in the Sandwich Islands.

On his voyage to this archipelago, Captain Golovnin
intended to sail first southward, to lat. 30°N, long. 135°W,
and then along that parallel of latitude to the west, in

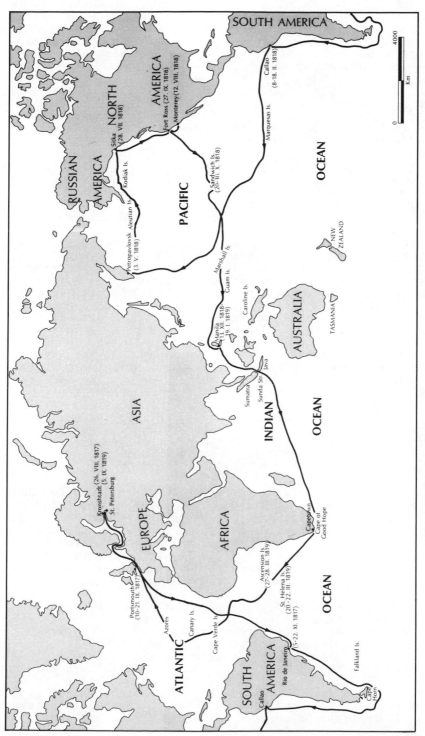

VOYAGE OF GOLOVNIN ON THE "KAMCHATKA" (1817-1819)

order to examine a position where two islands were supposed
to lie and where, as he knew, Lieutenant Podushkin, commander
of one of the Company's vessels, had earlier observed some
signs of land - though Laperouse, who had also passed near
the spot, had detected none.

Till October 7, the sloop proceeded with moderate
following winds. That day found her in lat. 28° 55'N and
long. 135°W: she should therefore have been near the
supposed land. However, there were no indications of
land, nor any shores to be seen.

Strong westerlies did not allow Captain Golovnin to
sail further west along that parallel, and he judged it
necessary to move south as far as the limit of the NE
trade winds which he encountered on October 11 in lat. 25°N.
From there, he set a course for Hawaii, and on the 20th
dropped anchor in Kealakekua Bay, having met nothing
remarkable on the way save an enormous swell from the NW
which had accompanied Kamchatka almost all the way from
the shores of California. Vancouver had noted the same
swell, when sailing from the shores of America to the
Sandwich Islands. Captain Golovnin remained in this bay
until October 25. He then called at Maui, Oahu, and Kauai
and, having purchased sufficient provisions, set off on
his voyage on October 30. With the aid of a fresh trade
wind, by November 4 he was in lat. 13° 30'N and long. 172°W,
whence he laid a course for the Marianas. On the 22nd,
he dropped anchor in Umatac Bay, Guam. Here too he took
on a sufficiency of supplies, putting to sea on the 25th.
The very next day, however, he nearly fell a victim to
fire, thanks to the lack of caution of one of his officers.
On December 5 he entered the China Sea. One week later
he dropped anchor in Manila Roads where he intended to
carry out certain repairs to the sloop and to prepare for
the voyage across the China Sea and to the Cape of Good
Hope.

By January 4, 1819, the sloop had been recaulked and
reladen, and her holds had been dried out. Over the next
two weeks she watered and provisioned. Captain Golovnin
put to sea on January 17, setting a course for the island
of Pulo-Sopato. On the 26th he crossed the Equator for
the third time, and on the 31st, by way of the Gaspar
Strait, he reached the Sunda Strait and entered the Indian
Ocean. He had been but 13 days crossing the China Sea.

The SW trade wind that crosses the Indian Ocean was
met on February 3, in lat. 11° 30'S, long. 256° 30'W.
However, it assumed its proper guise only on February 5,
and began to blow strongly from S by E. On the 11th, in
lat. 18° 50'S, long. 278° 56'W, a floating tree was
spotted from the sloop. Its branches and its bark were
fresh. The nearest land to windward was Australia, or
Amsterdam and St. Paul Islands. These places, however,
were very far off, and Captain Golovnin therefore believed
that there might be an unknown island not so far away.

On March 2, the sloop crossed the meridian of St.
Petersburg in lat. 34° 30'S. Soon afterwards (from the
5th to the 7th) she encountered a mighty westerly storm.
The Cape of Good Hope was passed on the 10th, and shortly
thereafter the Kamchatka called at St. James on the island
of St. Helena, to water and provision.

Finding only water on St. Helena, and finding himself
hampered by the extreme caution of the English guarding
Napoleon, Captain Golovnin trusted that he would manage
to find provisions on the island of Ascension. Here too
however he was disappointed and he continued towards the
Equator, which he planned to cross between 22° and 25°W.
But light variable winds and calms, beginning on March 28,
obliged him to enter the northern hemisphere in long.
18° 20'W.

Having crossed the Equator, Captain Golovnin bore
north as much as he could: he proposed to turn west near
the African coast to meet the NE trade wind as early as
possible. But on April 20, when reckonings indicated that
the sloop was still some considerable distance from the
coast, the water depth showed that she could not be far
from the mouth of the Rio-Grande. Captain Golovnin was
therefore obliged to hold off to the SW, and only a month
later did he enter the zone of the NE trade wind - in
lat. 9° 30'N, long. 17° 30'W.

The trade wind blew close to the meridian, and sometimes changed completely. Nevertheless, the sloop reached
Fayal Roads by June 9 after a passage from Ascension of
only 74 days. The average distance covered per diem had
thus been slightly under 40 miles.

Difficulties in obtaining fresh water and the slowness
with which fresh victuals were furnished him delayed
Captain Golovnin in Fayal until June 26. Proceeding thence
with variable winds, he entered the English Channel three
weeks later, dropping anchor in Portsmouth Roads on July
20. A few days later, there arrived at Portsmouth from
Kronshtadt four naval sloops, commanded by Captains
Bellingshausen, Lazarev, Vasil'ev, and Shishmarev. They
were bound for discovery in polar waters in both hemispheres.

Captain Golovnin finished his business in London and
put to sea once more on August 16. As far as the Kattegat
he had a following wind. Between Elsinore and Copenhagen,
however, he was detained about a week by contrary winds.
At last, on September 5, he reached Kronshtadt Roads. He
had suffered no serious damage during the course of a
two-year voyage, nor even lost any significant parts of his
spars or rigging.

An account of the voyage of the sloop Kamchatka may
be found in: The Voyage Round the World Completed, on
His Imperial Majesty's Instructions, by the Naval Sloop

41

Kamchatka, in the Years 1817, 1818, and 1819: St. P.,
1822. Part Two contains observations relating strictly
to navigation.

10

The Naval Sloops Vostok and Mirnyi
(Bellingshausen and M. P. Lazarev)
1819-21

A Sovereign command was promulgated in March 1819 to
the effect that two expeditions would be fitted out to
explore the polar waters of both hemispheres. The first
division, under the command of Captain Bellingshausen,
consisted of two sloops, the Vostok and the Mirnyi.
Lieutenant M. P. Lazarev was given the Mirnyi. This
division was bound on discovery in the Southern Polar
Sea. The Vostok was 130' in length and 33' in the beam
(the same dimensions as the sloop Kamchatka); the Mirnyi
was 120' long, 30' in the beam. Both vessels were
pine-built by the St. Petersburg shipwrights Stoke and
Kolodnin.

The second division, commanded by Captain-Lieutenant
Vasil'ev, similarly consisted of two sloops - the
Otkrytie and the Blagonamerennyi. Captain of the latter
was Lt. Shishmarev. The division was to investigate to
the north and north-east of Bering Strait.

Both expeditions were equipped for two years. Their
commanders had detailed instructions, relating both to
their maritime and to their scientific duties, from the
Naval Minister, the Admiralty and the State Admiralty
Department. According to these instructions, Captain
Bellingshausen was to commence his investigations with an
examination of South Georgia and the South Sandwich
Islands, then to penetrate as far south as proved possible.
The winter months he was to pass in searches through the
equatorial zone of the South Pacific Ocean.

Captain Bellingshausen left Kronshtadt on July 4,
1819. He was followed out by Captain Vasil'ev's
division. After four days at Copenhagen waiting for the
naturalists Mertens and Kunz, and learning that both had
declined to participate in the voyage, Captain Bellingshausen sailed. After a call at Portsmouth to purchase
instruments, maps, books, etc., he proceeded to Teneriffe
(September 15), where the sloops watered. On the 22nd
the sloops traversed the Tropic of Cancer to meet light
winds and calms. On October 8, in lat. 4° 52' 30"N and
long. 20° 30'W, they passed the place where a bank was
indicated on Purdy's chart, the bank having been discovered by the French in 1796. However, no bottom was
found at 90 sazhen. On that basis, and that of the water

42

color, Captain Bellingshausen concluded that the bank did not exist or was wrongly shown on the chart.

After nearly two weeks in the zone of calms, the sloops at last met with the SE trade wind, in 3°N, and on October 18 they entered the southern hemisphere (long. 22° 19'W). Thence they made for Cabo Frio reaching Rio de Janeiro on November 2.

Here, Captain Bellingshausen readied for the difficult voyage in the polar seas, and to South Georgia Island. On December 8, being in lat. 45°S, long. 43°W, he searched for the Grande Ile which Laroche had supposedly seen about that parallel of latitude, but he did not find it. On the other hand, however, flocks of birds and floating weeds were spotted for several days together.

On the 15th and 16th, Captain Bellingshausen passed to the south of South Georgia Island, and determined the positions of nearby Wallis and Annenkov Islands. The former lay in lat. 54° 4'S, long. 38° 22'W, the latter - named after the Mirnyi's Second Lieutenant - in lat. 54° 31'S, long. 37° 13'W. On the 20th he spotted ice for the first time, in lat. 56° 13'S and long. 32° 30'W. Two days later, as he approached the northern extremity of the South Sandwich Islands, he discovered a new group - the Marquis de Traversay Islands. Proceeding south through the Sandwich archipelago, by January 4, 1820, he had reached lat. 60° 25'S in long. 27° 58'W. Here ice obliged him to turn east. Continuing east among icebergs in the hope of finding a passage leading south, on January 18 (lat. 69° 21'S, long. 2° 15'W) he sighted solid and immobile ice-fields stretching away from east through south to west. Moving yet further east, to long. 1° 15'W, the sloops encountered a contrary wind. In view of this and of the floating icebergs, there was no further possibility of proceeding, so Captain Bellingshausen found himself obliged to turn north in order, having met with westerly winds, to make another attempt to go south.[1]

On February 2, Captain Bellingshausen did indeed turn south again, and the following day crossed over the Antarctic Circle for the third time. Neither in this longitude, however, was he able to penetrate further south than lat. 69° 6'S (in long. 15° 52'E). The frost increased to 4° on the Reaumur scale.

Turning north-east once more, they soon observed land birds which led them to suppose that land was near (lat. 68°S, long. 16° 30'W). By February 12 a westerly wind had sprung up, and they proceeded to the spot where, in January 1773, Captain Cook had been halted by ice (lat. 67° 15'S, long. 30° 35'E). The next day, in

---

[1] The Mirnyi was in great peril on this passage, having struck a submerged iceberg at night. However, she suffered no harm.

lat. 66° 50'S, long. 38°E, land birds were again spotted.
Since the closest known lands (Prince Edward Island and
Kerguelen Island) were not less than 1,200 miles off,
Captain Bellingshausen confidently concluded that some
other land must exist nearby, though icebergs prevented
his proving to himself the truth of the supposition.
(In 1831, Captain Biscoe discovered the posited land and
called it Enderby Land.)

Captain Bellingshausen observed that the position of
the solid ice had changed hardly at all since Cook's time,
and then turned north once more. On the 5th, and from
lat. 63°S, long. 42°E, he again bore east. On the 24th,
being 800 miles from the nearest known piece of land -
Kerguelen Island (lat. 62° 30'S, long. 57° 41'E) - he
again sighted land birds.

Passing by a number of ice islands, some extremely
high (as much as 350'), and having encountered a severe
storm, by March 8 the sloops had reached long. 89°E, in
lat. 59°S. From this position, Captain Bellingshausen
laid a course for Port Jackson 5° north of that taken by
Cook. Meanwhile the sloop Mirnyi followed a course to
Port Jackson 3° south of Captain Furneaux's. In this
as yet unexplored stretch of ocean, Captain Bellingshausen
believed that new discoveries might be made and, moreover,
he intended to seek the Company Island shown on Arrowsmith's charts as lying in lat. 49° 30'S, and long. 143°
4'E.

There followed a three-day storm (March 8-11) during
which the sloop lost all headway and was very nearly cast
onto an iceberg. Captain Bellingshausen passed beyond
the ice-limit in lat. 57° 30'S, and on the 22nd passed
over the supposed location of Company Island without
seeing it. He reached Port Jackson on March 30, after a
131-day voyage from Rio de Janeiro. The sloop Mirnyi
also reached Port Jackson, on April 7, after a vain
search for Company Island. However, land birds had been
spotted from the Mirnyi in lat. 54° 44'S and long. 115°
7'E, and the birds had reappeared on March 23 in latitude
49° 30'S, long. 142° 47'E, i.e., near the supposed location
of Company Island.

Captain Bellingshausen fortified the crews of his
sloop with rest and replenished his stores of fresh provisions, while in Port Jackson. He then put out to sea,
meaning to proceed to the tropics north of New Zealand
and by way of the island of Oparo, discovered by
Vancouver. From there, he planned to cross the Dangerous
(Tuamotu) Archipelago, in which he proposed to make care-
ful investigations. To such an extent, however, did constant northerly winds drive the sloops to the south, that
Captain Bellingshausen was forced into Cook Strait. On
May 28 he paused for a few days in Queen Charlotte Sound.
Going out into the ocean, on June 5, he encountered a
great storm with snow and hail. Proceeding in accordance

with the former plan, the sloops came up to Oparo on June
28 and determined its position: lat. 27° 37'S, long. 215°
45'E. A strong easterly wind did not allow them to
approach the shore closer than four miles. Nonetheless,
islanders came out to the sloop in several native craft.
They could furnish no supplies, unfortunately, but a few
roots. From here, Captain Bellingshausen laid a course
to the Dangerous (i.e., Tuamotu-GB) Archipelago and, over
a two-week period beginning on July 5, discovered or
examined the following groups of coral islands:

Name of Group	Latitude S	Longitude E
Moller (Amanu)	17° 49'	219° 20'
Arakcheev (Angatau)	15° 51'	119° 10'
Volkonskii (Takume)	15° 47'	217° 49'
Barclay de Tolly (Raroia)	15° 5'	217° 41'
Nihiru	16° 42'	217° 15'
Ermolov (Taenga)	16° 21'	216° 54'
Kutuzov (Makemo)	16° 36'	216° 35'
(Northeastern part)		
Raevskii	16° 43'	215° 49'
Osten-Saken (Katiu)	16° 28'	215° 42'
Chichagov (Tahanea)	16° 50'	215° 7'
Miloradovich (Faaite)	16° 47'	214° 47'
Wittgenstein (Fakarava)	16° 20'	214° 27'
Elizaveta	15° 56'	214° 4'
(2nd Palliser)		
Greig (Niau)	16° 11'	213° 44'
Third Palliser	15° 45'	213° 22'

All these groups together, from the Arakcheev to the Kruzenshtern Islands, are known as the Russian Islands (Ostrova
Rossiian).

On July 22, the sloops dropped anchor in Matavai Bay,
Tahiti, to water and to check chronometers. On July 27,
Captain Bellingshausen put out to sea again, and proceeding
northward, passed by Makatea Island; on the 30th he
examined Kruzenshtern (Tikahau) Island, determining the
position of its center as lat. 15° 00'S, long. 211° 52'E.
And he discovered Lazarev (Matahiva) Island (lat. 14° 56'
20"S, long. 211° 21'E), adding it to the Russian Group.
Next proceeding further north, to the tenth parallel of
southern latitude, and along that line to the west, he
decided to seek the Groeningen (Upolu) and Thienhoven
(Tutuila) Islands spotted by Roggeveen (in long. 156° to
159°W).

On August 3, in lat. 10° 5'S, long. 207° 43'E, Captain
Bellingshausen discovered little Vostok Island, and three
days later - another, inhabited, island, which he named
Grand Duke Alexander Island (lat. 10° 2' 25"S, long. 198°
57'E). Passing through the spot where Thienhoven Island

was shown on the Arrowsmith chart, he headed for Port Jackson.

On their way thither, the sloops passed (August 11) the islands of the Vava'u group which were reckoned to lie in lat. 18° 43'S and long. 186° 4'E, and Late Island (lat. 18° 26'S, long. 185° 26'E). According to reckonings made from the sloop Vostok, the latter was 1,320' high and some five miles in circumference.

Continuing between the routes of Cook and of Laperouse, Captain Bellingshausen then discovered yet two more small coral islands: Mikhailov Island (Tuvana-i-Tholo, lat. 21° 1'S, long. 181° 19'E) and Simonov Island (Tuvana-i-Ra, lat. 21° 2'S, long. 181° 13'E). Then, on August 20, he found the inhabited chain of hilly islands called Ono (Ono-i-Lau), in lat. 20° 39'S, long. 181° 20'E. The chain was about seven miles long. Near here, the sloops almost met destruction on a reef, the position of which was reckoned at lat. 20° 45'S, long. 181° 10'E. The bar had a circumference of as much as ten miles, and was named "Beregis'" ('Beware'). On September 5, the sloops came in sight of Lord Howe Island. After a severe storm, they dropped anchor in Port Jackson on the 9th.

While in port this time, the sloops were quickly dismasted. The process was necessary in view of the fact that the spars had sustained damage in various places. Having put the spars to rights and readied the sloops for a new voyage beyond the polar circle, which took 50 days, Captain Bellingshausen put to sea on October 31.

On November 17, they passed by Macquarie Island, where they remained until the 20th. The position of its centre was reckoned to be: lat. 53° 38' 40"S, long. 158° 40' 50"E.

On November 28, in lat. 62° 18'S and long. 164° 13'E, icebergs made their first appearance, 3° further south than the previous year. There was much floating ice amongst the bergs. Over the following five days, the sloops proceeded some 380 miles east around the fringes of icefields. Towards evening on December 2, and having observed signs of a storm, Captain Bellingshausen thought it best to go north and out of the icebergs. His caution saved the vessels from certain ruin; for on the 3rd and 4th, a wild storm blew, with snow. So bad was visibility that nothing could be seen at 25 sazhen. To steer was impossible. Thick snow and seaspray stuck to the rigging and sails and, freezing to 3° Reaumur, formed a 2"-thick ice-crust over everything. The winds eased on the 4th. The sloops then found themselves in lat. 62° 20'S, long. 178° 47'W. On the 13th, they crossed the polar circle for the fourth time, in long. 164° 34'W. The next day, and from lat. 67° 15'S, long. 161° 27'W, Captain Bellingshausen was obliged to sail north: for solid ice prevented

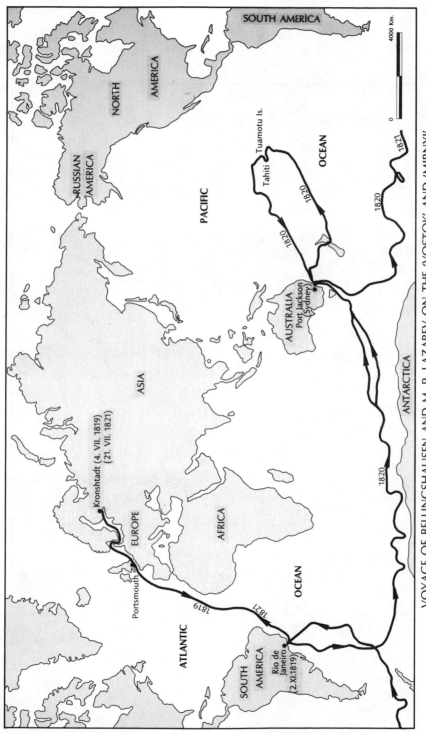

VOYAGE OF BELLINGSHAUSEN AND M. P. LAZAREV ON THE 'VOSTOK' AND 'MIRNYI'

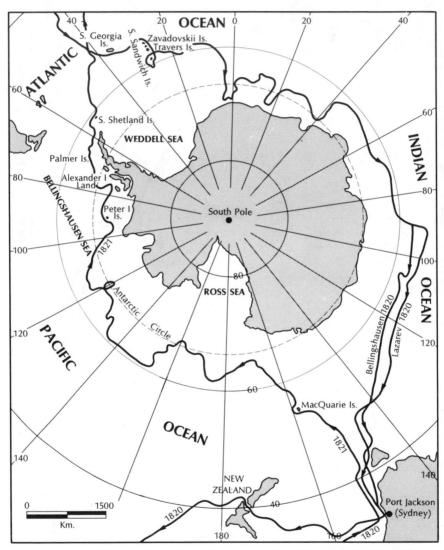

VOYAGE OF BELLINGSHAUSEN AND LAZAREV AROUND ANTARCTICA
1820-1821

his proceeding further to the south. Keeping to the fringe of the ice, first in an easterly, then a south-easterly direction, he succeeded in crossing the polar circle yet again in long. 119° 48'W: but in that region, the ice once more forced him northwards.

Again turning east, in damp and cloudy conditions, Captain Bellingshausen reached lat. 69° 48'S on January 7, 1821. On January 10, a coast appeared to the east; but ice prevented an approach of less than 14 miles. This newly discovered land, which seemed to be an island, was perhaps 9 1/2 miles long, and was named after the founder of the Russian Navy, Emperor Peter 1. Except for the capes, which showed dark from afar, the entire island was snow-covered. It reached a height above sea-level of some 4,200'. Its latitude - 68° 57'S, and its longitude - 90° 46'W (compass var. 36° 6'E).

Proceeding on their way east, the sloops attained a latitude of 69° 10'S and a longitude of 77° 43'W by noon on January 16, when an unusual change in the water color was observed (no bottom at 145 sazhen), as well as a few land birds. Sure enough, a shore was spotted the following morning. At its northern end stood a high hill (lat. 68° 45'S, long. 73° 10'W). The new land was named Emperor Alexander 1 Land. Its southern extremity lay beyond the horizon.

From here, Captain Bellingshausen laid a course to the South Shetlands, and intersected that archipelago in its south, from SW to NE, determining the positions of all capes and islands encountered on the way. It appeared that, in its entirety, the chain stretched 160 miles along a WSW-ENE axis.

Having examined and fixed the positions of a few more islands lying on that same course and in clusters, Captain Bellingshausen decided to conclude his exploration of those polar waters. He was induced to do so both by the poor condition of the sloop and by the approach of winter, with its attendant storms. On February 5, therefore, he bore north, intending to take on fresh provisions at Rio de Janeiro. On his way to that port, he again searched for Grande Ile, unsuccessfully as before. Proceeding between the routes once taken by Cook and Laperouse, he reached the aforementioned place towards the end of February.

On his voyage back to Russia, Captain Bellingshausen called at Lisbon to put ashore our Envoy, recalled from Brazil. Putting out from the River Tagus on July 28, both sloops returned to Kronshtadt Roads one month later. They had been absent 751 days.

This voyage is described in: Two Investigations in the South Polar Sea and a Voyage Round the World, During the Course of 1819-1821, Completed in the Sloops Vostok and Mirnyi by Captain Bellingshausen: St. P., 1831: 397 & 326 pp.

11

The Sloops Otkrytie and Blagonamerennyi

(Vasil'ev and Shishmarev)

1819-22

The expedition under Captain Vasil'ev was dispatched to explore the Arctic Ocean and, especially, to seek out a passage to the Atlantic Ocean from Bering Strait.

The sloops Otkrytie and Blagonamerennyi, placed under Captains Vasil'ev and Shishmarev and under the overall command of the former, were provisioned just as were the vessels comprising the southern division and destined for the South Polar Sea. The greater part of the provisions for both sloops were placed aboard the Blagonamerennyi. Also placed aboard her were the parts of a dismantled boat, to be employed in the surveying of shallow coastal waters.

Captain Vasil'ev's division sailed from Kronshtadt on July 3, 1819. Proceeding in company with the Vostok and Mirnyi, it called at Copenhagen and at Portsmouth, whence Captain Vasil'ev sailed on August 30. Ten days later he passed the latitude of Gibraltar and on September 20, a little to the north of the Tropic of Cancer, met with the NE trade wind, which at times veered to ESE and generally blew erratically. After nearly two weeks in the zone of tropical calms, he pressed on towards the coast of Brazil, first with the SE trade wind and later with a NE coastal wind. He anchored at Rio de Janeiro on November 1. Captain Bellingshausen's division arrived the very next day.

Captain Vasil'ev continued his voyage after three weeks, steering for the Cape of Good Hope. Taking advantage of strong westerly winds, he passed under that cape on December 24, at a distance of 12 miles. From there, his sloops proceeded, with the same W and NW winds, to Port Jackson, where they arrived in mid-February 1820.

Having refreshed his crew and taken on fresh stores of victuals and water, he sailed in mid-March and on April 23, crossed the Equator in long. $172^{\circ}E$. On this passage, the Blagonamerennyi came upon a group of 16 wooded and inhabited islands, which were given the name of that vessel and were reckoned to lie in lat. 8° 7'S and long. 178° 17'E.[1]

On May 13, then being in lat. 29°N and long. 162°E, Captain Vasil'ev sent the Blagonamerennyi to the island of Unalashka, there to find interpreters for use among the northern American peoples. Kotzebue Sound was designated as the rendezvous. On June 4, Captain Vasil'ev reached Petropavlovsk harbor. Captain Shishmarev had reached Unalashka on the 3rd.

At the end of June, Captain Vasil'ev left Petropavlovsk. On July 14 he passed through Bering Strait in sight of the American coast, reaching Kotzebue Sound on the 16th and rejoining the Blagonamerennyi, which had arrived five days previously. Not finding interpreters on Unalashka, Captain Shishmarev had four baidaras with their crews taken on board. On his way to Kotzebue Sound, he had passed over the spot where the chart showed Ratmanov Island (discovered by Captain Kotzebue on his first voyage). However, he had not seen that island even though he continued as far as the easternmost cape of Asia.

On July 18, Captain Vasil'ev put to sea with both sloops. Following the American coast northward, by the 29th he reached lat. 71° 6'N in long. 166° 8'W - and met ice. Though he did not consider the ice to be solid, nevertheless, not having a longboat or other small craft from which the shallow coastal waters might have been explored, and being pressed in by the mists, he resolved to go back.

On July 31 he headed south. Coming to St. Lawrence Island, he entrusted to Captain Shishmarev a definitive surveying of its coasts, and himself went on to the shore of America, whence however he withdrew in view of the shallowness of the sea. On August 19 he arrived at Unalashka, having examined St. Paul and St. George Islands on the way. Three days later, the Blagonamerennyi also reached Unalashka.

And with this, the first essay at a cruise in the Arctic Ocean ended. Convinced of the need to have with him a small sailing craft, Captain Vasil'ev set out for Novo-Arkhangel'sk, which he judged the most convenient place to assemble a boat from the parts in the Blagonamerennyi and where, besides, he hoped to find interpreters for employment among the natives of the Arctic shores of America. Both sloops reached Sitkha in mid-September.

---

[1] Later it appeared that this group was the same as the "Peieter Islands" discovered not long before. See Admiral Kruzenshtern, Atlas of the South Sea.

Captain Vasil'ev here entrusted Lt. Ignat'ev with
the building of the boat. He himself, on October 27,
proceeded with the division to the port of San Francisco.
Here he wintered, putting out to sea again in mid-
February 1821 to provision in the Sandwich Islands. On
his voyage to that archipelago, Captain Vasil'ev vainly
sought the Maria Laxara Islands shown on Arrowsmith's
charts, as had many other officers.

Remaining at Honolulu harbor from March 25 until
April 7, both sloops then proceeded to Novo-Arkhangel'sk.
Arriving about the middle of May, they found the boat
ready[1] and interpreters on hand. On the 30th of that
month, and taking the newly constructed boat along,
Captain Vasil'ev put out to sea.

On June 12 the sloops reached Unalashka island.
Among other things, the fact emerged on this passage that
the boat could not keep up with them. The Otkrytie was
therefore obliged to take her in tow.

Given the shortness of the time that remained for
a voyage in the Arctic Ocean, Captain Vasil'ev thought
it best to separate the Blagonamerennyi and to entrust
Captain Shishmarev with the investigation of the Asian
coast north of Bering Strait and the search for a passage
thence to the Atlantic. In the event of failure,
Captain Shishmarev would describe Chukotka. He himself
wished to describe the shore between Bristol Bay and
Norton Sound, then to proceed north along the American
coast, seeking a northern passage from that side. The
boat remained with him.

On June 26 the division left Unalashka, and the two
sloops set off on their respective missions.

Once more determining the positions of St. Paul and
St. George Islands (the Pribylovs-GB), Captain Vasil'ev
instructed Lt. Avinov, commanding the boat, to chart
the coast between Capes Newenham and Derbi (Denbigh),
then to rejoin him (by July 20) at Stewart Island in
Norton Sound. If he did not find the sloop, or if his
work had not been completed by that date, he should
proceed directly to Petropavlovsk harbor. Captain
Vasil'ev himself took his sloop into Norton Sound. On
his way there, on July 21, he discovered Nunivak Island,
which, however, he had no time to survey since he was
hastening up to the Arctic Ocean. Pressing northward,
he stopped by Cape Derbi (Denbigh), but continued, not
finding the boat there. On the 31st he sighted Cape
Lisburne.

---

[1] Its dimensions are not given, but from the log it is
evident that it drew about 4' of water, so it was probably
not more than 45' in length.

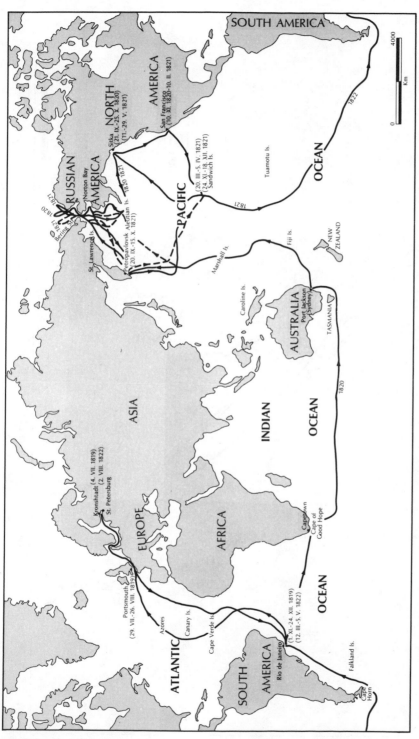

VOYAGE OF VASIL'EV AND SHISHMAREV ON THE "OTKRYTIE" AND "BLAGONAMERENNYI" (1819–1822)

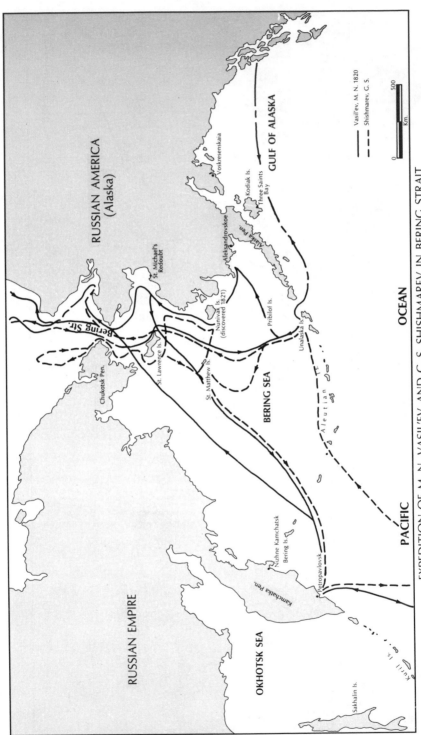

EXPEDITION OF M. N. VASIL'EV AND G. S. SHISHMAREV IN BERING STRAIT

RUSSIAN AMERICA
(Alaska)

RUSSIAN EMPIRE

GULF OF ALASKA

Voskresenskaia

Kodiak Is.
Three Saints
Bay

Aleksandrovskoe

Alaska Pen.

St. Michael's
Redoubt

Nunivak Is.
(discovered 1821)

Pribilof Is.

Bering Str.

Unalaska Is.

Chukotsk Pen.

St. Lawrence Is.

St. Matthew Is.

BERING SEA

Aleutian Is.

PACIFIC

OCEAN

Nizhne Kamchatsk

Bering Is.

Kamchatka Pen.

Petropavlovsk

OKHOTSK SEA

Sakhalin Is.

Kuril Is.

————— Vasil'ev, M. N. 1820
– – – – Shishmarev, G. S.

0   500
Km.

Continuing along the coast, with mists and variable
winds, by August 3 he reached lat. 70° 40'N, long. 161°
27'W. Here he again met solid ice, extending from the
west through north to the northeast. Wishing to examine
an icy cape, he bore to, and on August 4 fixed its
position: lat. 70° 33'N. The sloop then survived a
great storm, during which the surrounding ice all but
crushed her. Captain Vasil'ev turned south, leaving the
Arctic Ocean on the 9th and passing Cape Lisburne.

From here, he once more sailed to Cape Denbigh and
Stewart Island, where the natives informed him they had
seen no craft whatever and so on to Kamchatka. He
reached Petropavlovsk harbor on September 8. There he
found Lt. Avinov's boat. The lieutenant had, in the
allotted time, surveyed part of the coast north from
Cape Newenham, but had been obliged to break off his
work before completion because scurvy had made an
appearance among his people. Besides this, the boat
itself had proved to have poor qualities.

Captain Shishmarev, meanwhile, proceeding north
from Unalashka, had on June 4 and in lat. 62° 32'N,
long. 193° 11'E, sighted an unknown shore which, however,
shallow water had prevented him from carefully examining.
(It subsequently transpired that this had been Cape
Rumiantsev, lying to the south of the entry into Norton
Sound.) Having described the northern coast of St.
Lawrence Island, Captain Shishmarev had then entered
the gulf of that name on the (Asian) mainland and had
continued along the Asian coast. Often encountering icebergs and contrary winds, on July 21 he had sailed down
to the American coast, dropping anchor off Cape Mulgrave
in lat. 67° 34'N. Here he gathered firewood from drift,
and the very next day set out once again for the coasts
of Asia; but again ice hindered him and forced him to
the north. On August 1 the sloop was in lat. 70° 13'N.
On the 4th, Cape Serdtse Kamen' was sighted. Meeting
continual obstacles in the forms of ice, storms, and
contrary winds, Captain Shishmarev decided to proceed
into Mechigmenskii Bay, where he hoped to restore his
people with fresh supplies.

He indeed obtained there all that he needed from the
Chukchi, and in mid-August crossed over to St. Lawrence
Island to complete his survey of its northern shore.
From there he sailed to Kamchatka, reaching Petropavlovsk
harbor on September 21. On his way there, he fixed the
position of St. Matthew Island, discovered by Lieutenant
Sind.

His division complete again, Captain Vasil'ev prepared for the home voyage. He put to sea in mid-October
meaning to round Cape Horn. But three days after their
departure the sloops were separated in a mist. The
Otkrytie went on to Hawaii, the designated rendezvous.

Accompanied by fresh northerly winds as far as 30°N, she reached Honolulu harbor on November 27 and - found the Blagonamerennyi: who had arrived yet three days earlier.

Both sloops left Honolulu on December 20 and crossing through the torrid zone without particular incident, reached lat. 57°S in long. 281°E by mid-February. Here they encountered a four-day SW storm which was attended by snow and gloom. Crossing the Cape Horn meridian on the 18th, they started to bear north and reached Rio de Janeiro in mid-March.

By May 5, all those repairs to spars and hull which are inevitable after a long passage were complete. Fresh stores of victuals and water having been procured, the two sloops sailed. On May 19, they entered the range of the SE trade wind; exactly one month later they passed beyond the limit of the NE trade wind. Early in July the division passed along the English Channel. After a five-day stop at Copenhagen, it reached Kronshtadt on August 2, 1822.

We are indebted to this expedition for the investigation of a significant part of the American coast, namely, from Cape Newenham as far as Norton Sound; of the whole of that extensive sound; and from Cape Lisburne to the Icy Cape.[1] Also investigated was a sector of the Asian coast, up to Cape Serdtse Kamen'. But of course, its most important end - the northern passage - could not be achieved. Some information concerning the surveys made during this expedition are included in V. N. Berkh's Chronological History of All Voyages..., pt. 2, pp. 1-20.

12

The Russian-American Company Vessel Borodino

(Ponafidin)

1819-21

Lieutenant Ponafidin, who on another occasion had already been to Sitkha now found himself commanding a large Company vessel of some 600 tons, the Borodino. Her cargo was mainly comprised of iron, naval stores, and rigging, to a total value of 800,000 paper rubles. He had instructions from the Main Office of the Russian-American Company to call at Rio de Janeiro, there to sell a portion of his cargo, and then to proceed around the Cape of Good Hope to Manila and to Novo-Arkhangel'sk.

---

[1] Remarkably, Captain Vasil'ev's survey of the coast between these two capes is in perfect accord with that made by Captain Beechey, from the Blossom.

Sailing from Kronshtadt on September 29, 1819, Lt. Ponafidin first called at Copenhagen and Elsinore, leaving the latter port on October 16. Passing through the English Channel, he headed for Rio de Janeiro. Continuing under a helpful NW wind, he crossed the Equator in long. 25ºW and, entering the southern hemisphere, proceeded with the SE trade wind to lat. 15º 30'S, near which point he met with a moderate coastal wind, which blew from NE - NNW. On December 11 he reached Rio de Janeiro.

Having stood in that roadstead until February 7 of the following year while business transactions were completed and repairs made to the rigging, Lt. Ponafidin then laid a course for the Cape of Good Hope. On February 13, in lat. 29ºS and long. 41ºW, he lost the coastal wind which had hitherto accompanied him; the wind was replaced by variable but mostly south-westerly winds. When the storeroom was examined on March 4 it was found flooded. The ship's biscuit in it had been soaked. This biscuit was cast overboard. A damaged part by the stem was repaired as well as it could be.[1]

Four days after this incident the meridian of Greenwich was passed in lat. 37º 30'S. On the 14th, having rounded the Cape of Good Hope, they entered the Indian Ocean and proceeded until March 27 between latitudes 38º and 39ºS, with fresh westerly winds. They then (in long. 56ºE), set a course for the Sunda Strait. On April 24, by the Equator, they met with a SE trade wind. On May 6 they sighted the coast of the island of Java.

Between May 10 and 22, Lieutenant Ponafidin stood becalmed off the Dutch settlement of Angers (Anzher) (on the southern shore of Java). The calms, mixed with south-westerly winds, accompanied him to Manila itself. The weather was windy and wet. Such climatic conditions, together with the considerable heat, made themselves felt on the crew's health: as many as 20 men were sick on the Borodino's reaching Manila on July 31. Of these, however, most recovered ashore.[2]

Leaving Manila on August 3, Lt. Ponafidin crossed the Equator on the 19th in long. 130ºW, and on the 27th discovered two small islands, which were named, after the ship, the Borodino Islands (lat. 25º 56'N, long. 131º

---

[1] The constant and serious leakage of this vessel is noteworthy: there was seldom less than 20" of water in her hold. Was this perhaps the reason for the high mortality among her crew?

[2] On this passage, they lost their doctor, who was one of the first victims of the disease. A Frenchman, Dr. Plantain, was hired at Manila as his replacement.

15'E). On the 24th, they sighted a small rocky islet
which they at first took for Todos-Santos Island. Later
the significant difference between the islet's latitude
and that of Todos-Santos led them to consider it a new
discovery. In Admiral Kruzenshtern's Atlas of the South
Sea, the islet is given under the name of Ponafidin
Island (lat. 30° 32'N, long. 140° 24'E).[1]

From here, Lt. Ponafidin headed straight for Sitkha
and, proceeding in variable weather and with inconstant
winds, crossed long. 180° in lat. 42°N (September 14).
By October 1 he was already in sight of Mount Edgecumbe,
by the entrance to Sitka Sound; but easterly winds and
poor visibility kept the vessel another ten days within
sight of Sitkha itself. At last, on October 11, the
Borodina entered Sitkha harbor after a 69-day voyage from
Manila. The sick-list on that voyage contained twenty
names; five men died. In Sitkha roadstead, the Borodino
joined the Otkrytie and the Blagonamerennyi.

The transfer of items brought out and the stowing
of a new cargo of peltry prolonged Lt. Ponafidin's stay
at Novo-Arkhangel'sk until the January of 1821. He put
to sea on the 29th of that month, with Lieutenant de
Livron and 21 persons of various ranks as passengers.
Even when he did so, there were 25 sick men on board.

Making for Cape Horn, Lt. Ponafidin entered the
tropics on February 25 in long. 125° 30'W and at once
met with the NE trade wind, which accompanied him to
lat. 5° 30'N. For the twelve next days (March 5-17)
they struggled with the calms, squalls, and rain that
are usual in that zone. The SE trade wind blew fairly
steadily as far as the southern tropic, where it veered
to the east.

Until April 14 the voyagers proceeded (to 40°S) with
a moderate westerly wind and fairly good weather; but
starting on that day there blew westerly storms with
constant damp in the air. These conditions persisted
right to Cape Horn and even into the Atlantic Ocean.
This was the unhappiest part of the voyage: the number
of sick, which had been growing since the first day,
increased to 45 - about half of the crew - and many died.
(According to an eyewitness, Mr. Kashevarov, the disease
had certain of the symptoms of cholera.) Near the
Falkland Islands, which were rounded on the east (May 1),
the wind softened but at the same time blew from the
north, that is against the ship. Only three weeks later
(May 22) did she come to Rio de Janeiro.

---

[1] Lt. Povalishin saw this same island the following year
when on his way to Kamchatka from Manila. Not knowing
of Lt. Ponafidin's discovery, he called it 'St. Peter
Island', having reckoned that it lay in lat. 30° 32'N,
long. 140° 24' 40"E., Atlas of the South Sea, pt. II.

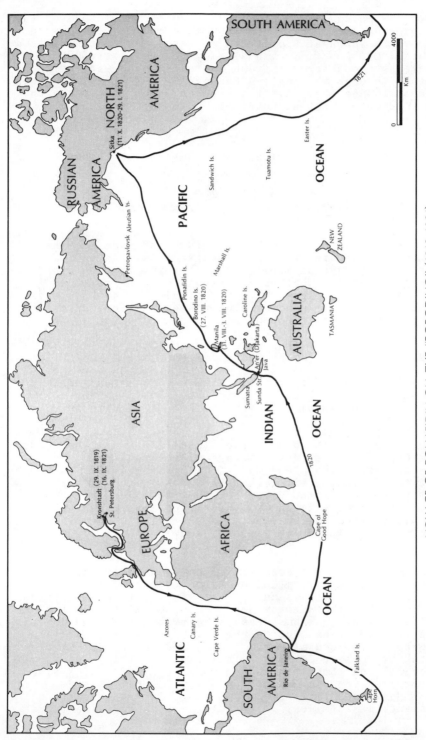

VOYAGE OF PONAFIDIN ON THE "BORODINO" (1819-1821)

SOUTH AMERICA

NORTH AMERICA

RUSSIAN AMERICA

Sitka (11. X. 1820-29. I. 1821)

Petropavlovsk Aleutian Is.

PACIFIC

Ponafidin Is.

Sandwich Is.

Marshall Is.

Tuamotu Is.

Easter Is.

OCEAN

Borodino Is. (27. VIII. 1820)

Manila (31. VIII.-3. VIII. 1820)

Caroline Is.

ASIA

Sumatra

Sunda Str.

Anjer (Djakarta)

Java

NEW ZEALAND

AUSTRALIA

TASMANIA

INDIAN

OCEAN

EUROPE

Kronshtadt (29. IX. 1819)
St. Petersburg (16. IX. 1821)

AFRICA

Cape of Good Hope

1820

OCEAN

ATLANTIC

Azores

Canary Is.

Cape Verde Is.

SOUTH AMERICA

Rio de Janeiro

Falkland Is.

Cape Horn

1821

4000

Km

0

The passage from Rio de Janeiro to Europe proved far
happier; and the crew's health had completely recovered
after a sojourn at Rio of two months. One month out from
Brazil, Lt. Ponafidin had already reached lat. 30°N;
there he encountered a fresh westerly wind, with which he
passed through the English Channel by August 28, and then
the North Sea too. After a five-day stop at Copenhagen,
he reached Kronshtadt Roads on September 16, 1821.

13

The Russian-American Company Vessel Kutuzov

(Dokhturov)

1820-22

Commanded by Lieutenant Dokhturov, the Kutuzov sailed
from Kronshtadt on September 8, 1820 and made for the
Company's colonies with passengers and with a cargo.
After a few days at Reval, Lt. Dokhturov went on his
way (the 16th). Near Pakerort, however, he collided
with a trading brig which tore off all his anchors and
starboard stream-anchors. The vessel was forced to put
in for two weeks at Copenhagen.

Lt. Dokhturov passed through the Zund on October 12
and, crossing the North Sea under moderate W and NW
winds, entered the Atlantic on the 28th. On November 6,
he passed Teneriffe at a distance of 200 miles and laid
a course for the Equator, which he crossed on November
21 (long. 26° 45'W). He reached Rio de Janeiro on
December 6.

Leaving this port at the close of January, he headed
for Cape Horn; taking advantage of a coastal wind, he
reached lat. 37°S, long. 50° 30'W by February 9. Throughout the following six weeks, SW and NW winds blew -
strong as far as the Cape, but soft or moderate beyond
it. On February 24 and 25, near Cape San Juan, a very
significant northward-flowing current was observed
(between 1 1/2 and 3 miles each hour) under a strong SW
wind.

Encountering a coastal southerly wind in lat. 33°S,
they continued north, and on March 30 passed 15 miles
to the west of the island of Massafuero or Juan-Fernandez.
On April 11, the Kutuzov dropped anchor in the port of
Callao. There was business to be transacted, and certain
repairs had to be made on the ship. They proceeded
thence at the end of April and sailed westward. On the
30th they passed Charles Island (lat. 8° 14'S); on May 7
they entered the northern hemisphere, 5 1/2 months since
first crossing the Equator. On May 23 they passed
Nublada Island (lat. 17° 54'N, long. 120° 45'W) at a
distance of 25 miles. A week later they left the tropics

in long. 128° 30'W. The NE wind obliged them to bear
NW as far as lat. 36°N, long. 140°W, whence they headed
for the coast of California.

On June 27, the Kutuzov reached Rumiantsev Bay. She
then went in to Monterey where part of her cargo was sold
and where provisions were bought. She returned to
Rumiantsev Bay towards the end of September. Once those
articles destined for the settlement of Ross had been
discharged, she continued on her way to Sitkha, which
was reached on October 23 - almost one year since her
departure from Kronshtadt.

At the close of January 1822, Lt. Dokhturov set out
on the return voyage to Russia with a cargo of peltry
to the value of some 1,100,000 paper rubles. He again
made for Cape Horn. On February 5, in lat. 46° 30'N and
long. 139° 40'W, the voyagers encountered a storm.
Thereafter, a light westerly wind blew until they met with
the NE trade wind. Crossing the Equator on March 19,
in long. 107° 30'W, they bore SW as far as lat. 26° 30'S
in long. 122°W. On April 2, passing beyond the limit
of the SE trade wind, they turned to the SE, towards
Cape Horn, and were followed by a strong westerly wind
and wet weather. The cape was rounded on May 3. A week
later, the Kutuzov passed the parallel of the Falkland
Islands in long. approx. 48° 30'W, and on the 21st was
already a mere 100 miles from the estuary of the River
La Plata. On June 2 she arrived at Rio de Janeiro.
Here they stayed about a month. On the passage to Russia,
they called at Portsmouth to pick up a [Channel] pilot,
and reached Kronshtadt on October 21.

14

The Russian-American Company Brig Riurik

and Ship Elisaveta

(Klochkov and Kislakovskii)

1821-22

In 1821 the Russian-American Company sent two vessels
to its colonies: the Riurik, 180 tons, under the command
of Navigator (12th class) Klochkov (who was also commander
of both vessels), and the Elisaveta, 220 tons, commanded
by Navigator (14th class) Kislakovskii. The brig Riurik
was the same in which Captain Kotzebue had sailed to
Bering Strait; the Elisaveta had been purchased at
Kronshtadt from the merchant Murash. Half the crews of
these vessels were foreigners on hire. They were to sail
by way of Cape Horn to the Sandwich Islands, whence the
brig Riurik was to proceed to the island of Atkha (in
the Aleutian chain) and so to Novo-Arkhangel'sk. Having
there unloaded her cargo and taken on peltry and a crew
from the Elisaveta, she was to sail back to Kronshtadt

61

by way of the Cape of Good Hope. The Elisaveta herself
was to proceed directly from the Sandwich Islands to
Novo-Arkhangel'sk, and remain in the colonial service.

Both vessels left Kronshtadt on September 13, 1821
and called at Elsinore, having encountered rather strong
contrary winds in the Baltic Sea. Remaining at Elsinore
till October 10 in view of the contrary winds, they left
the Skagerrak only to meet a strong south-westerly wind.
Mr. Klochkov, who had no cause to visit England, elected
to lay a course between the Orkney and the Shetland
Islands. By October 19, passing between those groups,
the two vessels had reached a latitude of 60°N in long.
3° 30'W, and bore south-west. Between October 22 and 26,
they encountered a fierce north-easterly storm, during
which Mr. Klochkov lost sight of the Elisaveta. He
himself proceeded until November 4 and lat. 50°N under
high SW winds; he then met with an even NE and then E
wind which turned into the trade wind. With it, he passed
in sight of the Azores on November 12 (São Miguel and
Santa Maria Islands) and on the 20th crossed the Tropic
of Cancer in long. 22° 7'W. On November 26 he dropped
anchor in Porto-Praia (Santiago Island). The following
day, the Elisaveta also arrived. During the storm of
October 22 her captain reported she had been in great
danger: though carrying only foresail and brails, she
had been laid on her side to such a point that her
leeward side had been in the water - and so she had
remained for an hour and a half, until the foresail was
cut... So unstable was she that even in a moderate wind
under topgallants, she had only to tack and one deck-
plank was under water.

On December 2, both vessels put to sea [from the
Cape Verde Is. - GB]. Accompanied by the fresh NE trade
wind, they had reached lat. 3°N in long. 19°W by the 12th.
But at this point the NE wind gave way to the faintest
SE wind, with which they crossed the Equator (December
16) in long. 23° 20'W. On December 25 the SE wind
itself veered ENE; and that wind accompanied them right
to the coast of Brazil, which came in view on January 1,
1822 in lat. 25°S. On the 3rd they reached Rio de
Janeiro.

Here stores were replenished and ten more men were
hired for the Elisaveta (to see her to Valparaiso). Both
vessels then left Brazil (January 28) and proceeded
towards Cape Horn with a strong south-westerly wind. On
February 7 they passed 230 miles off the estuary of the
La-Plata; on the 9th they found themselves in lat. 39°
40'S and long. 46° 20'W. That day the Elisaveta tele-
graphed that she was leaking badly (7" to 9" per hour)
and that the water was entering through parted frame-
spacings in the underwater section of the hull. To seal
it, it was essential to go to the nearest port; but
since the wind was blowing off the shore, and since the
nearest harbors were not altogether suitable for the

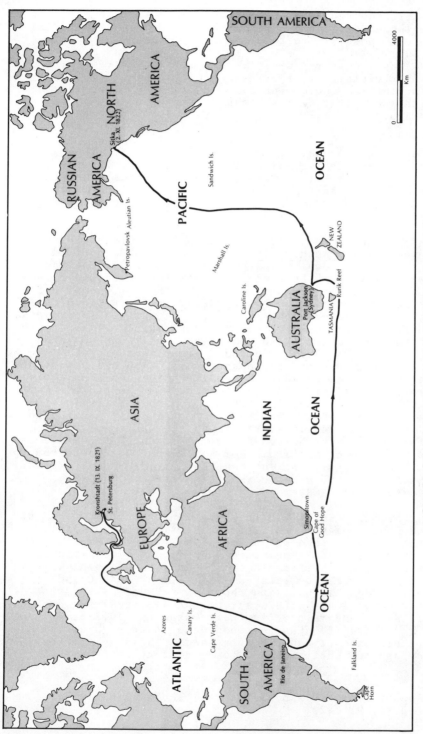

VOYAGE OF KLOCHKOV ON THE "RURIK" (1821-1822)

repair, the squadron commander decided to make straight for the Cape of Good Hope but by a route that passed as close as possible to the island of Tristan da Cunha.

Under westerly winds, fresh for the most part, and in poor visibility, they passed within sight of that island at the end of February and reached Simons Bay on March 17 - after no less than 46 stormy days from Rio de Janeiro.

To have the Elisaveta repaired, it proved necessary to sell part of her cargo and to dismast her. But all was done by the beginning of May and on the 7th the Riurik and the Elisaveta put to sea. It was proposed to cross the Indian Ocean and to round Australia. But hardly had the vessels left the coast before the corvette Elisaveta sprang so grave a leak that, by the morning of the 8th, the operation of all pumps scarcely kept the water in her hold at 15". An inspection of the vessel showed that her underwater parts were sound, but that in the parts above the waterline, particularly at the bow, almost every bolt was taking water, even under the sheathing... Through four bolts in the bow, water was not merely entering but was flowing in.'[1] Besides this, the upper reinforcement of the vessel was generally weak, and several beams and knees could be moved. Taking into account the length of the passage to Port Jackson and the high winds that prevailed in that season, Mr. Kislakovskii decided, in open counsel with his assistants, that the vessel could no longer keep the sea. He there-fore requested Mr. Klochkov to accompany him to the Cape of Good Hope once again. On May 9 both vessels again reached Simons Bay. And there, upon a close examination of the Elisaveta, it emerged that she was completely unfit for any further voyaging. That June, therefore, she was sold at auction. Her sailors were transferred to the Riurik, and those who had been hired were dismissed. Kislakovskii and his two assistants returned to St. Petersburg via Amsterdam, arriving in November 1822.

Mr. Klochkov, with the brig Riurik left the Cape of Good Hope on May 22 and, first steering south to avoid Agulhas Shoal, then proceeded along the 42nd parallel of southern latitude. He moved away from the Moçambique Channel, where hurricanes are often met. Accompanied by westerly storms, he reached lat. 42°S by June 6 and continued on his way with those same W and NW winds which were almost always strong and almost always brought hail and thunderstorms in their wake. On July 3, 43 days out from the Cape of Good Hope, they sighted the southern cape of Van Diemen's Land. The very same day, they spotted what appeared to be a stony outcrop in lat.

---

[1] Report from Kislakovskii to the squadron commander dated May 9, 1822.

43°S and long. 147° 42' 30"E.[1] The remainder of the
passage to Port Jackson, which was reached on July 15, was
completed with soft or moderate variable winds. Having
completed all the necessary repairs to the hull and rigging
of his brig, Mr. Klochkov went on his way at the beginning
of August. Taking into account the lateness of the
season, he decided to make straight for Novo-Arkhangel'sk,
not calling at Atkha Island. Accompanied by constant
northerly winds, on the 24th he passed within sight of
Ascension Island (at about lat. 29°S) and that same day
met with the SE trade wind, then blowing from the SSE.
On the 27th, the Riurik crossed the Tropic of Capricorn
in long. 192°E. On September 9, with a steady wind and
in fair weather, she crossed the Equator (long. 192°
12'E). From then until the 20th light variable winds
alternated with calms; but on the 20th, Mr. Klochkov met
with a fresh NE trade wind (in lat. 11° 40'N, long. 193°
40'E), which was attended by squalls and rain. The Tropic
of Cancer was crossed in long. 191°E on September 27.
On October 17, in lat. 39°N, the Riurik encountered a
severe SW storm. Thereafter, variable fresh winds prevailed from the SW and SE quarters with rain. On
October 28, the mountains of Sitkha appeared; but contrary storm-force winds kept the vessel at sea another
ten days. She entered Novo-Arkhangel'sk harbor on
November 7, having completed the last passage in 95 days.
The brig's complete voyage from Kronshtadt had lasted 14
months.

On instructions from the director of the colonies,
the brig Riurik remained there in the colonial service
while Captain Klochkov proceeded to Okhotsk with the
Company schooner Chirikov. From Okhotsk he returned to
St. Petersburg overland, arriving in November 1823.

(Based on reports by Klochkov and Kislakovskii and
the article concerning the voyage of the Riurik and the
Elisaveta, in vol. XXIV of Severnyi arkhiv (Northern
Archive), 1826.)

15

The Naval Sloop Apollon

(Tulub'ev and Khrushchev)

1821-24

At the beginning of 1821 there were fitted out at
Kronshtadt, to convey a mixed cargo to Kamchatka and Novo-
Arkhangel'sk, the 28-gun sloop Apollon and the brig Aiaks

---

[1] In Kruzenshtern's Atlas of the South Sea, this bank or
reef, which is 300 sazhen long, is shown as 'Riurik
Bank.'

(Ajax). On reaching the colonies, the former vessel was to cruise about the shores of Russian America to protect our commerce and halt contraband. Command of the squadron was given to the captain of the Apollon, Captain Tulub'ev; Lt. Filatov was captain of the Aiaks.

The two vessels sailed from Kronshtadt Roads on September 28, entered the Baltic Sea on October 1, were in the Zund by the 12th, and stopped at Elsinore. Having replenished stores of water and victuals, they continued. In the Skagerrak and in the North Sea, they met with a westerly storm that lasted seven days, in the course of which the brig was lost from sight and, as will be seen, came to grief. Captain Tulub'ev took refuge from the storm, on November 7, in the Downs. Remaining there until the 17th he then proceeded to Portsmouth.

Already he had noted the sloop's lack of stability. At Portsmouth, therefore, he thought it necessary to shorten masts and spars and, having reladen the hold, to add 80 tons of ballast. With the aid of the local Admiralty yard, all these operations were completed by the end of December and the sloop put out to sea on the 27th of that month.

Accompanied by a helpful following wind, Captain Tulub'ev reached the island of Porto-Santo by January 4, 1822. On the 10th he encountered the NE trade wind which blew for him till the 19th. Starting on that day, the trade wind gave way to the calms which accompanied the sloop on her passage across the Equator. He reached Rio de Janeiro on February 12. Here again supplies and fresh water were taken on, and Captain Tulub'ev put to sea once more in early March, laying a course for the Cape of Good Hope - for the lateness of the season did not permit him to round the Horn.

On March 31, the commander, who had suffered some considerable time already from consumption, which had worsened under the change of climate, died. Command of the sloop passed to the senior Lieutenant, Lt. Krushchev.

The voyage from Rio de Janeiro to the Cape of Good Hope and thence to Port Jackson was tolerably easy. Proceeding between latitudes 42° and 44°S, with fresh westerly winds, Lt. Khrushchev passed the meridian of the southern cape of Van Diemen's Land on May 13, and on the 27th reached Port Jackson, 87 days out from Brazil.

From Port Jackson they proceeded on their way about the middle of June. On this passage Lt. Khrushchev fixed the position of Balls Pyramid, which lies near Lord Howe Island in lat. 31° 48'S, long. 159° 20'E. On June 25, the Apollon crossed the Tropic of Capricorn in long. 169° 25'E and the following day stood near Walpole Island, which, however, was not sighted. They then

examined Mitre (Fataka) and Cherry (Anuta) Islands,
reckoning the SE top of the former to lie in lat. 11° 55'S
and long. 170° 20'E, and the northern extremity of the
latter - in lat. 11° 35'S, long. 170° 00'E. Some fresh
provisions were acquired by barter from the natives of
Cherry Island, and it was learned that the native name
of the place was 'Annuta.' They were five days in the
zone between the trade winds. During those five days,
they were subjected to almost continual rain. The NE
trade wind was met with only on the 19th, and even then
- by the parallel of St. Bartholomew Island (lat. 15°N)
and again between latitudes 18° and 20°N in long. 160°E
- it blew most inconstantly, even veering to the SE
quarter. Having steadied, however, the trade wind
accompanied the sloop to 36°N. On August 3, in lat.
41° 30'N, long. 165°E, indications of land were noted.
The sloop was at that time 45 miles west of the point
of intersection of Captains Clerk's and Kruzenshtern's
routes. But mists then descended and were with the
sloop right the way to Kamchatka which was reached on
August 13.

Having delivered the cargo brought for the place,
Lt. Khrushchev set out to execute his duties in the
colonies and dropped anchor, on October 10, in Novo-
Arkhangel'sk harbor.

The sloop passed the winter in San Francisco harbor:
a shortage of provisions and the poor state of her
crew's health made it impossible for her to remain at
Sitkha. Returning to Sitkha in mid-April 1823, however,
she cruised until September in the region of the sounds,
seeking out contrabandist traders.

On September 3, the sloop Apollon was replaced on
her station in the colonies by the frigate Kreiser,
commanded by Captain Lazarev. Her captain received instructions to return to Russia together with the sloop
Ladoga, which had arrived with the Kreiser and was then
in California. Lt. Khrushchev accordingly set off for
San Francisco harbor. Concerning the remainder of the
voyage of the sloop Apollon, see the voyage of the
Ladoga, below.

The voyage of the Apollon was described by Lt.
Khrushchev in pt. 10 of the Transactions of the State
Admiralty Department. That vessel's log was used for the
purposes of the present article.

Mr. Shabel'sky, who was on the sloop as interpreter,
composed notes on the subject of the voyage in the French
language, under the title: Voyage aux colonies russes
de l'Amerique, fait au bord du sloop de guerre l'Apollon
en 1821, 1822, et 1823: (St. P., 1826).

16
The Naval Brig Aiaks
(Filatov)
1821-22

As observed above, the brig Aiaks left Elsinore in
company with the sloop Apollon on October 15. Until the
30th the vessels proceeded together under strong north-
westerly winds; but on that day a storm and poor visibility separated them. The brig was then 200 miles north
of Zuid-Beveland. On November 12 she same within sight
of Calais but could not enter the Channel for the strong
and contrary wind. The incessant SW storms had driven
her far to the east, and on November 25 she began to
press against the coast of Holland. At 7 p.m. that day,
she grounded on a sand-bar near the island of Ameland,
in the bay between that island and the island of
Schiermonnikoog. In spite of her anchor, the brig
drifted further onto the bar until at last, for want of
water, she stopped. She then began to strike against
the bottom. At 9 p.m., after shots had been fired
continually, 12 sails appeared from the shore. Four of
the craft came fairly close to the brig, a six-oar was
put off: but the current took the six-oar by the bows
and she filled with water. The two men in her were
saved. After this, the brig's longboat was put off with
a hawser - but hardly had three seamen leapt into the
longboat before it was similarly caught up, and swept
off. Aiaks had no more rowing boats except a half-
broken four-man gig, so there was nothing with which to
aid the longboat. The sailing craft continued to tack
around the brig until 11 p.m., after which they returned
to the shore.

Fearing lest the brig be broken by the breakers in
the night, the crew began to make a raft from the booms.
To lighten the blows she was receiving, they also cut
down the foremast. It fell, bringing the topmast with
it. There was now 2 feet of water in the hold. It was
pumped out constantly. By 6:30 a.m. next day, the raft
was ready. The early light revealed three merchantmen
all grounded near Schiermonnikoog. At 7 a.m., two of
the previous sailing craft approached the brig. Five
sailors and an under-officer managed to leap onto one
of these from the stern. Since, however, this particular
sailing craft had a broken mizzen-mast, having fouled
against the brig's mainboom, she made off. The other
sailing craft requested that rowing-boats be launched,
since she had none herself; she did not stand closer.
The four-oar broken gig was launched from the stern. She
filled and sank at once. The one seaman in her managed
somehow to scramble out onto the sailing craft which,
having tacked round Aiaks a few more times, also went off.

At 9 a.m., fearing that the brig might fall on her

side at low-tide, the crew cut down the mainmast. The blows that resulted caused the rudder to disengage. Torn away from its supports, it fell and sank. About noon, the sailing craft in which were the brig's sailors again approached the scene of the wreck. She managed to pass a cable.

'The brig had not ceased to strike against the sea-bottom,' one reads in the log, from which this account is taken. 'Despite all the continual pumping, the water was rising, rather than sinking. And evening approached. Therefore, fearing the breakup of the brig and yet worse trouble for the crew, we asked the people in the sailing craft (who numbered as many as 20 and looked like fishermen), through a Danish pilot whom we had aboard, to summon more craft to take our heavy articles and State property, and to stay with the brig during the night. To our request, the fishermen replied that they could not stay a long time, and, moreover, that they should be paid for saving our crew. Being in a perilous situation, having to spend the night on the brig, and desiring to convince the fishermen that we did have money, we transferred the sealed box from our captain's cabin: the box contained money. We instructed the under-officer who was with the seamen in the sailing craft to look after it. But the fishermen would not let him near it, and menacingly took the money under their own protection.

With the consent of Captain and officers, the crew now began to transfer to this same sailing craft. It was their intention, if the winds quietened and there was no rocking, and if the brig remained intact in the morning, to attempt to draw her off the bar with help from the shore and from the local authority. At 2:30 p.m., when the officers crossed onto the sailing craft, the last box was taken out. It was dealt with as the first had been. Then, following signals made by the fishermen, three more craft came out to the brig.'

Despite all requests, the fishermen refused to stay with the brig at night: 'wherefore,' records the journal, 'we found ourselves constrained, with the general consent of captain and officers, to abandon the brig with much chagrin.' The brig Aiaks was subsequently taken off the sand-bar by pilots, and was taken to Harlingen to be repaired; from there, quite put to rights, she emerged on September 3, 1822. She returned to Kronshtadt on October 3.

17

The Frigate Kreiser and the Sloop Ladoga
(M.P. Lazarev and A.P. Lazarev)
1822-25

The 36-gun frigate Kreiser and the 20-gun sloop Ladoga were appointed to deliver cargoes to Kamchatka and to the Russian-American Company's colonies. The former vessel was commanded by Captain M. P. Lazarev, the latter by Captain-Lieutenant A. P. Lazarev. Both were equipped and provisioned for 18 months. Besides the usual spare tackle, the Ladoga carried an extra lower yard, in two pieces and a dismantled rudder.

The Kreiser and the Ladoga left Kronshtadt on August 17, 1822. Both stopped in Copenhagen Roads on September 5, having met with fresh contrary winds in the Baltic Sea. A store of wine was taken on in Copenhagen, and both made sail on September 16. On the 19th, on leaving the Skagerrak, the two vessels parted. The Kreiser arrived at Portsmouth on the 30th, the the Ladoga, which had encountered a SW storm near Galloper and suffered a broken cross-tree on the foremast, arrived only on October 6.

Having made certain alterations to his spars and rigging, and purchased astronomical instruments and charts in London, Captain Lazarev was minded to be off not later than November 5. However, the winds kept him at Portsmouth until the 28th of the month. The delay was recompensed by a successful passage to the island of Teneriffe: by December 10, a mere 11 days after leaving the Channel, the Kreiser and the Ladoga were already standing in the roadstead of Santa-Cruz.

Here the squadron watered and took on all that was needed. Captain Lazarev proceeded on his way on December 17, making for Rio de Janeiro. The weather remained clear almost throughout the passage: only near the Equator were there occasional showers. In Rio de Janeiro, the vessels took on grain, sugar, etc., and the holds were reladen. Consumed provisions were replaced by stone ballast of equal weight.

Not trusting to round Cape Horn, in view of the lateness of the season, Captain Lazarev judged it best to enter the South Sea by way of the Cape of Good Hope and Australia.

On February 23, 1823, the Kreiser and the Ladoga left Rio de Janeiro. On March 2, they passed at a distance of 33 miles from Stackelberg Island, the position of which is given by Arrowsmith at lat. 31ºS, long. 19ºW. It was not sighted because of poor conditions.

On March 6, near lat. 32° 25'S, the sloop drew away
from the frigate several times, to a distance of six miles
on a perpendicular course (E by N) from that of the
frigate. She sought an island shown on the charts in
long. 20° 41'W, but in vain. On April 22, Easter Day,
the squadron passed within sight of St. Paul Island.
The shores of Van Diemen's Land were sighted on May 16,
after an 85-day passage, and on the 18th the squadron
entered Hobart Town roadstead through the D'Entrecasteaux
channel. Here, both vessels' crews were put ashore and
the vessels were, inter alia, dried out, as well as
readied for the further voyage. The Kreiser and the
Ladoga put to sea again on June 9 and laid a course to
the NE. It was Captain Lazarev's intention to pass north
of New Zealand.

The following day during a SW storm a roller smashed
the Ladoga's gig, which was hoisted up at her stern, as
well as her stern-shutters and several gun-ports. That
night the vessels were separated: the Kreiser, the better
sailor, went ahead and out of sight and on July 9 she
reached Tahiti. The Ladoga, too, made her way there - it
was the designated rendezvous. On the 17th, she was in
sight of Three Kings Island and by July 8 actually in
sight of the island of Tahiti. But a strong NE wind
delayed her almost a week. Only on July 15 did she
rejoin the Kreiser, in Matavai Bay.

Five days later, on July 20, both the Kreiser and the
Ladoga proceeded thence. By July 24 they were in lat.
13° 36'S, long. 148° 58'N, which was the location where
they were to part. The frigate Keiser was to sail to Novo-
Arkhangel'sk, to replace the sloop Apollon on that station;
the Ladoga was to make for Kamchatka, and thence return
to Russia.

The frigate Kreiser reached Novo-Arkhangel'sk on
September 3. With the onset of winter she proceeded to
San Francisco, there to replenish her stores. After a
stay of about 2 1/2 months in that port (from December 1,
1823 to February 17, 1824) she returned to Sitkha and
remained, until the mid-October of the following year, at
the disposal of the Chief Manager of the colonies. She
was then replaced by the sloop Predpriiatie, lately
arrived from Russia.

Crossing the Equator, the sloop Ladoga had, on July
10, entered calms; in lat. 2° 30'N, however, she had
encountered a fresh ESE wind. The night following, she
had passed the island of Palmyra at a distance of nine
miles, without sighting it, however, although the night
was fairly bright. On August 21, in lat. 32° 26'N and
long. 189° 19'W, the Ladoga passed directly over the spot
where, on Arrowsmith's chart, is indicated the island of
Roco-de-Plata. Believing his chronometers to have been
accurate, Captain Lazarev thinks that this island's

71

position is quite erroneously given.[1] Next day, a number
of butterflies were observed about the sloop. No shore
was seen, however (lat. 33° 12'N, long. 191° 8'W). On
September 10, Captain Lazarev arrived in Petropavlovsk
harbor. From there, having unloaded the cargo destined
for Kamchatka and Okhotsk, he proceeded to Sitkha Island.
On his voyage to Novo-Arkhangel'sk, he intended to look
over a land the existence of which had been posited by
Bering himself, in lat. 49°N, and long. 172° 19'E. After
a futile three-day search between longitudes 170° and 174°E,
however, he abandoned the effort. Not the slightest
indication of land had been spotted. On November 9, the
Ladoga reached Novo-Arkhangel'sk and there found the
Kreiser, whose arrival date had been September 3.

     At Novo-Arkhangel'sk, the commander of the Ladoga re-
ceived instructions from the squadron commander to proceed to the port of San Francisco, and thence, in company
with the sloop Apollon, to return to Russia.

     Having encountered a two-day easterly storm near
Sitkha's coast, Captain Lazarev duly reached San Francisco
on December 1 and on January 12, 1824 left the California
shores together with the Apollon. Accompanied by a trade
wind, both vessels entered the southern hemisphere on
February 9. They crossed the Tropic of Capricorn, in
long. 239° 43'E, on February 24.

     Rain and storms set in on March 1. The crew,
perfectly healthy until now, began to sicken with
feverish colds. Cape Horn was rounded at a distance of
70 miles on March 22, 71 days out from San Francisco, and
the Falkland Islands were sighted on the 25th. Early in
April, in lat. 29° 30'S and long. 316°W, a steady north
wind was met. Scurvy then appeared among the crews of
both vessels. Fearing that the sickness might develop
further (there were 13 cases of scurvy in the Ladoga and
almost as many in the Apollon) but not hoping to reach
Rio de Janeiro in a short time because of contrary winds,
Captain Lazarev, on April 12, made his way from lat. 27°S
in long. 44°W to the island of Santa Catharina. Three
days later, both sloops dropped anchor opposite the
fortress of Santa Cruz. The day after their arrival in
this roadstead all the sick were transferred ashore
where their health soon mended.

     On May 17, the sloops went on their way. Having
stood off the shore as much as 3 1/2 degrees of longitude,
Captain Lazarev turned north towards the Equator and soon
met the SE trade wind. The passage through the torrid
zone proved highly successful: no protracted periods of
calm or of rain were encountered, nor did the thermometer

_____
[1] In Admiral Kruzenshtern's Atlas, the rock is shown as
lying in lat. 33° 50'N, long. 209° 15'W, and is not given
as doubtful.

72

rise above 24° Reaumur. The current was observed to flow
chiefly to the S or SW, and sometimes reached a rate of
20 miles per 24 hours.

But about the 24th parallel of northern latitude,
light northerly winds and calms considerably slowed the
progress of the sloops. Captain Lazarev descended to the
Azores from lat. 32°N, took on fresh stores of water and
victuals at Fayal, and continued on his way. The English
Channel was crossed on September 20, the Skagerrak on the
25th. A strong easterly wind held the sloops off Skagen
until October 2; on the 6th, however, they passed Copenhagen (where the Apollon halted for want of firewood) and
on the 13th the Ladoga reached Kronshtadt Roads. The
Apollon arrived there two days later.

. . . . . .

Captain of the 2nd rank M. P. Lazarev, of the frigate
Kreiser, who had been replaced on station by the newly
arrived Captain Kotzebue of the sloop Predpriiatie, had,
on October 16, 1824, left Sitkha and first sailed down to
California to take on fresh provisions. His passage along
the shores of California had been very long, thanks to
the high and contrary winds which, in the latitude of
Cape Mendocino, had kept the frigate nearly two weeks
under reefed trysails and only occasionally allowed the
use of a reefed main-topsail. But, at last, on November
18, the wind had changed, and on the 21st the Kreiser
dropped anchor in the port of San Francisco. The
Predpriiatie was also in port at the time. In the course
of a four-week stay at San Francisco, the frigate was
readied for her voyage round Cape Horn while her crew
picked up after their sojourn in the damp climate of Novo-
Arkhangel'sk.

On December 21, Captain Lazarev put to sea. Until
meeting the NE trade wind, he proceeded with light and
variable winds. On January 13, in lat. 3° 49'N, long.
242° 35'E, several land birds flew close to the frigate,
and they reappeared on the following day. No land was
sighted, however.

On January 24, the Kreiser passed over the very spot
where the island of 'Dudoza' is shown on Spanish charts
(lat. 17° 5'S, long. 122° 01'E). Against expectation,
Captain Lazarev now met with easterly winds which blew
nearly two weeks. On February 25, those winds veered to
the NW; the next day, the Kreiser came in sight of the
island of Diego-Ramirez. Cape Horn was rounded. On
March 23, they reached Rio de Janeiro. The ten men who
had fallen ill with swellings on this last passage were
immediately put ashore where most quickly recovered.

Captain Lazarev left Brazil in late April, proposing
to proceed directly to Kronshtadt. The contrary winds and
calms met by the Azores, however, obliged him to put into

Portsmouth to restore the crew and to see to certain repairs to the rigging. Departing from the coast of England
at the end of July and encountering a violent SW storm in
the Skagerrak (on the 25th of that month), the Kreiser
arrived at Kronshtadt on August 5. She had been abroad
nearly three years.

An account of the voyage of the Ladoga, sloop, was
printed in 1832 by Imperial instruction, under the title:
A Voyage Round the World in the Sloop Ladoga in 1822-1825:
St. P.: 275 pp. with a map. Regarding the voyage of the
frigate Kreiser, fragmentary information was published in
the Trans. of the State Adm. Dept., p. 6, pp. 457-66.
Here, additional use was made of her log-book.

18

The Naval Sloop Predpriiatie

(Kotzebue)

1823-26

The sloop Predpriiatie was built in St. Petersburg
early in 1823, expressly for the purposes of delivering
a cargo to Kamchatka and of cruising of the shores of
Russian colonies. A scientific object had also been in
view, namely, exploration in Bering Strait and further to
the north. Because of changed circumstances, however,
this last object was deferred and the captain of the sloop
was assigned merely to occupy himself with geographical
investigations on his voyage out - and not to deviate from
his principal ends. Commanding the sloop was Captain-
Lieutenant Kotzebue, well known for his voyage in the brig
Riurik.

Captain Kotzebue left Kronshtadt on July 28. On
August 10 he put in at Copenhagen, and on August 25
dropped anchor in Portsmouth Roads. Having here taken
on the instruments which had been specially ordered in
advance, on September 8 he put to sea; but a SW storm
forced him to return shortly after. Captain Kotzebue
finally did leave the English coast on September 11, and
by the 16th had entered the Atlantic Ocean.

Another storm was met in lat. 47°N, also from the SW.
On September 7, the Predpriiatie passed within sight of the
island Grandes Salvages, and on the 28th Teneriffe was
reached where the captain intended to take on fresh
provisions and to water. Met at the entrance to Santa
Cruz roadstead by cannon-balls, however (it subsequently
transpired that such an inhospitable reception had been
ordered by the island's governor, an ardent republican),
and not wanting to waste time in negotiations, he laid a
course direct to Rio de Janeiro. On October 8, in lat.
21° 51'N, the NE trade wind was lost and the voyagers

74

encountered variable SE and SW winds and calms, which continued as far as lat. 3° 30'N. On October 18, the SE
trade wind was met. Cabo Frio came in sight on November 1,
and Rio de Janeiro was reached the next day. Here they
remained until November 28, then proceeding along the
shores of South America towards Cape Horn. Two hundred
miles off the estuary of the River La Plata they observed
WSW sea-current of 33 miles per 24 hours. On December
23 Staten Land was passed. Three days later, the meridian
of Cape Horn was also passed, at a distance of 20 miles.
On January 17, 1824, the voyagers dropped anchor in
Concepcion Bay, on the west coast of South America.

From here, Captain Kotzebue laid a course for the
Tuamotu Archipelago, which he proposed to explore a
little. Towards the end of February, when in the zone of
the SE trade winds (lat. 16°S, long. 129° 30'W), the
Predpriiatie met with squalls that lasted almost without
a break for four days, with thunder and heavy rainfall.
On March 2, in lat. 15° 52'N, a low coastline was observed
from the sloop. The following day it emerged that it was
a small inhabited island with a central lagoon. By
reckonings made, the latitude of this little island, which
was named Predpriiatie (Enterprise) after the vessel, was
15° 58' 18"S. Its longitude was found to be 140° 11' 30"W.

Continuing his investigations, Captain Kotzebue
described the lately discovered island of Arakcheev
(Angatau) (lat. 15° 51'S, long. 140° 52'W) and, on the next
few days, determined the positions of the Karlhof Islands
(Aratika) (lat. 15° 27'S, long. 145° 31' 12"W); the
Palliser Islands (lat. of the southern tip of the first
island: 15° 34' 25"S in long. 146° 6' 49"W); and the
King George Islands. He also verified the locations of
other previously-discovered groups - the Rumiantsev,
Riurik, the Kruzenshtern groups.

On leaving this archipelago, on the night of March
10, the sloop very nearly struck on a coral reef against
which the current held her; only an unexpected squall off
the land saved her. On March 14, the voyagers dropped
anchor in Matavai Bay, Tahiti.

In the course of a nine-day stay here, a detailed
survey was made of Matavai Bay as of the neighboring bay
of Mataua. By observation, the true position of Point
Venus was reckoned at lat. 17° 29' 22"S. (Observations
on the spot; compass var.: 6° 50'E; var. of needle -
28° 30' to S.)

On his way to the Mariner Islands (Hamoa), which he
intended to examine, Captain Kotzebue next, on March 26,
discovered a group of islands which he named the
Bellingshausen group (approx. lat. of centre: 15° 48'S,
long. 154° 30'W). A few days later, he came upon yet

another small island, Kordiukov (in lat. 14° 32' 39"S, long. 168° 6'W).[1] On April 3, Oulu came in sight - the easternmost island of the Hamoa group. For the next four days, Captain Kotzebue occupied himself with the investigation of that group, surveyed several islands, and gathered much interesting information regarding the people who inhabit the Hamoa Archipelago.

On his way thence to Kamchatka, Captain Kotzebue called at the island of Otdia in the Radak group, to take magnetic readings. Becalmed another ten days near the Marshall Islands, he reached Petropavlovsk harbor on June 8. Here, articles brought out were unloaded. Captain Kotzebue then proceeded to Novo-Arkhangel'sk to replace the frigate Kreiser.

Early that October, the Governor of the colonies, Captain-Lieutenant Murav'ev, declared that until the following March he had no need of a warship. Captain Kotzebue, who wished to employ his remaining time in exploration, therefore put to sea, first calling at San Francisco to replenish stores.

Entering that port on October 27, he met such a powerful current (9 knots or more) that he could make no headway despite a following wind - until the tide flowed. On November 9, i.e., at about that time when St. Petersburg was flooded, a south-westerly storm raged in the port of San Francisco which tore roofs off houses and upturned everything in its path. The water rose up on the shore and covered the spot where the observatory tent stood: the instruments were barely saved.

From California, Captain Kotzebue sailed to the Sandwich Islands. On December 3, he crossed the Tropic of Cancer in long. 133° 58'W, and met with a NE trade wind. On the 4th, however, the wind suddenly veered to the SE. Next passing to the SW and NW, it blew freshly until December 8 and lat. 19° 30'N, long. 141° 30'W. This unusual variation of the wind in the trade wind belt had been observed by Captain Kotzebue, at about the same place, when he had been in the brig Riurik in 1816.

Again assisted by the trade wind, they reached Honolulu roadstead on December 14 and there remained until the following February. Captain Kotzebue occupied himself throughout that time with astronomical and other observations; the sloop, meanwhile, was readied for a winter voyage to Sitkha. By more than 300 lunar reckonings, the longitude of Honolulu was determined at 157° 56' 15"W.

---

[1] In Kruzenshtern's opinion, Kordiukov Island is the Rose Island found by Capt. Freycinet in 1819. By the latter's calculation, it lies in lat. 14° 33'S, long. 168° 5'W.

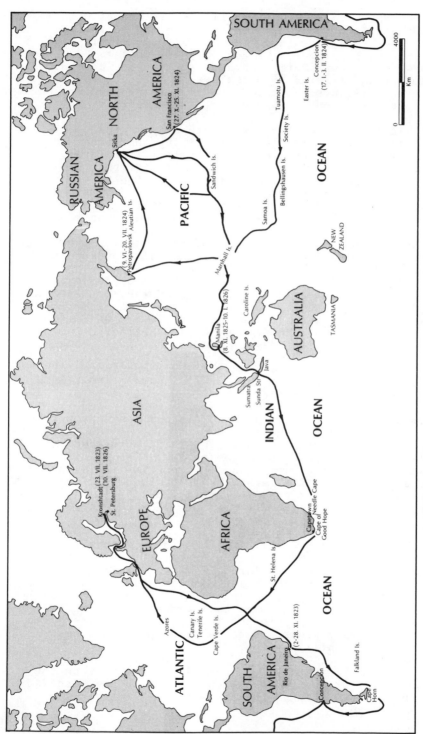

VOYAGE OF KOTZEBUE ON THE "PREDPRIIATIE" (1823-1826)

Wishing to shorten the time before he met with westerly winds, Captain Kotzebue laid a course due north from Oahu; but calms still detained him several days within sight of the Sandwich Islands. On February 14, in lat. 35°N, long. 155°W, the Predpriiatie passed a spot where, according to information gathered from whalers on Oahu, there should have been islands. However, not a sign of land was observed. The sloop reached Novo-Arkhangel'sk on February 24, 1825.

In the course of a five-month stay in that port, the voyagers made a detailed survey of the approaches to Novo-Arkhangel'sk and reckoned the fort itself to lie in lat. 57° 2' 57"N, long. 135° 33' 18"W. By the terms of a convention then concluded with the United States of America, the further presence of a Russian warship in the colonies was rendered unnecessary; therefore, wasting no time, Captain Kotzebue hastened his preparations for a return voyage to Russia. He was further induced to make haste by shortages or spoilage of provisions. The sloop Predpriiatie sailed from Novo-Arkhangel'sk on August 11, 1825, making for the Sandwich Islands. Keeping as far as possible away from the routes of the celebrated mariners, on September 4 Captain Kotzebue passed the spot where, on Arrowsmith's chart, was shown the island of Maria Laxara; but no sign of land was perceived. On September 14, the anchor was dropped in Honolulu harbor. They thence proceeded, after four days, towards the Radak group.

On September 26, in lat. 14° 30'N and long. 169° 38'W, clear signs of land were observed; however, the land was not sought. Similar signs were frequently observed on the whole passage to Radak, but overcast weather and rain prevented the making of any new discoveries. By October 6, the sloop was already in the vicinity of the Marshall Archipelago. Having fixed the position of Pescadores Island, Captain Kotzebue augmented the list of his discoveries by two more groups: the Rimsky-Korsakov group (in lat. 11° 26' 42"N, eastern limit, long. 192° 45' 40"W); and the Eschscholts group (Bikini) (in lat. 11° 40' 11"N, long. 194° 37' 35"W). All these islands belong to the Ralik chain.

Leaving the Marshall Archipelago on October 9, Captain Kotzeube then examined and fixed the position of Brown's Range Island in lat. 11° 20' 50"N, long. 197° 28' 30"W. He then paused at Guam for three days. Aided by a fresh trade wind, he entered the China Sea in early November. Approaching Manila, where Captain Kotzebue meant to rest his people and to put the sloop to rights, he met contrary winds and calms which postponed his arrival at that port until November 8.

By the beginning of January 1826, all work on the sloop was finished. She put out to sea on the 10th and on the 25th, by way of the Sunda Strait, entered the Indian Ocean.

In lat. 20°S, and long. 256°W, they met a violent
storm, which lasted for 48 hours; thereafter, moreover,
they struggled for two weeks with incessant westerly winds.
In those latitudes, where the easterly wind prevails,
such a wind is a rare phenomenon.

On February 22, the meridian of Isle-de-France was
passed. Several storms, from the NW and SW, were encountered in the following days, that of March 12 being
especially violent: the rolling and pitching broke the
helm, and the sloop would have been in great peril had
the helm not swiftly been replaced by a new one.

On rounding the Cape of Good Hope, Captain Kotzebue
thought of calling in at Table Bay for water, but indications of an approaching storm from the north obliged him
to abandon that intention. Eleven days after rounding
the cape, he reached St. Helena. There he stayed nine
days, leaving on April 7. The Equator was crossed on
April 17, the Azores rounded in mid-May, and they reached
Portsmouth on June 9.

After two weeks here, the proceeded and, having
stopped at Copenhagen a few days because of contrary winds,
dropped anchor in Kronshtadt Roads on July 10.

An account of this voyage, written by Captain Kotzebue,
was printed by the Scientific Committee of the Navy, under
the title: A Voyage Round the World in the Navy Sloop
Predpriiatie: St. P., 1828: 200 pp. with 4 maps. The
results of the voyage as far as natural science went were
published by Mr. Lenz, in the book: Physicalische
Beobachtungen, angestellt auf einer Reise um die Welt unter
dem Commando des Capitans Otto von Kotzebue, in den Jahren
1824-1826: St. P., 1830.

19

The Russian-American Company Vessel Elena

(Chistiakov and Murav'ev)

1824-26

The Russian-American Company's vessel Elena, which was
fitted out for the voyage to Sitkha on the lines of previous
vessels and carried a mixed cargo, was under the command
of Captain-Lieutenant P. E. Chistiakov. Chistiakov left
Kronshtadt on July 31, 1824, and, having encountered high
south-westerly winds on the Baltic crossing, paused at
Copenhagen. He proceeded thence on the 22nd and, losing
his following wind in the Skagerrak, was accompanied by
SW storms on his whole passage across the North Sea. But
he again met with a following wind on September 6, when
about to enter the Channel, and on the 10th dropped anchor
in Portsmouth roadstead. Having here taken on a supplementary

cargo, Lt. Chistiakov put to sea on October 4. Again, until the 17th, he met south-westerly storms (as far as lat. 45°N, long. 12°W); and after that, contrary winds still persisted for a week. The Elena encountered the NE trade wind on October 27, in lat. 29° 50'N, and with it now made a fairly good passage. The Equator was crossed on November 18 in long. 27° 8'W, Cabo Frio was sighted on December 2, and five days later they reached Rio de Janeiro, after a 64-day voyage from England.

In Rio de Janeiro, Lt. Chistiakov took on all necessary provisions for the coming passage and completed business affairs. He weighed anchor again on January 6, 1825. Followed constantly by strong W winds, the Elena, on February 4, crossed the meridian of the Cape of Good Hope (lat. 43°S) and on March 13 reached the southern cape of Van Diemen's Land, in lat. 45° 49'S. In the Indian Ocean, Chistiakov had closely followed the route taken by Captain Golovnin in the Diana. On March 23, the Elena reached Port Jackson after a 76-day passage from Rio de Janeiro.

The passage from Port Jackson to Sitkha Island was completed in 78 days, and in the happiest circumstances. To check the chronometers, Lt. Chistiakov passed within sight of Norfolk and Rotuma Islands. Crossing the Equator on June 10, in long. 171° 40'E, he reached his destination - the harbor of Novo-Arkhangel'sk - on the 29th of that same month. Here he handed his vessel over to Captain Murav'ev, the former Governor of the colonies, and himself assumed that post in his place.

By November, the Elena was ready for her return voyage with a cargo of peltry worth 200,000 rubles, and on the 4th of that month Captain Murav'ev made sail for the settlement of Ross, where the rest of the cargo was to be picked up. On this passage, which was generally a stormy one, he met two violent storms (on November 11 and 12); moreover, the continual humidity affected the health of the crew, so that as many as 13 men fell sick. Three times Captain Murav'ev approached the settlement of Ross but was unable to take on his cargo, so strong were the winds. Eventually he was obliged to proceed to the port of San Francisco, whither the cargo in question was sent from Ross settlement. Having completed his fitting out at San Francisco, Captain Murav'ev put to sea on January 2, 1826. One month later he crossed the Equator, on March 6 he reached the meridian of Cape Horn, and on April 5 he dropped anchor in Rio de Janeiro roadstead, with not a single man sick.

The passage from Brazil to Europe was completed without particular incident. From August 22 to 28, the Elena stopped at Elsinore and Copenhagen, before reaching Kronshtadt Roads on September 1.

L.V. Hagemeister

V.M. Golovnin

I.F. Krusenstern

Lu.F. Lisinskii

M.P. Lazarev

O.E. Kotzebue

F.F. Bellingshausen

M.N. Vasil'ev

G.S. Shishmarev

F.P. Wrangell

F.P. Lütke

I.I. von Schantz

Men of Vostok and Mirnyi in New Zealand, 1820.

20

The Naval Sloop Smirnyi

(Dokhturov)

1824-25

The sloop Smirnyi (520 tons), commanded by Captain-Lieutenant Dokhturov, was sent with a cargo to Petropavlovsk as the other ships had been. Dokhturov left Kronshtadt on September 27, 1824, reaching Copenhagen on October 1 after a Baltic Sea crossing with strong NE and SE winds. On October 20 he left Copenhagen and took on a pilot at Elsinore for the North Sea passage. Till November 1, this passage proceeded under high NW and SW winds. Starting now, the Smirnyi labored under violent storms which caused her such damage that Captain Dokhturov was forced to put in at the closest port, and afterwards to return to Kronshtadt. One storm especially raged from November 3 on. We here reproduce the account of the subsequent misfortunes by Lieutenant M. M(iroslavi)ch who was one of the participants in this voyage. (The account appeared in Severnaia pchela, 1846, nos. 83-86).

'At midnight on November 3, a storm raged from the NW, with enormous rollers. The sloop was on a starboard tack under one maintopsail. Then, at 4 a.m., a huge breaker descended onto the sloop from windward, flooding the longboat which was standing on the booms, and covering the vessel from stem to stern. The officers of the watch, Lieutenant Bodisko and Midshipman Istomin, and steersmen were thrown onto the quarterdeck and very nearly washed overboard; the leadsman was flung onto the deck from the chain-wale and broke his arm. From the weight of the water on her, the sloop sank down and could have flooded, had the netting guards not risen. Nevertheless, so much water had crashed onto the decks that the holds contained 5' of it. The blow of the same huge breaker had damaged the forward channel-wales, the ship's head, the martingale-boom and the netting, and had torn a spare top-yard away from the channel-wales while destroying binnacle-lamps and compass and breaking the tiller at the helmhead. The binnacles were replaced by little kegs, and a jury-rudder was made from capstan-bars.'

During the night preceding November 4, the wind, from the WNW, hardly lessened. At dawn, the coast of Jutland was sighted - the pilot said it was near the village of Hanstholm, but in Captain Dokhturov's opinion the sloop was further south. The reckoned noon-time latitude of 55° 48' demonstrated the pilot's error: the sloop was in

fact near Hornsreef shoal (south of it). Had the pilot
been heeded, the Smirnyi would probably have grounded on
it. But to round the shoal from the west, it was necessary
to turn onto the port tack - a questionable manoeuver in
view of the rolling and the wind-strength. Against
expectation, however, the turn was made, under double-
reefed topsails and mizzen. It was only a fortunate
incident, however, which assisted the completion of this
manoeuver: at the very instant when the sloop came up to
the wind and paused, the wind veered from WNW to W. The
turn was completed, and it proved possible to move off
into open water. After this, the storm continued with
renewed force. The sloop bore north and on the morning
of November 6 found herself close to the Norwegian coast.
Captain Dokhturov thought it best to put in at Kristiansand.
He was led to think it by the damage sustained by the
sloop, and especially by his lack of binnacle-lamps.
Learning from the pilots who came out that Kristiansand
was to windward, however, he entered Arendal, the nearest
harbor. The Smirnyi returned to Kronshtadt on May 17 in
the following year. (From log and account of M. M--ch,
Sev. Pchela, 1846, No. 83-85.)

21

The Naval Transport Krotkii

(Wrangell)

1826-27

Captain-Lieutenant Wrangell left Kronshtadt with the
transport that had been entrusted to him, the Krotkii, on
August 23, 1825. He was to convey a cargo to Kamchatka
and the Company colonies. The transport had been
expressly built for the voyage, had a length of 90' and a
beam, minus sheathing, of 29'. Captain Wrangell entered
the Zund on September 1 and, in order not to lose a
following wind, did not stop at Copenhagen. On the 15th,
he entered Portsmouth Roads. Work on the transport and
the purchasing of chain-cables held him here about a month.

The passage from Portsmouth to Brazil took 46 days
and passed without special incident. Replenishing his
stores of water and victuals at Rio de Janeiro, Captain
Wrangell went on his way towards Cape Horn. After meeting
with protracted storms about the cape, by January 26 he
had reached lat. 58° 49'S in long. 70° 23'W, whence he
turned north and, on February 19, dropped anchor in
Valparaiso roadstead.

Having reladen the holds and made certain repairs,
he put to sea again on the 28th of that month. On April
7, he put in at Port Chichagov, Nuku Hiva, being short of

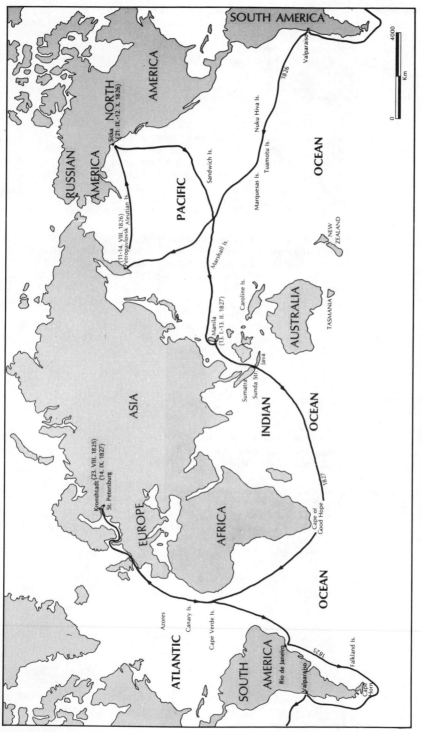

VOYAGE OF WRANGELL ON THE "KROTKII" (1825-1827)

fresh water.[1] For the first eight days of their sojourn
in that harbor, relations with the natives were constantly
amicable; then, on April 16, occurred the incident that
resulted in the deaths of one officer and three seamen.
The incident is described as follows in the Krotkii's
logbook:

'On April 15, the islanders' priest was held
on board because of deceit in the bartering of
pigs. At 7.30 a.m. on the 16th, the detained
priest was put ashore and left one of the natives
with us as a hostage, promising to send the pigs
on. An hour later, the launch returned to the
transport (evidently empty). A little later, the
same launch was sent back to the shore under
Midshipman Deibner. In the launch, Midshipman
Deibner and two sailors were killed; the remaining
two sailors and an interpreter of the Nukuhivan
language swam back to the transport, but one of
them was struck and wounded. As soon as we observed the natives' hostile acts, we sent a longboat off with Lt. Lavrov and 12 armed men. One
of the men in the longboat was killed by a bullet
in the chest. The longboat having returned, the
transport was held on a spring and canister was
fired into the crowd of assembled natives.
Before this, they were firing at us with their
rifles. Our fire, from cannon and rifles, and
their fire also, lasted until 7 p.m. We then
slipped our mooring and, still under fire from
the shore, pulled out of the harbor to sea,
leaving four men and four rifles with their
appurtenances in the savages' possession.

We entered open sea at 8 p.m., having lost
a stream-anchor in the narrows, and all night
long we heard cries and saw fires on land.'[2]

From the Marquesas Islands, Captain Wrangell laid a
course straight for Petropavlovsk harbor, which he
reached on June 11. The articles brought out were unloaded,
and he then proceeded to Novo-Arkhangel'sk, arriving on
September 21. Since, in the opinion of the colonial
Governor, a warship was not required there, Captain Wrangell
prepared his transport for the home voyage to Russia. On
October 12, he left the shores of Sitkha, meaning to take
on fresh provisions in the Sandwich Islands.

---

[1] Water was, in fact, so short that each man received only
four cups per 24-hour period.

[2] Taking the various factors into account, Captain Wrangell
believes that it was the natives' intention to seize the
transport - and that the onslaught on the launch was but
the beginning of a general attack.

On his way to that archipelago, as just as unsuccessfully as his predecessors, Captain Wrangell sought Maria Laxara Island, given by Norie in lat. 27° 6'N, long. 139° 20'E. Passing over that spot, not even a sign of the proximity of land was observed. After one week's stay in Honolulu harbor, Captain Wrangell set a course for the Philippines, attempting to keep to those regions where, according to whalers, there should have been unexplored islands and shoals. Over the entire voyage, however, nothing resembling a sign of the proximity of land was spotted. Entering the China Sea in late December and between the islands of Sariguam and Anatahan, he dropped anchor at Manila on January 13, 1827.

The preparing of fresh provisions and the construction of a new boat, replacing that left on Nuku Hiva, detained the transport about four weeks at Manila. Putting out to sea in mid-February, Captain Wrangell passed through the Gaspar and Sunda Straits and, on March 14, entered the Indian Ocean.

On April 6, he lost the SE trade wind (lat. 24° 30'S, long. 297°W). Off the Cape of Good Hope, the transport several times met protracted storms, especially in late April and in lat. 29° 30'S and long. 314°W, when there was a storm from the east, which was accompanied with heavy thunder and at times hail and even snow.

Having rounded the Cape of Good Hope, Captain Wrangell put in at the island of St. Helena for a week, before Pressing on and, on June 18, crossing the Equator for the last time and in long. 23°W. After nine days in the zone of variable winds and calms, he met with the NE trade wind on June 28 and by July 11 had reached lat. 30°N. Accompanied on his way by a SE wind, he reached Portsmouth on the 31st. Here he stayed, for various purposes, until August 22. He dropped anchor in Kronshtadt Roads on September 14, having spent more than two years outside the confines of Russia.

Ship's log; Severnyi arkhiv (Northern archive), 1828, part 36, pp. 49-106, and Zapiski Uchenago Komiteta (Notes of scholarly committee), pp. 144-149.

22

The Naval Sloop Moller

(Staniukovich)

1826-29

At the beginning of 1826, and on the pattern of earlier expeditions, two warships were to have sailed with cargoes for Petropavlovsk harbor and Okhotsk; they were also to have cruised off the Russian-American Company's colonies.

Since, however, in consequence of a treaty concluded at about this time with the United States of America, the colonies no longer needed any warships, the commanders of the sloops in question were instructed that the year to have been in cruising duties should be employed in surveying and exploring the north-east coasts of Asia and the north-west coasts of America, and in investigating that portion of the Pacific Ocean which lies between those coasts.

The sloops sent on this mission, the Moller and the Seniavin, had been built on the Okhta at St. Petersburg and had identical dimensions (length - between perpendicu-lars - 90'; beam - minus sheathing - : 29'; internal depth: 12' 9"). Commander of the former, and of the squadron, was Captain-Lieutenant M. N. Staniukovich; captain of the Seniavin was Captain-Lieutenant O. P. Lütke. Early in the June of 1826, both these sloops were brought to Kronshtadt and armed as barks. Besides the usual stores for three years, they were equipped with all means of preserving the crews' health, also with instruments and other aids for hydrographic and scientific work. The commanders were instructed to purchase certain of these items in Copenhagen and London. In addition to their full complements, each sloop carried 15 men, of the lower ranks, being sent out for service in Okhotsk or Petropavlovsk ports.

The vessels' commanders and the scientists of the expedition received detailed instructions from the State Admiralty Department.[1] The sloops were to proceed in company to Unalashka, whence each was to sail to her work area. Hydrography completed, they were to rejoin each other at Petropavlovsk, and thence sail together to Kronshtadt. On the return voyage, it was envisaged that they would examine the shores of New Ireland, the Solomon Islands, and New Hanover and so, entering the Indian Ocean by one of the straits between the Moluccas, continue on their way around the Cape of Good Hope.

Captain Staniukovich's orders were to make a detailed examination of the Aleutian chain and the Alaska Peninsula with its adjacent islands. He was to employ the months of winter in an investigation of that part of the ocean which stretches to east and west of the Sandwich Islands, particularly in the direction of the chain formed by those islands. Explorations among the Marshall and Gilbert groups were also to be one of his objects; and on his home voyage to Russia, he was to examine the islands of Bonin-Sima, which had yet to be looked over.

Once the cargo destined for Okhotsk, Petropavlovsk, and the Company's colonies had been stowed, on August 20,

---

[1] These were printed in pt. XI of ZGAD (Trans. of the Admiralty Dept.).

1826, Captain Staniukovich left Kronshtadt in company with
the sloop Seniavin. The very next day, however, the sloops
parted in a mist. Light and changeable winds slowed
their passage across the Baltic Sea, so that it was not
until August 30 that they even reached the parallel of
Riga Bay. But there the Moller encountered a strong SW
wind, from which it proved necessary to take shelter in
Arensburg Bay. Four days later, they proceeded thence and
on September 10 dropped anchor in Copenhagen Roads, where
the Seniavin stood already.

In Copenhagen, Captain Staniukovich bought his crew
rum and a complete supply of warm clothing. On September
15, he proceeded into the Kattegat with both sloops.
They crossed the North Sea under a moderate NW wind and
on the 24th reached Portsmouth. Here, the purchase of
instruments, charts, and other articles detained them
about a month. Captain Staniukovich put to sea again on
October 22.

Having waited 24 hours in the Channel for Captain
Lütke, who had remained a few hours longer in Portsmouth
roadstead, and supposing that he had passed on straight
to Teneriffe (since Seniavin had not been sighted from
the sloop), Captain Staniukovich also laid his course for
Teneriffe. Accompanied by moderate NE winds, he approached
the entrance to Santa Cruz roadstead on the evening of
November 2. Not to lose a following wind, however, he did
not stop but proceeded towards Rio de Janeiro - the other
rendezvous agreed to with Captain Lütke.

Crossing the Tropic of Cancer and encountering light
variable winds instead of the NE trade wind, Captain
Staniukovich sailed between the Cape Verde Islands and
the African coast, keeping closer to the islands than the
coast. This part of the ocean he traversed with light
SW and NW winds. But meeting with the SE trade wind, on
December 1, he proceeded with it straight to Rio de
Janeiro, which he reached on December 16.

Here he was rejoined by the sloop Seniavin. He then,
with both sloops, headed for Cape Horn. The voyage proved
easy as far as the Falkland Islands; but on February 4,
1827, in lat. 55°S, a hitherto moderate SW wind began to
increase in strength, and soon developed into a storm.
In the poor visibility that ensued, the sloops were
separated. The wind quietened after 48 hours, but continued to blow from the SW, and weather conditions were
bad. Still hoping to rejoin the Seniavin, Captain Staniukovich proceeded southward and, having reached a southern
latitude of 61°, laid his course for Valparaiso - the
designated rendezvous with the Seniavin. He waited two
weeks at Valparaiso; but the Seniavin did not come. As
he was leaving, he met her: she was only then coming up
to Valparaiso. Captain Staniukovich gave Captain Lütke
orders to proceed in accordance with his previous instructions,
and himself went on.

From Valparaiso he sailed towards the Tuamotu Archipelago (Pomatu) and through that archipelago to Tahiti. On April 27, he sighted the island of Lito (Ahunui) and, having determined its position astronomically (the western extremity lay in lat. 19° 38' 40"S, long. 140° 25' 35"W), continued through the archipelago, dropping anchor in Matavai Bay on the 29th.

A two-week stay at Tahiti was employed in checking chronometers and in making various repairs on the sloop. Weighing anchor on May 15, Captain Staniukovich made for the Lazarev (Matahiva) Islands, discovered by Captain Bellingshausen in 1820. He determined their longitude (148° 37' 5"W), then laid a course for Kamchatka. On June 14, the Moller passed between Hawaii and Kauai in the Sandwich chain, and on July 13 Petropavlovsk port was reached.

Here, materials brought out were unloaded and the discharged cargo replaced by stone ballast. Captain Staniukovich then sailed for Unalashka. Unbroken rain and mists, together with a very high wind, kept him right at the entrance to Illiuliuk harbor until August 30. Here, a baidara, needed for the surveying of shoaly coasts, was taken on, and on September 5, Captain Staniukovich sailed for Unimak, where he proposed to commence his hyrdographic work. But strong winds and mists delayed the beginning of that work until September 8, and then, on the 9th, the hitherto moderate wind acquired storm force. Foreseeing the onset of bad weather and of autumn storms, the captain decided to break off his work and go to Novo-Arkhangel'sk, where he was yet to deliver a part of his cargo. He arrived there on September 21.

As he left the coast of Sitkha, where he had remained four weeks, Captain Staniukovich intended to occupy himself with an examination of the portion of the ocean which lies to the east of the Sandwich Islands. High SW winds and mist detained him for another week in the latitude of Novo-Arkhangel'sk, so that he set out on his proper course, with a following NW wind, only on October 28.

In his search for the islands in question, Captain Staniukovich proved no more fortunate than his predecessors, even though he passed the very places where they should have been. These islands, which the Spaniards allegedly discovered, were supposed to lie to the east of the Sandwich Islands; but they have yet to be found although those waters have been crossed by numerous mariners. They are not shown on the latest charts.

In the course of these investigations, the Moller reached a latitude 9°N, and thence proceeded in to the Sandwich Islands, reaching Honolulu harbor on December 6, 1827. There Captain Staniukovich remained until February 9 of the following year, both for repairs to the Moller's rig and to rest her people.

In accordance with instructions, Captain Staniukovich proceeded thence to the NW along the chain of the Sandwich Islands. Continuing over one and a half thousand miles of longitude, he examined and established the positions of the following islands (all longitudes reckoned by lunar observation):

Name of Islands	Point Fixed	Latitude N.	Longitude E.
Niihau (Onigio)	E. tip	21° 55' 19"	199° 48' 40"
Orehua	middle	22° 02' 45"	199° 42' 40"
Necker	middle	23° 34' 16"	195° 09' 03"
Gardner (Pinnacles)	middle	25° 03' 00"	191° 57' 49"
Lisianskii	middle	26° 04' 21"	185° 56' 18"
French Frigate (reef)	N. tip	20° 54' 52"	193° 37' 53"
Pearl and Hermes	SW tip	27° 45' 05"	184° 00' 02"
Maro (reef)	N. tip	25° 32' 16"	185° 15' 08"

Besides this, he also rediscovered the Moller Islands, lying in lat. 25° 45' 59"N and long. 188° 9' 59"W.

At the end of March, having experienced very high winds for several consecutive days which made it both dangerous and useless to proceed with the surveying, Captain Staniukovich sailed for Petropavlovsk harbor. He arrived on April 11. In Avacha Bay he still found much ice.

On April 27, he again proceeded to the Aliaska Peninsula. To check chronometers and pick up a baidara, he meant to call at Unalashka. A number of the Aleutian islands were examined, and their positions determined, during the passage.

The chronometers checked, and having gathered all possible information about the Aliaskan coasts from hunters, Captain Staniukovich set out for Unimak Island and, rounding it from the north, on June 3 began his survey of the shores of Aliaska (Peninsula) north from Isanakh Strait. When necessary, he dropped anchor and had the survey conducted from rowing-boats or skin craft.

In this fashion, the whole northern coast of Aliaska (Peninsula) as far as the mouth of the Naknek River was examined. From there, on July 13, the sloop returned to the island of Amak, supplementing the survey enroute. Captain Staniukovich stayed a day at Amak to search for a chain and anchor that had been left on the previous visit. The search was unsuccessful, however. At this point, a high wind sprang up which obliged the captain to go down to Unimak Island, on the south shore of which the sloop was held till July 22 in expectation of suitable weather for the continuation of the survey. But an easterly wind, which blew into Isanakh Strait starting on that day, made it impossible to continue. Therefore, and also because the store of dry provisions was low and the crew tired out, Captain Staniukovich was obliged to abandon his surveying. He returned to Unalashka on July 26, surveying part of the northern coast of Unimak on his way.

On Unalashka, the chronometers were again checked and corrected: it was found that an error had been made in reckonings of longitude. Captain Staniukovich then, on August 3, sailed to Kamchatka, closely following the Aleutian chain. Because of the continuing mist and poor visibility, it was impossible to take any bearings.

The stay at Petropavlovsk, of more than two months, was employed in preparations for the return voyage to Kronshtadt. After one month, Captain Lütke also arrived, and on October 30, 1828, both sloops left the shores of Kamchatka. Manila was agreed on as the rendezvous point.

Until November 6, the voyage was a fairly easy one. On that day however, when in lat. 40°N, long. 161°E, the vessels met a high SE wind, which turned into a storm. They were separated, in the wretched visibility that ensued, and the Moller proceeded to the island of Luzon. Passing close to the Bonin and Alexander Islands on November 23, Captain Staniukovich fixed their positions. That done, he continued under variable winds. On December 2, he entered the China Sea between the Babuyan Islands. Nine days later he dropped anchor in Manila roadstead.

Here the sloop was unrigged and Captain Staniukovich at once looked to the repairing of spars and rigging, which had suffered a good deal from the last storm. When this was done, and when Captain Lütke had arrived (on January 1, 1829), he again put to sea (January 18). The Sunda Strait was passed by February 2. But now light and variable airs and calms held both sloops back for a full ten days, during which signs of cholera made several appearances amongst the crew of the Moller: such was the heat. Not one of the sick crewmen died, however. On February 9, the Moller touched on an unknown bank; but she soon re-entered deep water, having suffered no damage. This bank was at the time reckoned to lie 1 1/2 miles SE of the northern extremity of Pulo-Krakatua.

On March 21, in lat. 32°S, long. 37°E, they met with extremely high SW winds, which accompanied them almost to the Cape of Good Hope. Captain Staniukovich, who intended to put in at Table Bay, instructed Captain Lütke to proceed to the island of St. Helena. He stayed one week at the Cape, and himself arrived at St. Helena on April 24. Both sloops proceeded thence on the 28th of that same month. On May 10, they crossed the Equator for a fourth time. Stopping one day at Fayal, they called at Le Havre on June 30.

Having here put the sloops' rigging to rights, Captain Staniukovich sailed straight for the Zund on July 21, while Captain Lütke proceeded to Greenwich for comparative readings with the constant pendulum. Captain Staniukovich vainly waited for Captain Lütke two weeks at Copenhagen. Supposing that he must have passed straight by and into the Baltic, he left the Zund on August 11 and reached Kronshtadt on the 23rd, three years since his leaving that port.

See: Log book; extracts from the journals kept on the voyage to the NW of the Sandwich Islands, and reports of the surveys of Aliaska (Peninsula). In Zapiski of the Hydrographical Department, part 1, are printed three reports by Capt. Staniukovich about the voyage of the sloop Moller from Kronshtadt to Kamchatka and Novo-Arkhangel'sk.

23

The Naval Sloop Seniavin

(Lütke)

1826-29

According to instructions given him by the State Admiralty Department, Captain Lütke was to occupy himself with exploration of the coasts of Chukotka and the Aliaskan Peninsula, also to survey the northern and southern shores of the Sea of Okhotsk, together with the Shantar Islands. To fulfil this mission, he was to follow this plan: commencing his investigations at Bering Strait, he was to sail along the coasts of Chukotka, putting into all bays. In particular, he was to examine the Bay of Anadyr and the mouth of the river of that name. He was to conclude the work of the first summer with a survey of the Kamchatka coast from the mouth of the Anadyr to Avacha Bay and to Cape Lopatka. The next summer he was to occupy himself with a survey of the coasts of the Sea of Okhotsk, starting from the northern tip of Sakhalin and proceeding as far as the Uda stronghold and the Shantar Islands. He was then to cross over to the north coast and, having described the bays of Tauisk, Penzhinsk, and Izhiginsk, to return to Petropavlovsk along the west coast of Kamchatka, fixing his position astronomically on all possible occasions. The plan was an extensive one, and hardly feasible even by two or three vessels in the space of two years. However, it was observed in both commanders' instructions that 'neither in one, nor perhaps even in two years will you manage to complete the survey above. Still, the plan is presented to you in full.'[1] As to the winter season work, which was to be undertaken in the tropics, it was left to Captain Lütke's discretion. It was suggested, however, that he seek out and examine the Bonin-Jima Islands and inspect the Caroline Archipelago from the

_____
[1] Zapiski of State Admiralty Dept., Part XI, p. XLVI.

Marshall group as far as the Pellew group. For the return voyage to Kronshtadt, Captain Lütke was to rejoin the sloop Moller in Petropavlovsk harbor.

Captain Lütke intended to engage not only in hydrographic work but also in experimental work with the constant pendulum and magnetic observations. There were natural scientists aboard the Seniavin.

On August 20, 1826, Captain Lütke left Kronshtadt together with Captain Staniukovich, reaching Portsmouth on September 25 after a one-week stop at Copenhagen. A strong contrary wind in the Baltic slowed the passage greatly.

Work on the sloop, especially the alteration of chain-cables bought in England before they could be fitted, and observations made at Greenwich Observatory by Captain Lütke, held the Seniavin at Portsmouth about a month. Putting out to sea only a few hours after the Moller, he no longer found her in the Channel so, continuing with a fresh NNE wind, he entered the ocean the following day and reached the parallel of Cape Finisterre within five days. On November 2, he called at Teneriffe, expecting to rejoin the Moller there; but not finding her in the roadstead, he made sail after two days and met SW winds which blew for ten whole days. Finally encountering the NE trade wind in lat. 21° 20'N, the Seniavin moved quite swiftly towards the Equator until November 23, when the trade wind gave way to light airs, which continued, except for brief intervals, two weeks.[1]

On December 13, already sailing with the SE trade wind, Captain Lütke crossed the Equator (long. 24° 27'W), forty days after leaving Santa Cruz. On the 26th, he passed within sight of Cabo Frio, and the next day he dropped anchor at Rio de Janeiro next to the Moller.

The two sloops proceeded thence together, and, for the most part, they met moderate following winds as far as Cape Horn. On February 2 they passed in sight of the Falkland Islands and on the 4th reached the parallel of Staten Land, in long. 60°W. But they were separated that same evening in a strong westerly wind and poor visibility.

These westerlies, often strong, continued to blow for ten days. Taking advantage of their every change, Captain Lütke passed the meridian of the Horn on February 13, meeting a severe storm the very next day; he then proceeded under moderate winds. Cape Horn was rounded by the 24th, in the parallel of the Straits of Magellan. Cold and wet weather persisted throughout this whole passage, the

---

[1] Near the Cape Verde Islands, the trade wind blew with extreme force; there was torrential rain. Cf. Voyage of Capt. Lütke, pt. 1, p. 29.

thermometer generally showing no more than 2° or 4°
Reaumur.

Not having been given a definite rendezvous by Captain
Staniukovich, Captain Lütke now made for Concepcion Bay,
a resting-place indicated in the Admiralty instructions,
and on February 27, in lat. 45° 30'S, he met with a
southerly coast wind. He dropped anchor on March 4 at
the entrance to the bay. But he did not find the Moller
there, so hastened out to sea again, only to be detained
until March 8 by calms.[1] The same calms, together with the
lightest NE winds, accompanied him right to Valparaiso,
where work of various kinds and the replenishing of
stores held him until the beginning of April.

On leaving Valparaiso, he struggled for five days and
nights with a strong NW wind. At last, it veered a little
to the west and allowed him to hold closer to the
meridian. Continuing with light SE and SW winds, and
meeting the SE trade wind on April 14, the Seniavin
crossed the Tropic of Capricorn in lat. 10°S, long. 116°
16'W, on the 16th. On the 30th, Captain Lütke laid a
course to the NW in order to cross the Equator in
longitude about 125°W. The chosen course led through an
expanse of water - between latitudes 13°S and 15°N and
longitudes 115°-140°W - that was still little known, since
it lay to the side of the usual paths of vessels visiting
the Pacific Ocean. Knowing that a number of his predecessors
had observed signs of land in those latitudes, Captain
Lütke hoped to make some discovery. But in any event,
the course would conduce to the solution of the problem
of the magnetic node in the Pacific - Hanstein proposed
that the node lay in long. 130°W or thereabouts.

On May 1, the sloop intersected the former route of
Captain Golovnin about that place where he had observed
signs of the proximity of land; neither on that day, nor
on later days, however, were shores sighted. At noon on
the 4th, the magnetic Equator was crossed (lat. 2° 21'S,
long. 123° 41'W). From this point, Captain Lütke was
intending to continue westward a little in order, having
crossed the magnetic Equator twice more, to determine its
three points, i.e., both sides of the node. The SE trade
wind soon changed, however, and a NE head-current forced
him to postpone his intention and hasten to the limits
of the NE trade winds.

The zone between the trade winds was crossed quite
successfully. Meeting the NE trade wind in lat. 8° 10'N,

---

[1] During the night of March 6-7, when held at the bay
entrance by a stream-anchor, the sloop was nearly thrown
by a squall onto some rocks which lay only 1 1/2 cable's-
length off. The stream-anchor cable was successfully cut,
however, and the sloop moved under sail.

Captain Lutke proceeded north and, on May 22, intersected Captain Vancouver's route of 1793-94 (lat. 18°N, long. 138°W). He thereby entered a part of the ocean that was well known already.

On the whole passage from the southern tropic, not even an indication of land had been observed. Captain Lütke believes, it may be added, that he would have been more fortunate in his explorations if calms and an easterly current in latitudes 5°-8°N had not forced him two degrees to the east of the course that he had originally planned. On the entire voyage across the tropics, very few live organisms were met; but starting in lat. 30°N, various sea-worms began to appear in great masses. It was noted that certain of these were encountered in great belts stretching in the direction of the current. It is note-worthy that the greatest heat recorded on this passage (23°R) was not at the Equator itself, but some distance away from it to north and south. The same thing is noted by certain other mariners.

The NE trade wind, which imperceptibly changed into a steady easterly, bore the sloop rapidly northward till June 3 (lat. 45°N); after this, the voyagers encountered light winds from the SE and NE quarters. On the 11th, the shores of America were sighted, and the next day the Seniavin entered the port of Novo-Arkhangel'sk.

The five weeks passed there were employed in unloading the sloop and in making the usual repairs after a ten-month voyage. All this work was complete by mid-July, and on the 19th Captain Lütke sailed for Unalashka, there to take on a baidara and Aleuts for his coastal surveys.

High winds and windless periods delayed the sloop more than a week at Unalashka (August 10-19). When he did leave, Captain Lütke made for St. Matthew Island. On the way he examined the Pribylovs. From August 26 to September 1 he busied himself with a survey of St. Matthew, deter-mining the position of its southern extremity as: lat. 60° 18'N, long. 172° 4'W.

The lateness of the season made it impossible to con-sider work in Bering Strait, and the autumn gales, which soon arrived, forced Captain Lütke to desist even from the work on which he was engaged. He arrived at Petropavlovsk on September 19. The unloading and transmitting of articles brought out, and preparations for a winter voyage, lasted till the middle of October. On the 19th of that month, Captain Lütke put to sea with the intention of first calling at Ualan Island, easternmost island in the Caroline Archipelago, to make observations and then begin an examination of the archipelago.

Accompanied by a fresh NE wind, by September 29 he reached lat. 39°N. Next day, he encountered a storm from

the south. Then, the winds were light till November 8.
On that day, they met with the NE trade wind, strong
initially, but soon losing force. It accompanied the
Seniavin to her destination.

On November 17, the Brown group of coral islands was
examined. Moving on to the south, they next (on the 22nd)
saw Ualan. The trade wind died, however, and light airs
did not permit the sloop to enter La Coquille harbor till
the 27th. On entering this port, a sudden squall almost
threw the sloop on a reef.

On his voyage from Kamchatka to Ualan, Captain Lütke
sought the islands of Kolukas, Beniovski, Dexter, Vulcan,
Lameer, and St. Bartholomew, most of which had become
known through American whalers. Not only did he see none
of them, however, but he even observed no signs of their
proximity.

Leaving Ualan on December 20, Captain Lütke fixed
another point on the magnetic Equator: lat. 4° 7'N, long.
197° 6'W. Proceeding westward, on January 2, 1828, he
discovered an inhabited coral group, the Seniavin Group,
some 50 miles in circumference.[1] Completing a survey of
the group, he went still further west, to the Mortlock
Islands, where he stopped a few days (January 22-27) to
make observations. He then determined the positions of
the islands: Quiros (Freycinet's Hohole), Pisserar
Maryr' (Mague), Onoun (Onon)(Pigailoe), Faieu (Pikelot)
and (Fayu), then setting a course for Guam in the
Marianas. He needed to call there because of a shortage
of provisions and for experiments with the pendulum.

After three weeks in Luis de Apra harbor, Guam,
Captain Lütke returned to the Caroline Archipelago. Over
the next three weeks (from March 8-30) he examined and
determined the positions of these island clusters:
Namurek (Namorik), Elato, Namoliaur (Namoluk), Farrolayp
(Faraulep), Olimarao, Pfaluk (Ifalik), Eurypig (Eauripik),
and Uleay (Woleai). On this last island group, he stopped
for three days to make observations (March 25-28).

On March 30 he left the Caroline Archipelago for
good and headed north, intending to examine the Bonin-
Jima group. On April 11, in lat. 22^oN, the NE trade wind
gave way to light winds from the SW and NW quarters. On
the 18th he inspected Rosario and Failure Islands and,
proceeding to the east, next day he observed four groups
of fairly high islands. Approaching the second of these
from the south, Captain Lütke soon learned from two
Englishmen who came out to him (seamen from a wrecked

---

[1] Between lats. 6° 43' and 7° 6'N, and longs. 201° 30'
and 202^oW. The largest island in this group, Ponape,
rises to a height of 2,930'.

whaler), that these groups were in fact the sought-for Bonin-Jima Islands, also that a year before his own arrival they had been examined by Captain Beechey in the sloop Blossom.

Going into the nearest bay, which was Port Lloyd, Captain Lütke remained there, taking observations, until May 3. On his way from Port Lloyd to the north, he examined two more groups, the Keter and the Parry, which also belonged to the Bonin-Jima group. He then sailed for Kamchatka.

On the passage thither, on May 7, he sought islands in lat. 29° 40'N and long. 217°W which had supposedly been found by Americans' but in vain. A little further on, however, in lat. 45° 30'N, long. 202° 30'W, signs of land were in fact observed,[1] and Captain Lütke believes that an unknown island may exist to the east of that spot. On May 20 (lat. 47° 30'N, long. 198° 54'W) calms set in, which lasted till the 27th, when Kamchatka became visible through the mist. Petropavlovsk harbor was reached the next day.

On June 15, Captain Lütke again put to sea and made for Bering Strait. Following the coast of Kamchatka, he fixed all the main points along it from Avacha Bay to Karaginskii Island, which he surveyed in the course of one week. Pressing on in sight of the coast, he fixed several more points; but strong easterly winds, which set in from July 5 bringing bad weather, forced him to stop work for a time and to hasten to Cape Chukotsk. Such were the fogs and visibility conditions that the Seniavin did not enter Bering Strait till July 15. Next day, she paused in St. Lawrence Bay, where observations were made while the rigging was set to rights: it had been somewhat damaged by the high winds over the last passage.

Proceeding thence to the south, Captain Lütke examined the mouth of Mechigmenskii Bay, and on the 28th discovered the hitherto unknown Seniavin Strait, formed by the shore-line and Arakamchechen and Ittygran' Islands. Until August 5, he occupied himself with the surveying of strait and islands. Then he examined the shores to the south. On the 10th, he entered the Sea of Anadyr', on the 16th - stopped in Holy Cross Bay. The surveying of this extensive bay took a long time (from August 16 to September 7). In consequence, it was not possible to send a launch party in to the mouth of the Anadyr'. Nor, indeed, did the bad weather and a wind blowing straight on-shore permit the fixing of that mouth from the sloop herself. Taking

---

[1] Little water movement despite a strong SE wind, and a few land birds. Capt. Golovnin had noted the same thing on his voyages in the sloops Diana and Kamchatka.

advantage of a short interval of clear weather, on the voyage back to Kamchatka, Captain Lütke managed to fix the positions only of Cape St. Thaddeus and Cape Oliutora (on Sept. 12 and 14 respectively). On the 23rd, he reached the port of Petropavlovsk, where the sloop Moller had been waiting more than a month.

Preparations for the return voyage to Kronshtadt were completed, and both sloops put to sea on October 30, proceeding together with a favorable wind till November 5 when a SE storm and poor visibility separated them. [1] Not finding it necessary to put in a Manila, the rendezvous with the Moller, till the January of 1829, Captain Lütke devoted the time remaining to him to investigation of the northern part of the Caroline Archipelago where, according to information previously acquired, several more unexamined groups might be found. With that object in view, he laid a course that would take the Seniavin to the latitude of Pisserar, two degrees east of the imagined islands, in about long. 24°W. On November 15, in lat. 27°N, he encountered a trade wind. By the 25th he was in lat. 8° 30'N and thereupon turned west.

Over the following 17 days, Captain Lütke sought and described these groups in the Caroline Archipelago: Murillo, Namolikiafan (i.e., Fananu, Namonuito and Feis); he also checked the positions of the Farrolaip (Faraulep), Uleai (Woleai), and Ulithi groups. At the conclusion of these investigations, on December 11, he made for the China Sea. Accompanied by light moderate winds, he passed by the Bashi Islands on December 23 and entered Manila Bay on January 1, 1829.

The voyage of the sloops from Manila to Le Havre, by way of the Cape of Good Hope, was described in the preceding section. From Le Havre, Captain Lütke went to Sheerness, where he stayed 17 days while he repeated experiments with the pendulum at Greenwich Observatory. He arrived at Kronshtadt on August 25, 1829, three years and five days after leaving that port.

The principal results of Captain Lütke's voyage were these: a) Geographical. In the Bering Sea: (1) the most important features along the Kamchatka coast from Avacha Bay northward were fixed astronomically; the heights of many knolls were measured; the Karaginskii Islands, previously unknown, were described, as were St. Matthew Island and Chukotka from Eastern Cape almost as

---

[1] During this passage (in lats. 46°-44°N, on Nov. 3), land birds and other indications of land were sighted from the Seniavin. Bearing in mind similar observations made by Kruzenshtern, Capt. Lütke believes that another, as yet unknown, island may exist in about lat. 40°N, long. 180°-195°W.

far as the mouth of the River Anadyr' and the positions of
the Pribylov as of many other islands were fixed. (2) In
the Caroline Archipelago: the expanse of water from the
island of Ualan to the Ulithi or Mackenzie group was
investigated; 12 islands or island clusters were found
and a total of 26 described. (3) The Bonin-Jima Islands
were found and most of them described. (4) A Marine
Atlas was compiled, comprising 51 charts, with views of
coastlines. (5) In addition, much information was
gathered whereby the positions of places visited by the
sloop might be determined, as was much information regarding
currents, tides, etc.
        b) Physical. Experiments were made with the
constant pendulum, from which it was deduced that the earth
is compressed 1/288. (2) Magnetic observations were
made by land and sea, mostly in the northern part of the
Pacific Ocean. The results harmonize to a remarkable
extent with Hanstein's theorem. (3) Observations were
made regarding hourly fluctuations of the barometer.
Between lats. 30°N and 30°S, readings were taken every
half-hour on two sympesometers, and by the barometer,
over a 12-month period. (4) Observations of the surface
water temperature were recorded daily.
        c) Natural Science. (1) In zoology: more than
one and a half thousand specimens of various creatures
were collected, e.g., birds, fish, insects, crustacea.
A significant collection of shellfish was made. A new
species of seal was observed, etc. (2) In botany: a
large quantity of plants was assembled and cased. (3)
In geodesy: as many as 330 specimens of rock were
collected in all places that the sloop stopped by.
        d) Ethnographical. A rich collection of clothing,
weapons, utensils, and ornaments. Most of these objects
were sketched - more than 1,200 sketches were made during
the expedition - and the collections themselves were
handed over to the museums of the Academy of Sciences.

        Captain Lütke's voyage and its results were described
in the following works: 1. A Voyage Round the World,
Completed on the Instruction of His Imperial Majesty
Nicholas 1, by the Sloop Seniavin in 1826-1829, Under the
Command of Navy Captain Fedor Lütke. Historical Section,
with Atlas and Lithographs from Original Sketches, by Mr.
A. Postel's and Baron Kittlits: St. P., 1834-36: in 3
pts., of 294, 282, ix and 270 pp. In Russian and French.
        2. The same: Maritime Section, with atlas: St. P,
1835. vi+356 pp. Included in this section are meteorological and route tables, comments on passages from one
location to the next and on currents, and a hydrographic
description of the Bering Sea.
        3. Experiments with the Constant Pendulum, Made on
the Voyage Round the World by Captain O. Lütke of the Naval
Sloop Seniavin, 1826-1829: St.P., 1833: 232 pp.
        4. Observations on the Variations and Strengths of
the Magnetic Needle, Completed During a Voyage Round the
World in the Sloop Seniavin, in 1826-29, by Naval Captain
F. Lütke: Examined and Computed by E. Lenz: St.P., 1836.

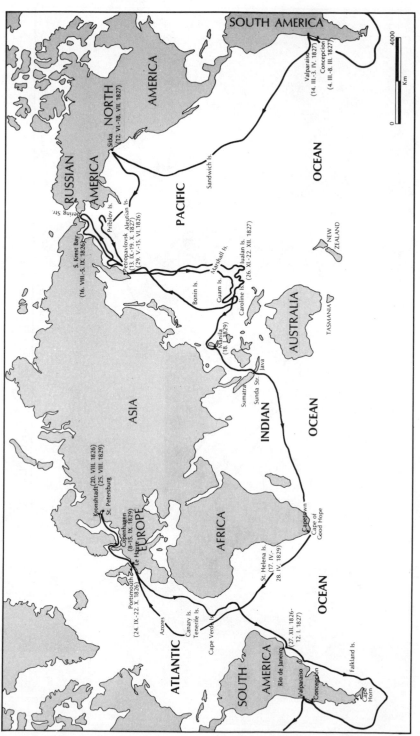

VOYAGE OF LUTKE ON THE "SENIAVIN" (1826-1829)

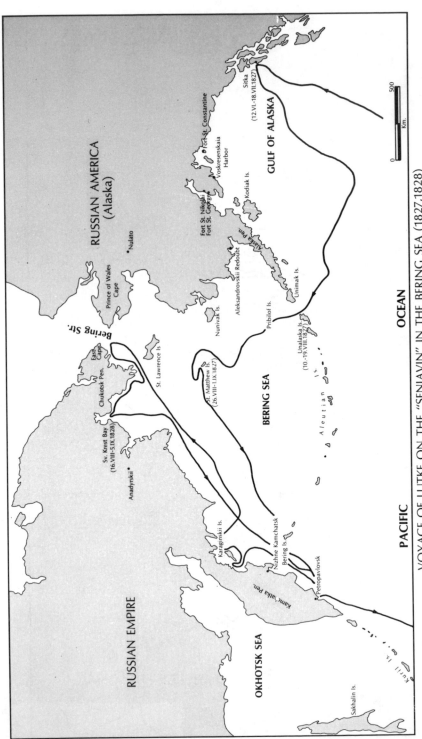

VOYAGE OF LUTKE ON THE "SENIAVIN" IN THE BERING SEA (1827, 1828)

Translated from the German by Naval Lieutenant B. Glazenap.
5. Barometric, Sympesometric, and Thermometric
Observations Made on Captain Lütke's Voyage Round the
World: computed by Professor H. Helstrom of the University
of Helsingfors: St. P., 1838: 37 pp.

24

The Russian-American Company Vessel Elena

(Khromchenko)

1828-31

At the beginning of 1828, the Elena was again
appointed to carry a cargo from Kronshtadt to Sitkha, this
time under the command of Lt. Khromchenko, who had already
participated in one such voyage, namely, that by the brig
Riurik, under Captain Kotzebue.

Lieutenant Khromchenko weighed anchor from
Kronshtadt Roads on August 4, 1828. He stopped for ten
days at Copenhagen, then struggled with high westerly
winds for two weeks in the North Sea, before dropping
anchor on September 5 in Portsmouth roadstead. He sailed
from there on October 4, accompanied by variable winds,
and on the 25th crossed the Tropic of Cancer in long. 24°W.
Having crossed the zone of the NE trade wind in a mere
three days and nights (October 27-November 1), he encountered
a SE wind in lat. 2°N, long. 23° 28'N and in that same
area observed many land birds. Rio de Janeiro was reached
on November 30.

Light southerlies prevailed for the most part on the
passage from Rio de Janeiro to the meridian of Greenwich,
which was passed on January 24 and in lat. 37° 30'S. They
then entered the zone of westerly winds and of north-
westerlies, proceeding with them to the Cape of Good Hope
and beyond, into the southern Indian Ocean. On February
8, in lat. 43°S and long. 49° 39'E, icebergs were observed
at dawn to the southward. Eight of them were counted, and
some estimated by eye to be 200' high. About noon, 25
miles away from this place, they were lost from view.
Over the entire passage to Port Jackson, a strong tail
current was observed: it carried the vessel almost 1,200
miles to the NE.

Leaving Port Jackson at the end of April, Lt.
Khromchenko headed NE. On April 28, he passed within
sight of Norfolk Island, and on May 3 crossed the southern
tropic in long. 172° 30'E. Continuing northward, on the
9th he passed Rotuma or Grenville Island at a distance of
15 miles. He reckoned its position as: lat. 12° 30' 50"S,
long. 178° 54'E.

On May 11, he discovered a wooded and inhabited islet, four miles in length and about a half a mile in breadth, with an elevation of 80'. He named it after the senior lieutenant in the _Elena_, Levendal' (Loewendal). This island lies in lat. 7° 13'S and long. 177° 14' 30"E.[1] Next day, flocks of land birds were seen flying to the SW, but no shores were seen. Passing the island of Grand Kokal' (Coqual) on May 14, Lt. Khromchenko reckoned it to lie in lat. 6° 12' 30"S, long. 176° 13'E.[2] Between May 22 and 26, passing through the Marshall group, he fixed the positions of the following island clusters: Mille, in lat. 6° 4' 30"N, long. 171° 55' 50"E; Mediuro (Majuro), in lat. 7° 8' 57"N, long. 171° 18' 26"; Eregup (Erikub), southern tip in lat. 9° 0'N, long. 170° 18'E; and Ligiep (Likiep), center in lat. 9° 55'N, long. 169° 15'E. A chart of this group was drawn by navigator Kashevarov. On June 1, the Tropic of Cancer was crossed in long. 167° 40'E, and the NE trade wind was lost. But N and NE winds, interspersed with calms, took the vessel to lat. 32°N. On June 18, in lat. 42° 30'N and long. 187°E, land birds and a floating trunk were observed; however, no land was found. On July 4, the _Elena_ reached her destination, the port of Novo-Arkhangel'sk.

After three and a half months had elapsed, in the unloading of the cargo at Sitkha, the receiving of a cargo of colonial peltry, and in consequence of the contrary winds that prevailed, Lt. Khromchenko set out on his return voyage on October 15. Sixteen days after leaving Sitkha, he dropped anchor in San Francisco harbor to wood and water. On December 13, he again put to sea, and one month later (on January 11) he crossed the Equator in long. 234° 48'E. The voyage continued happily in the southern hemisphere. On February 16 he passed the meridian of Cape Horn, in lat. 57° 53'S, and on March 13 he arrived at Rio de Janeiro - 90 days out from San Francisco. Rounding the Horn, scurvy had begun to make an appearance among the crew; but the speed of the following passage had not allowed any development of the illness, nor was there a single man sick when the _Elena_ left Rio de Janeiro on May 5.

Proceeding mostly with a following wind, Lt. Khromchenko passed through the English Channel on June 28, reached Elsinore on July 2 after two days at Copenhagen, and

---

[1] This same island was found in 1825 by Koerzen, the commander of a Dutch frigate, on his way from Nuku Hiva to the Moluccas. He named it Nederlandsch Eyland and found it to lie in lat. 7° 7'S, long. 177° 36'E. Not knowing this and thinking that he had made a fresh discovery, Mr. Khromchenko named the island after his First Lieutenant. Cf. supplement to Atlas of the South Sea, p. 19.

[2] This longitude reading was arrived at by observations with 8 chronometers.

dropped anchor at Kronshtadt on July 10, one year and
eleven months after leaving the port.

This was one of the most successful of voyages: not
only was not a single member of the crew lost - the vessel
herself suffered no damage in hull or rigging. The value
of the cargo brought from the colonies proved to be, at
the time of sale, 1,200,200 paper rubles.

Based on Commander's report and notes, now in the
archive of the Hydrographic Department; and ship's log.

25

The Naval Transport Krotkii

(Hagemeister)

1828-30

Captain-Lieutenant Hagemeister, known already for two
voyages out to the colonies of the Russian-American Company,
was early in 1828 appointed commander of the transport
Krotkii, lately returned from a voyage round the world.
She was now sent to Kamchatka and the colonies with a
mixed cargo, viz.: rigging, iron articles, carpenters'
and joiners' tools, etc. She was also to cruise about
the colonies.

Captain Hagemeister left Kronshtadt on September 10,
1828, stopped three days at Copenhagen, and two weeks
later arrived at Portsmouth. During a ten-day stay here,
he inspected his vessel and put her fully to rights. An
examination of her sides revealed, inter alia, several
blunders: these had been committed under the chain-plates,
and had resulted in a considerable leak. Another anchor
was purchased to replace the spare one. The new anchor
had a chain-cable, and all necessary alterations were
made to the main-hatch to accommodate it. At the same
time, astronomical instruments, three chronometers, and
charts were purchased in London.

On October 14, Captain Hagemeister sailed from the
shores of England. He proposed to enter the South Sea
by way of the Cape of Good Hope. On November 3, he passed
Teneriffe, and two days later he encountered the NE trade
wind. On November 11, he dropped anchor in Porto-Praia,
Santiago Island. Thence he proceeded, on the 16th, towards
the Cape of Good Hope. Passing swiftly through the zones
of both trade winds, by December 25 he was in lat. 34°S
and long. 20°W. Here, he met a violent storm.

By December 31, the transport was already in the
parallel of the cape, and some 1,700 miles to its west.
The meridian of Greenwich was crossed for the second time
on January 5, 1829, and on the 14th the Krotkii called in

at Simons Bay to water and for repairs to rigging damaged in a storm.

When all this was done, Captain Hagemeister put to sea again on the 26th. On the passage to Port Jackson, in lat. 41°S, long. 313°W, many birds were seen, but no land was sighted - possibly because the horizon was obscured. On March 13 they passed 40 miles off Cape Pillar (Van Diemen's Land), and on the 26th they reached Port Jackson, exactly two months after leaving Simons Bay. Over the whole passage, the winds had blown mainly from the SW and NW quarters.

In Port Jackson, the Krotkii's hold was dried and provisions were taken on. Captain Hagemeister left on April 19. He intended at first to examine the Loyalty and Brown Islands; learning, however, that Captain Dillon had already been on them, and that Captain Dumont-D'Urville had likewise visited the Loyalty and the Malikolo island groups, he decided to pass east of them, along the western fringe of the Fiji or Viti Islands. Having examined these, he would determine the latitude and longitude of Giunter or Farewell Island, with which the Fiji group terminates on the north.

On April 27, they crossed the meridian of Norfolk Island, then being 200 miles to its south, and on May 5 they crossed the Tropic of Capricorn in long. 181° 58'W. On the afternoon of the 7th, the island of Meivull (D'Urville's Candaboque) came in sight. Over the next two days, the island was surveyed and its position astronomically reckoned: lat. 19° 7'S, long. 177° 58'E.

On May 12, the transport crossed the parallel of Rotuma Island; and on the 24th, when near the Equator, she passed through the spot on which Ocean Island is indicated on charts, with an elevation of 1,804'. This island was not sighted, however, nor were any signs of land observed in spite of the clear conditions, which would have made it possible to see land at a great distance.[1] Throughout the following night, Captain Hagemeister kept the Krotkii under small sail, supposing that he was near the island. But nothing emerged.

On the morning of May 29 (lat. 4° 30'N, long. 171°W) a cluster of low islands were sighted from the cross-trees. Several small craft soon came out from them towards the transport. A few knives, beads, and the little mirror given to the elder in the first craft immediately brought all the other craft over. According to Captain Hagemeister,

---

[1] Thus in Capt. Hagemeister's notes. But according to the log, Ocean Island was passed at a distance of 42 miles. In ASS, the island is named among those whose positions are doubtful. It is given there as: lat. 6° 48'S, long. 170° 50'E, on the basis of Arrowsmith.

the natives of this cluster (which was probably the Boston (or Ebon) Island discovered in 1824 by the American ship-master Wray), in many ways resembled the inhabitants of the Radak Islands, investigated by Captain Kotzebue. By Captain Hagemeister's reckoning the group lies in lat. 4° 39'N and long. 168° 50'E.

Continuing northward, Elmore (Namu) and Princess (Lib) Islands were passed on June 2. The next day, at noon, a group of ten inhabited islands appeared. They stretched about 19 miles from E to W and about four miles across the meridian. A high wind and breakers made it impossible to make the closer acquaintance of the islanders, though their craft could already be seen from afar. The southern extremity of the most westerly of the newly-discovered islands was reckoned to lie in lat. 9° 5' 38"N, and long. 167° 22' 18"E.

Approximately 20 miles to the west of this cluster another was found, extending seven miles across the parallel. The southern tip of this second group was found to lie in lat. 9° 17'N, long. 167° 3' 40"E. Together, the two clusters form a single chain and belong to the Marshall Archipelago. Captain Hagemeister called them the Prince Menshikov Islands.

Having, on June 5, fixed the geographical position of the Eschscholtz Islands discovered and described by Captain Kotzebue, Captain Hagemeister made for the shores of Kamchatka. One week later he passed beyond the limit of the NE trade wind. Accompanied by variable winds and by poor conditions of visibility, he sighted the Kamchatka coast, near Petropavlovsk, on July 7. On July 10 he dropped anchor, after a ten-month voyage out from Kronshtadt.

When materials brought out had been discharged, and the Krotkii's hold dried out, Captain Hagemeister made preparations for his passage to Novo-Arkhangel'sk. During an examination, much damage to the transport's rigging had been noted, as well as to the spars. All this was attended to as well as possible and towards the end of September, fitted out according to the means of the place, the transport was ready to put to sea. Captain Hagemeister left Kamchatka on October 3,[1] and set a course along the southern face of the Aleutian chain in keeping with his instructions.

The 19-day passage to Novo-Arkhangel'sk was performed under high winds and in constantly poor conditions of visibility. On October 10, in lat. 47°N and long. 183° 45'W, many birds were seen flying to the NE, and certain indications of land were observed. At this time the nearest

---

[1] At Petropavlovsk, the Berlin Professor, Erman, was taken on as a passenger for Russia. The professor had been making magnetic and meteorological observations in Kamchatka and, particularly, had been determining magnetic force.

known land, Amytygasak Island, was 300 miles off to the NE at 37°. The conditions made it impossible to examine the horizon. Nor did the constantly cold and wet weather remain without effect on the crew. Many of the lower ranks suffered from colds. However, only one man died - and he had long suffered consumption.

On the afternoon of October 25, and through the deep gloom, Cape St. Lazarus came into view; but signs of an impending storm obliged the captain to put out to sea. The precaution proved to have been very timely; that night, the wind rose high, veered several times, and finally blew straight on-shore, in a thick mist. The mercury in the barometer fell from 29.18 to 28.34. In the morning Cape St. Lazarus again emerged through the mist and, steering by it, Captain Hagemeister entered Sitkha Sound towards midday.

Upon being informed by the Governor of the colonies, Captain Chistiakov, that the colonies did not stand in need of a warship, Captain Hagemeister left for San Francisco harbor, there to purchase provisions. He arrived on November 24 but could buy no provisions because of a poor harvest, caused by drought.

Leaving California, Captain Hagemeister headed south, nearly down the meridian of San Francisco itself, and on December 28 crossed the Tropic of Cancer in long. 238° 38' 30"E. With the intention of determining the magnetic node's position, he then set a course to the location where, according to Hanstein's calculations and Captain Freycinet's observations, it was to be sought. On the basis of observations with various inclinators, both Captain Hagemeister and Dr. Erman convinced themselves that, between longitudes 236° 42' and 218°E, the magnetic Equator does not intersect the earth's Equator, but runs south of it at a distance varying between 1° 48' and 1° 52'.

Being short of water, Captain Hagemeister was obliged to discontinue his investigations and proceed to the island of Tahiti. He intended, on his way thither, to occupy himself with surveys of Fly and Prince of Wales Islands, which had not yet been examined by contemporary mariners.

On January 28, 1830, after noon, a shore appeared which was quickly recognized as the island of Vaterland: its NE extremity was found to lie in lat. 14° 17' 20"S and long. 145° 54' 45"W. Proceeding on his way, Captain Hagemeister on the 27th passed Palliser Island and the northern part of the Riurik chain. On the night of the 28th he bore north; the following morning, he saw Fly Island. The light wind, occasionally broken by squalls, did not allow him to go closer to its shores than 3 1/2 miles. Smoke was observed on one of the islets near it, but no natives came out.[1]

_____

[1] Nothing more is said of these islands in the journal; probably the weather prevented the making of observations.

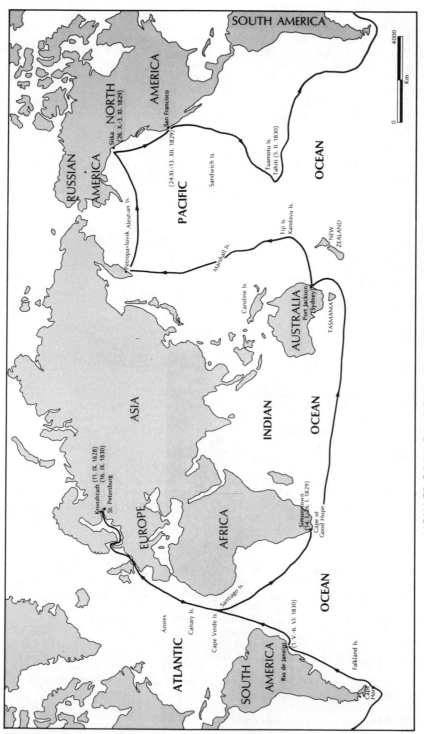

VOYAGE OF HAGEMEISTER ON THE "KROTKII" (1828-1829)

SOUTH AMERICA

RUSSIAN AMERICA

NORTH AMERICA

Sitka (26. X.-3. XI. 1829)

San Francisco (24.XI.-13. XII. 1829)

Petropavlovsk Aleutian Is.

PACIFIC OCEAN

Sandwich Is.

Tuamotu Is.
Tahiti (5. II. 1830)

Marshall Is.

Fiji Is.
Kandavu Is.

NEW ZEALAND

Caroline Is.

AUSTRALIA
Port Jackson
Sydney

TASMANIA

ASIA

INDIAN OCEAN

EUROPE

Kronshtadt (11. IX. 1828)
St. Petersburg (16. IX. 1830)

AFRICA

Simonstown (14. I.-26. I. 1829)
Cape of Good Hope

Azores

Canary Is.

Cape Verde Is.

Santiago Is.

ATLANTIC

SOUTH AMERICA

Rio de Janeiro (1.V.-6. VI. 1830)

OCEAN

Falkland Is.

Cape Horn

0   4000
Km

On January 31, they sailed with a NW wind past the
Kruzenshtern Islands. Their north-eastern cape was found
to lie in long. 148° 41' 33"W. On February 5, Captain
Hagemeister dropped anchor in Matavai Bay. But the north
wind which prevails in that season at Tahiti rendered a
sojourn in the bay extremely risky. Hagemeister therefore
made haste to water and to take on fresh provisions:
but for three whole days and nights he could not even
establish contact with the shore - the north wind was pro-
ducing such waves that when she pitched, the Krotkii took
water through her stern windows, and when she rolled -
through the gun-ports. In fact, the transport's position
became extremely dangerous. Surrounded by breakers not a
cable off, she could easily have been cast ashore, where
the natives had already gathered more than once, in
expectation of a shipwreck. The island itself was suffering
from this storm: many houses were destroyed, roofs were
torn off, trees torn out by their roots, and the breakers
actually washed over part of Point Venus. The place where
the observatory-tent stood was flooded with water and the
tent itself was pulled out of the sand the next day. The
astronomical instruments, however, were saved. The captain
himself very nearly drowned on returning to the transport
from the shore: he fell into the breakers from his launch.
During this storm, the transport lost a rowing-boat, which
had been filled to the deck with water.

Captain Hagemeister resolved to take advantage of the
first favorable wind to leave this dangerous roadstead,
even though water and firewood had been stowed only in
sufficient quantity to last two months. On February 11,
he put to sea. When the anchor was weighed, the Krotkii
was almost thrown onto Dolphin Reef.[1] Once again saving
himself from danger, Captain Hagemeister passed north of
the island of Eimeo, in order to avoid the calms prevailing
to the leeward of the larger islands.

As far as lat. 45°S, they had mostly a SE wind and
fine weather. From that latitude, however, and in mid-
March, they encountered bad conditions with storms, which
considerably damaged the transport's spars and rigging.

On March 31 they passed the meridian of Cape Victory
in lat. 56° 30'S. They entered the Atlantic Ocean on
April 6, which was Easter Day. About Cape Horn there blew
moderate winds, chiefly from the NE or SE quarters. The
greatest inclination of the magnetic needle was observed
in lat. 58° 33'S, long. 70°W: it was of 66° 16' to the
south. The greatest compass variation was observed in
lat. 56° 45', long. 73° 53'W: it was of 26° 9' to the
east. By Cape Horn, the inclination (the mean reading from
observations with two instruments) was 60° 38'.

---

[1] Upon weighing the anchor the transport began to drift
because of the negligence of a seaman, winding the chain
on the capstan; it fouled just as the anchor was about
to separate from the bottom.

On May 1, Captain Hagemeister reached Rio de Janeiro. When work on the transport was completed, he put to sea again (June 6); with a NE coast wind, he reached lat. 21°S by the 19th of that month. Here, calms delayed the vessel for a week or so. Then meeting with the SE trade wind, Captain Hagemeister had a very easy passage to the Equator. After three days in the calms, between latitudes 4° and 10°N, he entered the zone of the NE trade wind. On July 24 he left the tropics, proceeding with moderate SW winds. On August 17, the coast of England became visible near Cape Stuart (Start Point): that same day he entered Portsmouth Roads.

After five days at Portsmouth, they made for the Baltic Sea. A stop of two days and nights at Elsinore because of contrary winds, and on September 16 they arrived in Kronshtadt roadstead.

Notes on the Krotkii's voyages, prepared by Capt. Hagemeister, are held in the archive of the Hydrographic Department; they comprise only extracts, however, from an account of the whole voyage. The log-book has been used to fill in gaps.

26

The Naval Transport Amerika

(Khromchenko)

1831-33

Under the command of Captain-Lieutenant Khromchenko, the transport Amerika was, in the spring of 1831, sent to Kamchatka and the colonies with a mixed cargo. The commander also had orders to engage in hydrographic work to the extent that he was able; but the main end of the voyage was the delivery of the cargo. The Amerika was laden with 6,500 puds of State materials and Company goods and articles to a weight of 17,500 puds. Captain Khromchenko left Kronshtadt on August 26, 1831, carrying with him naval stores and provisions for two years. Certain items, however, were to be supplemented at Copenhagen and Portsmouth.

At Copenhagen, the Amerika was placed in quarantine because of the cholera which had raged in St. Petersburg. The period of quarantine, which was seven days, was employed in final preparations for the voyage: the purchasing of rum, wine, and antiscorbutics.

Making sail on September 16, Captain Khromchenko enjoyed a following wind into the Channel; but there he encountered a fresh south-westerly wind, and only on October 7 did he reach Portsmouth, standing by Mother Bank.

They proceeded thence in mid-November, making straight
for Rio de Janeiro - a stop at the Canary Islands was not
planned. As far as lat. 40°N, they sailed with moderate SW
winds; but about that parallel they met a SW storm, which
lasted several days. On December 6, they passed Porto
Santo. With the NE trade wind they swiftly traversed the
torrid zone, reaching Rio de Janeiro on January 3, 1832.
Over the last few days, they had a northerly coast wind
with them.

Once the rigging of the transport had been adjusted
and a store of fresh provisions and water stowed, Captain
Khromchenko went on his way (early February). The lateness
of the season obliged him to choose a route round the
Cape of Good Hope and Australia; and Port Jackson was
selected as the resting point on that voyage.

With the northerly coastal wind, the transport had
soon reached the 32nd parallel of southern latitude; by
February 28 she was already in the meridian of Tristan
da Cunha (lat. 34° 30'S). Now proceeding with W or SW
winds, they found themselves by the meridian of the Cape
of Good Hope, where they encountered a SW storm (lat.
41° 30'S), on March 9.

Repairing as best he could the considerable damage
which this storm had done to the rigging, Captain Khromchenko
continued westward between parallels 40° and 49°S, with the
strong westerly winds prevailing in that part of the
ocean. He crossed the meridian of Van Diemen's Land, in
lat. 44° 30'S, on March 31; on April 24, from long. 209°W,
he set a course straight for Port Jackson. On May 9 he
dropped anchor before the town of Sydney.

The protracted storms on this last passage had considerably damaged the rigging of the Amerika. Almost a
whole month was spent in putting it to rights. But at the
same time, all needed stores were taken on. They sailed
on June 10.

On June 20, they crossed the Tropic of Capricorn, and
the next day they reached the parallel of Hunter or Fearn
Island - westernmost island of the New Caledonia group.
They left it 270 miles to their west. During the next
ten days, the transport traversed the western side of the
Fiji Islands without sighting them; on the 28th, she
approached the Peister Group. From noon observations,
this group was found to lie in lat. 8° 0' 23"S, long. 178°
21' 25"E.

Just before sunrise on June 30, in lat. 6° 30'S, a
false sun was observed - a rare phenomenon in that zone.
That same day, the transport passed within sight of the
islands of Gran-Kokal (Grand Coquail) and St. Augustine;
she passed to their east. At 6 p.m. on July 8, in lat.
0° 15'S, long. 174° 1'E, an inclination of the magnetic

needle of 18° 30' to the north was observed. At the time, the _Amerika_ was 15 miles from the Henderville and Vuddl' (Waedle) groups in the Gilbert Archipelago.

Taking advantage of the unbroken fair weather, Captain Khromchenko decided to take a little time to examine this archipelago. At 10 a.m., when the _Amerika_ was three miles from the southern island in the Henderville group, several craft appeared bearing natives. The transport hove to, awaiting them. The little craft soon came alongside. There were two or three men in each. The savages immediately began to barter coconuts and bread-fruit for pieces of old iron hoops, which they greatly valued. The craft made off after an hour and Captain Khromchenko, having reckoned the center of the Henderville group to lie in lat. 0° 10' 30"N, long. 173° 36' 57"E, went on to the Vuddl' (Waedle) Islands. When five miles from the westernmost of these, he observed about 10 craft. Both the craft and the natives themselves proved to be very like those in the Henderville group. Having bartered a few more pieces of iron for provisions and native artifacts, he moved on north. By evening both groups were lost from view.

The following day, Captain Khromchenko determined the positions of these groups: the Hall group (S extremity in lat. 0° 50' 2"n, long. 173° 0' 17"E); the Cook group (SW extremity in lat. 1° 20' 30"N, long. 172° 56'E); and the Charlotte group (W extremity in lat. 1° 55' 2"N, long. 172° 54' 11"E).[1] Towards evening, he went out into open water.

Passing through the Marshall Archipelago on July 12-18, Captain Khromchenko further surveyed and fixed the positions of the following islands: Mulgrave (lat. 6° 4'N, as also reckoned by Captain Duperrey); Arrowsmith (lat. 7° 9'N, long. 171° 18'E); the Muskillo group (S. tip of Odia Island, 7° 15'N, long. 168° 46'E, and S. tip of Namu Island, 7° 46'N, long. 168° 23'E); and Prince Menshikov Island (SE extremity in lat. 8° 45'N, long. 167° 45' 30"E).

When he had concluded these observations, Captain Khromchenko laid a course for Petropavlovsk harbor. The Tropic of Cancer was crossed, on July 24, in long. 164° 30'E. From there to Kamchatka itself, the _Amerika_ was accompanied by moderate winds and fair weather - though the latter turned misty and gloomy the closer she came to the shore.

At dawn on August 13, Avacha Hill became visible; the transport approached the entrance to the bay the next morning. But at 5 p.m., when rounding Signal Cape, she grounded on a bank. Not for three days and nights did she

---

[1] All longitudes reckoned by three chronometers; the long. of Hall Island - by lunar distances besides.

get off it, when 3,000 <u>puds</u> of her cargo had been discharged onto the shore or into a brig sent out from the port.

As soon as the transport was brought off this bank, work began on the repairing of damage suffered by her spars and rigging: but this was inevitable, after so long a voyage. At the same time she was unloaded and the State materials brought were transmitted to the port authority. On September 7, a violent squall from the north threw an anchor into the water. Mooring lines went too, and the transport was carried towards the shore. However, she was quickly brought to a halt by another anchor, which had immediately been thrown out.

Captain Khromchenko proceeded hence to Novo-Arkhangel'sk on September 13. On the passage, he had constant high NW winds, with rain and mists. The Company goods discharged at Sitkha were replaced by 13,000 <u>puds</u> of stone ballast and 2,500 <u>puds</u> of various wares from the Company magazines. Also taken on at Sitkha were several passengers for Kronshtadt: Commercial Counsellor Khlebnikov, Navigator Obriadin, and several persons of lower rank. After standing four days in Sitkha Sound, for lack of wind, Captain Khromchenko went on his way to San Francisco harbor, there to water and provision for the return voyage to Russia.

Light airs and calms accompanied him to lat. 44° 30'N. On December 11 the transport passed within sight of Ross settlement; the next day, anchors were dropped in San Francisco Bay.

Having here taken on all that he needed, Captain Khromchenko put to sea again (January 1833), intending to round Cape Horn. One month later he was already in the southern hemisphere. On February 9, in lat. 24° 30'S, long. 127°W, a land bird was seen, though the nearest land (Elizabeth Island and the suspect Bond Island) was at least 120 Italian miles away. Two days later Pitcairn Island appeared - an island remarkable for its European colony. Approaching it to a distance of four miles, the transport hove to. Shortly afterwards, a number of craft came out, bearing the islanders. Three islanders remained on the transport till the following morning. They were then sent back ashore with Lt. Bodisko, who returned with a fair quantity of potatoes and other foodstuffs. The island was reckoned by three chronometers to lie in long. 229° 50' 33"E,[1] while its highest elevation was estimated at 1,109 English feet above sea-level.

Captain Khromchenko went on his way that same day. In lat. 40°S, he met with strong SW and NW winds which quickly carried the transport into the Atlantic Ocean. By April 7, he was already in Rio de Janeiro roadstead.

---

[1] Captain Beechey gives the longitude as 229° 51' 37"E.

Again adjusting the standing rigging here, and replenishing provisions, Captain Khromchenko put to sea again
with a gentle NE-NW wind which, after a few days, took
on the form of the true trade wind. One month later he
passed beyond the limit of the SE trade winds, and on July
4 he reached the parallel of Corvo Island. On the 20th,
he approached the entrance of the English Channel; but a
high north-easterly wind encountered here forced him
to take shelter in the Downs. He then crossed the North
Sea with a strong NW wind, paused at Copenhagen, and reached
Kronshtadt Roads on September 13. In the course of a two-
year voyage, he had lost only one man in his crew.

27

The Naval Transport Amerika

(von Schants)

1834-36

In the following year, 1834, the same transport, the
Amerika, was sent to Kamchatka and the colonies under the
command of Captain-Lieutenant (now Admiral) von Schants.
She carried a mixed cargo of some 25,000 puds weight.
Certain alterations and improvements were made to the
transport's rigging and other parts, on the basis of
experience gained during her previous circumnavigation.

Captain von Schants left Kronshtadt on August 5,
1834. He stopped for a week at Copenhagen. Proceeding
thence on the 22nd, the next day he met with a strong west
wind and cloudiness (by Skagen) which lasted throughout
the North Sea crossing. On September 3, the wind at last
veered to SE and the transport entered Portsmouth Roads
on the 5th.

At Portsmouth there were loaded 60 tons of woolen goods
bought by the Russian-American Company for its colonies.
They sailed on September 20, making for Rio de Janeiro
direct.

Accompanied by variable but frequently high winds, on
October 4 they passed Madeira at a distance of 17 miles
and on the 8th entered the zone of the NE trade wind. For
two days (October 13-14), this blew from the north (by
the Cape Verde Islands). By the 17th they had reached the
calm zone: for ten days and nights the rains and squalls
were almost incessant. Nor did the wet and overcast
weather even end then: it stretched as far as the coast
of America where, in sight of Cabo Frio, calms delayed the
transport more than ten days more. During this period
the longitude of Cabo Frio was reckoned by three chronometers at 41° 32' 6"W from Greenwich.

Taking advantage of the slight change of wind for the

113

better, and even using a tow-boat occasionally, Captain von Schants at last entered the roadstead of Rio de Janeiro - 60 days out from Portsmouth. From there he headed for the Cape of Good Hope. Strong NE winds accompanied him until the January of 1835, lat. 33° 30'S. From that parallel to the cape, the meridian of which was passed on January 17 at a distance of 360 miles, variable northerlies prevailed.

From the meridian of the Cape of Good Hope onward, they proceeded between latitudes 40° and 44°S. The following week (January 18-24), they encountered a very high N wind. On February 7, from the meridian of the southern tip of Van Diemen's Land (lat. 45° 48'S), Captain von Schants laid a course for Port Jackson. The coast of Australia came into view on the morning of March 6, and the following day the Amerika dropped anchor opposite the town of Sydney.

Having watered here, they put to sea and headed east between the 33rd and 35th parallels of southern latitude, under (often high) northerly winds. On April 22 they passed the northern extremity of New Zealand and on the 27th, in long. 179°E, headed for Petropavlovsk harbor.

On May 2, after a storm from the NE and a resultant heavy swell, the wind veered to the west; on the 9th, the SE trade wind was met. It was held, in constantly bad weather, till the 16th. The passage between trade winds, which lasted nearly two weeks, was performed under light winds from the NE and SE; they alternated, now and then, with squalls and showers. This protracted passage, which is usually so pernicious for a crew, was completed very happily, probably because of the steps taken in good time to preserve the health of the Amerika's company. Altogether no more than four men were sick.

From lat. 30°S, Captain von Schants sailed between the routes of Captains Golovnin and Hagemeister. The NE trade wind was met on May 28. The transport was then within sight of the Princess group (lat. 6° 30'N). Natives came out in several craft but soon returned to the shore after a little insignificant barter. The transport went on her way. The next day, a shore showed to W and NW. Since no known land was to be expected in this direction, Captain von Schants immediately bore west. He soon perceived that the shore was in fact a group of islands of coral formation. Whilst a survey was being undertaken from the transport, several native craft came out and approached her to within a cable's length. They soon returned to the shore, however, and all the means tried to induce the natives to come on deck proved ineffectual. The party themselves attempted a landing; but Lt. Berens, who was sent, was forced back - breakers made it impossible to near the shore.

The newly-discovered group was reckoned by observations
to lie in lat. 10° 5'N, long. 166° 4' 10"E. The group
consisted of 13 coral islands, most of them inhabited, and
belongs to the extensive Marshall Archipelago. In Admiral
Kruzenshtern's atlas they are called the Schants Islands.

Having completed the survey, by the evening of May 30,
Captain von Schants continued north. On June 5 he crossed
the Tropic of Cancer, in long. 158° 39'E, and thereafter
he struggled with extremely high NW winds, especially near
lat. 42°N, on June 19. The constant rain and mist, which
set in starting then, had a significant effect on the
crew's health: on this passage, as many as 10 men fell
sick. Most recovered only on arrival in Kamchatka. The
shores of Avacha Bay became visible through the mists on
June 25, and the Amerika reached Petropavlovsk harbor on
the 27th, 67 days since leaving Port Jackson.

Here the materials brought out were transferred to the
brig Elisaveta and a mixed cargo (mostly of worn out iron
and copper articles), of 2,000 puds weight, was taken on.
Captain von Schants then (August 21) set sail from
Petropavlovsk, and reached Novo-Arkhangel'sk on September
13. A violent easterly storm was encountered on the
passage. The unloading of the Amerika and the stowing of
articles from the Company magazines for delivery to Russia
detained him at Sitkha till October 11.

On leaving Sitkha the voyagers made for the Sandwich
Islands: it was proposed to take on provisions there for
the voyage into the Atlantic Ocean. After a stormy 26-
day passage, they at length sighted the heights of Maui.
Shortly thereafter, they entered Honolulu harbor, in Oahu.
Deceived in his hope of obtaining here a sufficient
quantity of provisions (though very kindly received by
the king), Captain von Schants sailed on November 13 for
the Tahitian group, where he expected to supplement his
stores.

For the first eight days of this passage, the Amerika
was accompanied by the NE trade wind. This, however, then
gave way to light winds from the SE and to calms; finally,
in lat. 4° 30'S, the wind veered to the SW. On December
6, the island of Tahiti came into sight; but the transport
was becalmed within sight of it for another four days.
They finally entered Talu Bay, on the island of Eimeo on
December 10, where the king of Tahiti was at the time.

Various repairs to the rigging, the loading of
provisions, and watering kept them here till the following
January (1836). Then, leaving the Tahitian group, they
headed for Cape Horn. On January 9, they crossed the
southern tropic in long. 211° 14'E. On the 15th (in lat.
33° 30'S, long. 220°E), poor weather set in, with high
winds from the E and SE, and later from the W. On
February 1, the transport then being in an estimated
latitude of 53°S, and a longitude of 262° 34'E, an iceberg

was sighted some ten miles to the south. A strong SW wind
blew, the horizon was obscure. The temperature was 50°F
(8° Reaumur). They hove to throughout the next night, for
fear of other comparable encounters with icebergs; but
ice appeared no more. Rounding Cape Horn, they met
frequent SW and W storms between February 4 and 9. However,
these did not especially harm the vessel.

W and SW winds accompanied the Amerika even in the
Atlantic Ocean until February 16 (lat. 43°S, long. 311°E),
and the weather remained mainly poor. But fair weather
and a coastal wind (from SSW-SE) were encountered on
February 26, and with that wind the transport reached Rio
de Janeiro on April 7. She remained there one week, being
readied for her further voyage.

They left Rio de Janeiro on April 13. Until the SE
trade wind was met, they had NE or NW winds, sometimes
strong. The weather was bad at times. In general, the
trade wind itself blew irregularly and alternated with
squalls, particularly about the Equator.

Leaving the tropics at the end of May, they made for
the English Channel. Encountering a strong NE wind in the
parallel of the Lizard, however (June 2, 450 miles out),
Captain von Schants decided to proceed around Great
Britain in order not to lose time in tacking. By the 14th
the Shetland Islands had been sighted and rounded.
Copenhagen was reached on the 21st. Having watered here,
they went on (July 9) and dropped anchor in Kronshtadt
Roads on the 15th.

28

The Russian-American Company Vessel Elena

(Teben'kov)

1835-36

On August 5, 1835, Lieutenant Teben'kov left Kronshtadt,
with the Company vessel that had been entrusted to him,
the Elena, the same ship on which Captains Chistiakov,
Murav'ev, and Khromchenko had sailed. After meeting with
strong contrary winds on his way to Copenhagen, he reached
that port only on the 14th, and entered the Kattegat on
the 19th. On his passage over the North Sea, he encountered
light winds, but on entering the Channel he found a strong
WSW wind, from which he was obliged to shelter for 48 hours
at Deal. He was then nearly two weeks tacking round to
Portsmouth, where he arrived at last on September 9. By
the 15th the vessel was ready to put to sea, but contrary
winds detained her in the roadstead till the 21st. She
finally entered the Atlantic on the 26th and, meeting a
north wind which imperceptibly turned into a trade wind,
proceeded to lat. 10°N. Here, the trade wind failed and

116

variable winds prevailed: so far did they carry the Elena
to the west that she could not traverse the Equator before
28°W. Accompanied by the SE trade wind from lat. 4°N, she
reached Rio de Janeiro on November 15, 55 days out from
Portsmouth.

Up to now, the condition of the crew's health had
been most satisfactory. Immediately before the Elena was
to have put to sea, however, on November 29, 16 men
suddenly fell ill - they were attacked by cholera. Over
the ensuing five days, almost the entire ship's company
fell sick. However, the illness soon passed: on
December 3 the Elena put to sea with a fit company.[1]

Proceeding under a light following wind, Lt. Teben'kov
reached the Falkland Islands in three weeks and on
December 24 came in sight of Salvages Island. Three days
later, he was already in the parallel of Cape San Juan;
on December 30 he crossed the meridian of Cape Horn, and
on January 9 came into the parallel of Cape Victory. The
Horn was rounded in 13 days, throughout which the vessel
had a heavy swell from the west but only light winds from
the SW and NW. The thermometer showed about 6° Reaumur.
The greatest inclination to the south had been in lat.
58° 13'S, and to the west - in long. 80°W.

The passage up the west coast of America was accompanied
by a moderate wind from the NW quarter; on January 24 the
Elena dropped anchor in Valparaiso roadstead.

Lt. Teben'kov left that roadstead at the beginning of
February, and arrived at Novo-Arkhangel'sk on April 16,[2]
having completed the voyage from Kronshtadt in 8 months
and 11 days. The Elena was left in the colonies and the
greater part of her crew entered the Company's service.
The remainder returned to Kronshtadt via Okhotsk.

In accordance with a prior arrangement between them
and the Company Main Office, Lt. Teben'kov and his people
received 6,000 rubles by way of a prize for their swift
passage from Kronshtadt to Novo-Arkhangel'sk.

From reports by the commander.

---

[1] Lt. Teben'kov thinks that the cause of the sickness was
the extreme heat and the abrupt changeover to a fresh diet.

[2] No data have been found regarding the passage from
Valparaiso to Sitkha.

29

The Russian-American Company Vessel Nikolai
(Berens)
1837-39

The vessel Nikolai, fitted out by the Russian-American Company to deliver a mixed cargo to the colonies, left Kronshtadt on August 8, 1837. She arrived at Copenhagen on the 17th, having met two great storms in the Baltic Sea, and there remained until the 22nd, for various necessities. On the 24th, she went into the Kattegat with a following wind, but when passing Skagen she met with strong SW winds, which prevailed over the whole North Sea. At last, on September 9, after the stormiest of crossings, the Nikolai dropped anchor in Portsmouth Roads.

A nine-day stay in the roadstead was employed in preparing the vessel for her ocean crossing. Captain Berens put to sea on September 18. But he had hardly lost the shores of England from view when he encountered a SW wind, which blew steadily throughout the next ten days (as far as lat. 45°N). He then met with a N wind, which gradually developed into a trade wind. The Equator was crossed on October 23. The remainder of the passage to Rio de Janeiro was more successful. Cabo Frio was sighted on November 4 and Captain Berens dropped anchor in the bay of Rio de Janeiro the next day, having made the passage from Portsmouth in 48 days.

Captain Berens weighed anchor from Rio de Janeiro on November 22 and set a course designed to take him between the coasts of Patagonia and the Falkland Islands. By December 13, he was already in the parallel of the latter; and here he encountered a brief but violent storm, from the SW.

On December 16, he passed the parallel of Staten Land; on the 19th, when in lat. 58°S, he crossed the meridian of the Horn, and there met with another, 48-hour, storm. From that day on, the Nikolai fought with constant storms, from W, SW, and WNW. So steering as to move as close as possible to the parallel, on January 3, 1838, Captain Berens was in lat. 60°S and long. 80°W. And there, against expectations, he encountered a wind from the SSW. It accompanied as far as the range of coastal winds. Taking advantage of all this, the vessel made excellent progress and by January 17 stood at anchor in Valparaiso roadstead, after a 50-day passage from Rio de Janeiro.

The Nikolai set out from Valparaiso at the beginning of February, safely reaching Novo-Arkhangel'sk on April 14.[1]

---

[1] Captain Berens' report of this part of the voyage could not be found in the company archives.

The voyage from Kronshtadt had been completed in 8 months and 6 days (three days less than in 1836 by the Elena). On November 8, the Nikolai left Sitkha for Kronshtadt with a cargo of peltry to the value of 300,000 rubles.

While in the colonies, this vessel took the Governor, Captain Kupreianov, on an inspection of the settlement of Ross. There now returned in her to Russia a number of officials whose terms of service in the colonies had expired, as well as the crew of the Elena who had arrived in 1836. To replace the latter, part of the Nikolai's crew remained at Sitkha.

After a stormy 43-day passage, Captain Berens arrived in Honolulu harbor, Oahu, on December 22. He remained there twelve days, i.e., till January 2, 1839, to rest his people. Then putting out to sea, he made for Cape Horn. An unusually swift and easy passage through the zone of variable winds, together with fresh trade winds in both hemispheres, so speeded the Nikolai's voyage that Captain Berens thought it possible to stop for a few days at one of the islands of the Tahitian archipelago. On January 29 he dropped anchor in Opunohu harbor, Eimeo.

A four-day stop here sufficed to replenish stores and to ready the ship for her further voyage. On February 2, the Nikolai left the island of Eimeo and, favored by fresh winds from the SW, W, and NW, made such good time that by February 28 she was already on the meridian of Cape Horn. The parallel of Staten Land was passed on March 5, that of the Falkland Islands on March 9, and on the 29th they dropped anchor in Rio de Janeiro roadstead. The last passage had been performed in 54 days, without a single sick man and without the slightest damage to the vessel, though a few storms were met while rounding the Horn.

On April 10, the Nikolai left Rio de Janeiro. After a swift voyage of 48 days, she was already in the Channel and in sight of Falmouth. Putting in here for a few hours, to purchase fresh provisions, Captain Berens went straight on to the Zund. Stopping four days at Copenhagen, he reached Kronshtadt on June 22. He had completed the voyage from Novo-Arkhangel'sk in 7 months and 14 days, only 32 days of which had been spent at anchor.

30

The Russian-American Company Vessel Nikolai

(Kadnikov/Voevodskii)

1839-41

On her return from Sitkha, at the end of June in 1839, the Nikolai was once again - and in the same year - sent to Novo-Arkhangel'sk, now under the captaincy of Lieutenant

Kadnikov and the overall command of Captain Etolin, who had
been appointed Governor of the colonies in place of Captain
Kupreianov.

Of the Nikolai's voyage out to Novo'Arkhangel'sk,
nothing has been uncovered either in Admiralty or in Company
archives. It is known only that she left Kronshtadt on
August 19, 1839 and reached Novo-Arkhangel'sk safely on
May 1, 1840. Lt. Kadnikov remained on duty in the colonies,
while the vessel passed under the command of Captain-
Lieutenant Voevodskii and the overall command of Captain
Kupreianov, who returned to Russia in her.

Captain Voevodskii prepared to sail late in September
(1840). He made sail on the 30th, having a cargo of
peltry on board to the value of 57,200 rubles. Proceeding
under moderate winds, he came into view of Ross settlement
two weeks later. Taking on a cargo there, he continued
to the port of San Francisco, which he reached on October
16. When final preparations had been made here, Captain
Voevodskii put to sea again (November 17); twelve days
later, when in lat. 28° 30'N, he met with the NE trade
wind. From here, he so steered as to cross the Equator
in long. 105°W. Continuing in this direction with a
highly irregular and gentle trade wind, he reached lat.
9°N in long. 247°E by December 12. Constantly changing,
the wind veered SE and, blowing from that quarter for
some time, turned at last into the regular SE trade wind.
With it, the Nikolai crossed the Equator on December 22
in long. 118° 45'W, and left the tropics on January 1.
The following day, the trade wind was lost and for several
days thereafter light northerly airs and calms prevailed.
These developed into a topgallant wind from the N and NW.
On January 23, the Nikolai passed in sight of Juan Fernandez
Island; on the 26th she dropped anchor in Valparaiso Roads.

Here she remained till the middle of February, 1841.
On her passage thence to Cape Horn she was at first
accompanied by a light SE wind, later by moderate winds
from the NW and SW. The meridian of Cape Horn was passed
on March 8 and, continuing under moderate but variable
winds, they reached Rio de Janeiro on the 27th.

The voyage from Rio de Janeiro to Europe was likewise
a happy one: by May 25, the Nikolai was already outside
the tropics and beyond the range of the NE trade wind.
Accompanied by light variable winds, they, on June 9,
passed 67 miles to the south of Flores Island (in the
Azores). On the 19th, they paused for 24 hours at the
Isle of Wight. Entering the North Sea on the 23rd, they
stopped for five days at Copenhagen before arriving at
Kronshtadt roadstead on June 13, 1841.

The Russian-American Company Vessel <u>Naslednik-Aleksandr</u>
(Zarembo)
1840-41

Captain-Lieutenant Zarembo left Kronshtadt with the ship <u>Naslednik-Aleksandr</u> on August 14, 1840, and made for Sitkha. His mission was the usual one - the delivery of a mixed cargo to Novo-Arkhangel'sk, where the cargo would be surrendered; the vessel and part of the crew were to remain in the colonies on service.

On August 24, this vessel arrived at Copenhagen; there she stayed until September 2. Proceeding thence, on September 4 she went out of the Skagerrak and on the 8th neared the approaches to the English Channel. There she encountered a strong SW wind, from which she was obliged to shelter in the roadstead at Deal. She went on from here on September 13 and, tacking through the Channel, entered the Atlantic on the 21st. Captain Zarembo made for Rio de Janeiro.

Continuing with following winds, he crossed the Tropic of Cancer and on October 9 (long. 25°W), met with the NE trade wind. It stayed with him till the 15th of that month when he reached lat. 8° 40'N, long. 24°W. From the 15th to the 25th, they were delayed by calms or light airs; but in lat. 5° 20'N, they met the SE trade wind. On October 25 they crossed the Equator in long. 24° 10'W, and on November 7 they reached Rio de Janeiro, having performed the last passage in 55 days.

From Rio de Janeiro, Captain Zarembo made sail on November 23. Proceeding round the Horn, he stopped in Valparaiso Roads on January 13, 1841. Having remained there about two weeks, he continued on his way with the SE trade wind until February 18 (lat. 3° 10'N, long. 117°W). He crossed the Equator, on February 17, in long. 116° 5'W. He reached Novo-Arkhangel'sk in safety on April 3.

Based on the private notes of a participant in the voyage, G. V. Bazhenov. No official data have been uncovered.

The Naval Transport Abo
(Iunker)
1840-42

The transport Abo, which was to deliver a mixed cargo to Kamchatka, was built in the Abo yards expressly for a voyage round the world. (She was 131 1/2' long and 33 3/4' in the beam). Command of her was given to Captain-Lieutenant Iunker.

The Abo left Kronshtadt on September 5, and reached Copenhagen on the 15th. She sailed again on the 26th, and entered the North Sea on October 6. Crossing that sea with a strong west wind, she stood at anchor in Portsmouth Roads by the 10th. Preparing for the coming passage, Captain Iunker here altered the Abo's rigging and replaced the stays that had split on the North Sea crossing (on October 7).

On November 12 he entered the Atlantic Ocean and made for the island of Teneriffe under light or moderate winds. On the 23rd, the Abo passed in sight of Madeira. They stopped at Teneriffe for four days to purchase fresh provisions, then proceeded along a course between the coasts of Africa and the Cape Verde Islands. They sailed with the NE trade wind, in overcast weather. On December 8 they passed the parallel of Cape Verde. Between the 11th and 18th of that month, they crossed the waters between the trade winds: as usual in that zone, winds were variable. On January 1, 1841, the transport crossed the Tropic of Capricorn in long. 24° 50'W. At 11 a.m. on this day, a sudden squall broke the foretopmast, in place of which the spare was raised. She then made for the Cape of Good Hope. The passage thence was accomplished under light or moderate northerly winds. On the 13th, when passing the parallel of the Cape itself at a distance of 1,130 Italian miles, the Abo moved onto an ESE course. Then, on the 22nd and in lat. 37°S, long. 8° 50'E, she moved NE. The voyagers dropped anchor in Table Bay on January 24. A three-week sojourn here was employed in repairing the rigging and renewing supplies of water and of victuals.[1]

Proceeding to lat. 39°S, Captain Iunker then sailed east, between latitudes 39° and 41°S, until March 14: he had strong SW and NW winds. That day, when in long. 90°E, he began to move NE and N; the following day, the Abo crossed the meridian of the islands of St. Paul and Amsterdam, being nine miles to the north of the former. Meeting

---

[1] Under the tension of the fore-mast backstay, the bolt on the chain of the water-stay broke, and the bowsprit was cracked.

with the trade wind in about lat. 28ºS, the transport went
with it towards the Sunda Strait and by March 31 was in an
estimated latitude of 13ºS, (long. 92º 30'E). There and
then, the Abo encountered a vicious hurricane, which did
much damage and was perhaps one of the main causes of the
subsequent high mortality. The hurricane is described as
follows in the logbook:

> 'Midday. March 30. Wind ESE., topgallant;
> cloudy. Bar. 29.97.; Symp. 29.84. Freshening.
> Midnight, March 31. Wind ESE., topgallant;
> cloudy and dark, occasional rain, course - NNE.
> Bar. 29.82.; temperature 19 1/2º Reaumur. Symp.
> 29.65. Therm. 20º Reaumur. Water temp. 19 1/2R.
> Topgallants still up, (foresail and mainsail
> brailed, mizzensail reinforced.) Shortly after
> midnight, the wind strengthened: barometer
> standing at 29.62. Symp. 29.50. Towards 1 a.m.,
> the wind grew higher and higher: bar. reading -
> 29.50. All hands aloft to take in reefs. But
> while reef-tackle being drawn out, the maintop-
> gallant split, after which the foretopgallant
> tore. Order given to strengthen sails, but it
> was impossible to do so without losing men. Wind
> still growing, with incredible force. Perhaps
> 11 1/2 knots headway. At 1.30 a.m., the wind swung
> in the briefest space of time from ESE, through
> SE, to SW., with hurricane force. On the captain's
> orders, we sailed by the wind on the port tack.
> A little later, the furling lines and brails to
> the mizzen and foresail split: these were in-
> stantly torn. At 1.45 a.m., the fore-topmast
> fell, then the main-topmast. Fifteen minutes
> later, the jib-boom and the side-beams where the
> boats hung broke. While the hurricane blew, heavy
> and almost parallel rain fell amidst constant
> thunder; but such was the cruel whistling and noise
> that the thunderclaps themselves were inaudible.
> At the height of the hurricane, the barometer
> fell below 29.38. Symp. 29.36. It began to
> rise 15 minutes later. At 4 a.m., there was
> 10 1/2" of water in the hold, (there had been 9"
> at midnight.) At 4.30 a.m., the wind was at its
> strongest, with mighty gusts and lightning:
> barometer at 29.55; Symp. 29.54. Temp. at bar.
> 21º; air temp. 20º, water temp. 21º Reaumur. At
> 5.30 a.m., the wind began to moderate, bar.
> showing 29.81. 11" of water in hold by 8 a.m.
> Lat. reckoned at 12º 30'S, long. at 92º 24' by
> three chronometers at noon.'

At 9 a.m., the wind quietened, and topgallants were
carried throughout the 31st: the weather was fair. As
soon as the hurricane had passed, the Abo's company set to
repairing the damage as well as they might, and by April
4 all was in good order. Meanwhile, the transport had
proceeded with light or moderate winds towards the Nicobar

Islands. On April 22, the coast of Sumatra became visible with the islands around, and on the 26th they dropped anchor in the roadstead of Nancowry, one of the Nicobar Islands. There, the transport's rigging was put completely to rights, and all available supplies were taken on. But there also appeared the fever which quickly spread in most virulent form.

On leaving this place, Captain Iunker made for the Straits of Malacca. Frequent calms and the unbroken heat further spread the sickness, and within a short time the company had lost five men. More than 20 were ill. Stopping at George-Town and Penang on the way through the Straits of Malacca, the Abo reached Singapore on June 2. The sick were immediately sent ashore; but in the one-month sojourn here, only half of them recovered. Several died.

The passage across the China Sea to Manila was completed in ten days, under moderate SE and SW winds. The Abo left Manila on July 22 and entered the Pacific Ocean on August 2. On August 9-11, she met a storm in lat. 28° 30'N and long. 128° 30'E, which gradually swung from ENE to S and to SW.[1] After this, she encountered light airs and calms with a heavy swell, which lasted until she reached lat. 25°N on September 2. She then met with a moderate following wind, and with it, by the 15th, came in sight of Kamchatka's shores. Anchors were dropped in Petropavlovsk harbor on September 20, a year and two weeks since the transport had left Kronshtadt. Thirteen men had been lost on the last passage.

The unloading of materials and readying for a return voyage to Kronshtadt kept the Abo at Petropavlovsk till the end of November. Captain Iunker made sail on the 24th of that month, cutting a path across the entrance to Avacha Bay, which was already frozen, and heading for Cape Horn. At first, he attempted to keep to the 40th parallel of northern latitude in order to remain within the range of westerly winds: he wished to cross the Equator about long. 105° or 110°W.

But the twelve-day passage from Kamchatka to the Tropic of Cancer proved a most difficult one, because of almost incessant storms, cold, and wretched weather.

'Seldom was it possible to carry two top-gallants even with three reefs,' says an eye-witness.[2] 'Top gallants were shown with two reefs

---

[1] During this storm a wave tore the gig from the stern davits.

[2] A. I. Butakov. See Zapiski of the Hydrographic Department, part II, p. 270.

124

only twice, and then only for a few hours: after
that, the wind again forced us to take in canvas
and still take in. Sometimes, at night, the
storms were accompanied by snow-squalls: enormous
flakes of wet snow swirled around in the air,
clinging to the spars and rigging and then falling
to the deck in balls. On occasion, the squalls that
blew were almost of hurricane strength; and after
them, the wind would suddenly fall off, creating such
a swell that the end of the mizzen boom was dipping
in the sea.'

Especially remarkable was a SW storm that struck on
December 11 at 8 p.m. A huge breaker crashed onto the
transport from the stern (she was on a SE course and making
8 knots).

'It first struck the four-oared gig, which was
slung over the stern, and smashed it in half against
the spanker-boom. The stem of the gig hung from its
tackle, while the bow, together with the broken right
davit, was flung around the mizzen mast and fell on
to the left side of the quarter deck. One of the
10-oar cutters was smashed to smithereens; the other
was somehow repaired later... The lieutenant of the
watch, the master, and the helmsmen were swept toward
the mainmast. The only hatchway which had been left
unbattened, had been closed with a cover. The mass of
water struck it, wrenched loose the copper bracing,
broke the ribs, and precipitated itself below. It
struck the doors of the captain's pantry so hard that
the doors were torn from their hinges and broke inwards
even though they opened outwards. The hatchways to
the captain's quarters and the wardroom were smashed
in and the windows were broken. One of the carronades
was picked up by the force of the water and the
coil of the main topsail brace was swept under it.'

However, no serious damage was sustained by the
rigging or other parts of the vessel generally. The dampness in the decks, which resulted from the great quantity
of water that had flowed in, later joined other causes
in provoking the development of scurvy aboard the transport.

The storms ceased about December 20, and the Abo proceeded with light winds and fair weather. In the trade
wind zone, the sudden change of the NE wind to SE was
remarkable. This phenomenon occurred on the morning of
January 13 in lat. 14°N, long. 119°W, at a great distance
from all known land. By 2 p.m., the NE trade wind was
blowing again. It is difficult to say what may have
caused such a swift and abrupt change in the trade wind.
Possibly it was a nearby, unknown island.

On crossing the Equator, in long. 125°W, they immediately encountered the SE trade wind; but it often played false both in strength and in direction, and died away altogether in lat. 19°S (on February 6). Then, between February 22 and 26, a strong equatorial current bore the transport to the NW at a rate of some 60 miles per 24 hours.

The passage from the southern tropic to Cape Horn was accomplished with variable, sometimes high, winds, and in bad weather. On February 10, Henderson Island was passed - a small, uninhabited island - and then 48 hours were spent vainly tacking towards Pitcairn Island. On February 20, in lat. 35°S, the first signs of scurvy manifested themselves. The sickness quickly worsened on board, as the cold and damp increased. On March 8, the parallel of Cape Horn was passed in long. 92°W; the cape itself was rounded over the next ten days, winds being fairly light in the main and sometimes even dying away. On the 18th, the parallel of the Horn was reached on the eastward side, in long. 57°W. The scurvy, meanwhile, had been growing exceedingly in strength, in the absence of many things: as many as 30 men were sick, or more than half the transport's crew, and there were deaths. Six men perished on the short passage from the Horn to Rio de Janeiro.

A rest of two and a half months was needed at Rio de Janeiro for the health of the Abo's company to recover from the 138-day passage from Kamchatka. Few Russian mariners had made a slower passage;[1] but, on the other hand, no single passage had been so surrounded by misfortunes - with the possible exception of one by the Borodino, when many had similarly died of scurvy.

Leaving the shores of Brazil on June 26, Captain Iunker soon met with the SE trade wind, and sailed with it as far as lat. 2°N (July 18). The whole expanse between the trade winds was traversed with a SW wind, in rain. In lat. 15°N, they encountered the NE trade wind, which then accompanied them to lat. 30°N. On August 30 they reached the Portsmouth Roads.

Sailing thence, Captain Iunker crossed the North Sea without particular incident, called at Copenhagen for five days, and reached Kronshtadt roadstead on October 13, 1842.

The voyage of the transport Abo is described in the Zapiski gidrograficheskago departmenta (Transactions of the Hydrographic Department), pt. 11, pp. 164-222. Accounts are also in Otechestvennye zapiski (Fatherland notes), 1844 (article entitled, 'The Memoirs of a Naval Officer'), and in Sovremennik for 1849, (article entitled,

---

[1] Capt. Lisianskii took 142 days from Canton to Portsmouth.

'A Passage from Portsmouth to Capstadt'). Here, use has
chiefly been made of the transport's log.

33

The Naval Transport Irtysh

(Vonliarliarskii)

1843-45

The transport Irtysh, a reconfigured merchantman
bought in England (length 89' 9", beam 23' 9"), was sent
out to Okhotsk, there to join the local flotilla and to
deliver a mixed cargo. Command of the vessel was entrusted
to Captain Vonliarliarskii.

Having taken on cargo weighing 17,000 puds and a 13-
month supply of provisions, Captain Vonliarliarskii sailed
from Kronshtadt on October 14, 1843. Meeting strong SW
winds in the Baltic Sea, he reached Copenhagen two weeks
later and from there, having replenished his provisions,
proceeded - still with constant fresh winds. On November
18, the hatches to the captain's own quarters and to the
wardroom were broken by a breaker in the course of a
passing storm (which had frequently changed direction by
as much as 8°). The steering control, binnacles, and
a 6-oar boat were also smashed, and the stern reinforce-
ments were somewhat damaged. The entrance to the Channel
was reached on November 22. Meeting a fresh and contrary
wind with cloud, they sheltered in the roadstead of Deal.
They reached Portsmouth on the 29th, 45 days out from
Kronshtadt.

The Irtysh was detained here till the end of January,
1844, while anchor-chain was purchased for Okhotsk, the
chain was loaded (which necessitated the relading of the
whole hold), and while various repairs and preparations
were made aboard her. High winds also contributed to the
delay. At last entering the ocean on January 30, 1844,
Captain Vonliarliarskii bore to the south-west. Followed
by a moderate wind, on February 12 he passed the islands
of Porto Santo and Madeira and on the 16th, to replenish
stores, stopped for 24 hours at Teneriffe.

Continuing under the NE trade wind, they passed within
sight of the island of San Antonio on February 25 and on
March 13 crossed the Equator, in long. 21° 44'W. From the
19th on, the SE trade wind became steady, first blowing
from SE but then gradually veering to E. Cabo Frio was
sighted on April 4, and anchors were dropped in the
roadstead at Rio de Janeiro on the 6th. On the passage
from Teneriffe to this port, the barometer had fallen no
lower than 29.93, nor had the air temperature exceeded
22 1/2° Reaumur. In general, the weather had been fair
even on the passage between trade wind zones.

Taking into account the lateness of the season, Captain
Vonliarliarskii preferred to proceed from Brazil towards
the Cape of Good Hope, entering the Pacific Ocean by way
of the Sunda and Macassar Straits.

Putting to sea at the beginning of May, he set a course
to the SW; on the 21st he passed in sight of Tristan da
Cunha. From there, he so steered as to round the Cape of
Good Hope in approximately lat. 40°S. The meridian of the
cape was passed on May 31, in lat. 39° 10'S, and they
continued along that parallel to long. 41°E, then gradually
rising in latitude and inclining towards the Sunda Strait.
The coast of Java came into sight on July 9. On the 11th,
they entered the Java Sea and, being short of fresh water,
made for Batavia, where they dropped anchor on July 16.

On the passage from Rio de Janeiro to Tristan da
Cunha, moderate following winds had prevailed; but thence
and until the SE trade wind had been met, the winds had
been always high, from the SW or NW quarters and sometimes
reaching storm force. But nothing remarkable had occurred
save on June 9, when a breaker had torn down the stern
wheelhouse, parts of which, to clear the rudder, were
then destroyed and thrown overboard. The sea-current was
in their favor and fairly significant: the estimated
point of arrival in the Sunda Strait was 14° to the SW,
or 840 miles, at variance from the position actually
observed there.

Captain Vonliarliarskii put to sea again on August 1
and laid a course for the Gaspar Strait. While at Batavia,
he had come to think that a passage through the Macassar
Strait would be unsuitable, in view of the lack of exact
charts. He therefore found himself obliged to alter his
original plan, and to enter the Pacific by way of the
China Sea.

Until August 13, the voyage was performed with light
winds from the SW or NW. But the winds on that day swung
to the NE. At first they remained gentle, but on the
20th a violent squall broke the foretopgallant mast (which
carried no sail), broke off the fore-yard, and reduced
the mizzensail to tatters. This squall was of short
duration, but constantly changed direction (from N through
NE and to WNW).

From then until August 24, Captain Vonliarliarskii
bore towards the Formosa Strait: the wind was constant,
from the NE quarter. At midday on the 26th, the Bashi
Islands were in view. It was then noticed that the main-
yard had a transversal crack. The steady NE wind convinced the captain that the time when the monsoon changes
had already arrived. Besides, the poor state of the spars
deprived him of hope of reaching Okhotsk in the 1844 sea-
going season. Therefore, since there was not one port
on the passage from the China Sea to Kamchatka where one
might have waited for favorable weather and found all the

provisions needed by a company, he thought it best to make for Manila. There he arrived on September 4.

During the Manila sojourn, the weather was generally good, but there were often violent storms. So the transport was hove to in 20' of water, with 80 sazhen' of rope. Several slight earthquakes were felt. On February 1 they left Manila, following the west coast of Luzon to the Formosa Strait. Until the 8th they had light winds. But on that day, every quarter of an hour or even more frequently between 9 p.m. and 6 a.m. the following morning, the shocks of an underwater earthquake were felt. The first shock proved so strong, says Captain Vonliarliarskii,

'that it occurred to me that the transport had gone onto a reef; I was in my cabin at the time, and most of the furniture in it shifted. Although I was quite certain of our position and of the absence of danger from any reef, still all necessary precautions were taken in that moment. But the deep sea lead found no bottom at 90 sazhen, and the repetition of shocks convinced me that it was an earthquake.'

At the time of the first shock, the vessel lay in lat. 19° 57'N, long. 120° 40'E. No fluctuations were observed in the barometer, which showed 30.2, throughout the period of earthquakes. There was a light, topgallant wind (between N and E). A few water-spouts were observed the following day.

At noon on February 12, the Irtysh entered the Pacific Ocean. Till March 3, she tacked towards the Bonin-Jima Islands in winds from the NE quarter. On that day, she passed the location of Burnyi (Stormy) Island (on Sarychev's map), and on the 5th dropped anchor in Port Lloyd, Peale Island.

Intending to remain here the whole of March, Captain Vonliarliarskii occupied himself with the checking of his chronometers and with the stowing of water and firewood. On the island, he found a little colony of 40 persons, formed by settlers of all nationalities. They lived without government of any kind. The island is often visited by whalers.

Leaving Port Lloyd, Captain Vonliarliarskii crossed the Bonin-Jima group, to the south of Ketter Island, on April 4; wishing to examine the islands of St. John and St. Margaret, shown on Sarychev's chart, he laid a course to the NNE. The next morning he passed over the very spot where the former was supposed to lie, without observing any sign of land. Mist made it impossible to verify the existence of the latter. [1]

---

[1] The islands are not shown on the latest charts by Kruzenshtern (1839) and D'Urville (1845).

For three days (April 12-14) between latitudes 35° 4'
and 36° 52'N and longitudes 148° 9' and 151° 11'E, they
passed through belts of reddish dust, saw many bunches
of seaweed, and noticed an overall change in the color
of the water: it turned from deep blue to green. On the
14th, a brown turtle was spotted.

They continued northward until April 25, with variable
winds. The shores of Kamchatka were sighted on that day,
through the mists: it was the second hill on the peninsula. But on the night of April 27, the Irtysh came upon
a solid mass of ice. At dawn it was seen that the ice,
now solid and now floating, stretched to the horizon.
Over the ensuing days, they moved through the ice, bearing
to the north as much as possible. On May 2 they entered
Avacha Bay. With assistance from the port, they proceeded
thence into Petropavlovsk harbor by the 15th of the month.

Having here surrendered the materials that he had
brought, Captain Vonliarliarskii put to sea again on June
20 and, passing between the third and fourth Kurile
Islands, laid a course for Okhotsk, where he arrived on
July 1. The entire voyage, from Kronshtadt to the
destination, had been completed in 594 days.

From log-book and commander's despatches. Brief
information about the voyage of this transport appears
in Zapiski of Hydrographic Department, parts I and II.

34

The Naval Transport Baikal

(Nevel'skoi)

1848-49

The transport Baikal (length 94', beam 24' 6"), built
by a private Helsingfors yard to an order from the Naval
Ministry, was destined for service in the Sea of Okhotsk
and was designed to carry a mixed cargo thither and to
Kamchatka. Captain-Lieutenant Nevel'skoi was named her
commander. Fitted out as a brig-type schooner, the
Baikal was brought to Kronshtadt. On August 17, already
fully prepared, she went out into the roadstead. On the
21st, she went out to sea, towed by the steamboat Izhora.
Before the floating London beacon was reached, the steamboat released the towing-line and the transport proceeded
under sail. At sea, the Baikal met a fresh contrary wind.
Having tacked in vain for 24 hours, on the 22nd Captain
Nevel'skoi dropped anchor on the east side of Seskar'
Island. There he stayed for another 48 hours, until more
favorable winds all the way to Copenhagen, which he
reached on September 8. Only for a few consecutive hours
had he enjoyed a following wind, with which a rate of 5
to 7 1/2 knots was attained.

Stores were supplemented in Copenhagen. The transport put to sea again on September 9 and, accompanied by light following winds, entered the North Sea on the 11th. On the 15th she entered the English Channel and on the 16th dropped anchor in Portsmouth Roads. Here she stood for 14 days while necessary work was carried out both to her hull and to her rigging. She proceeded on her way on September 30.

Until October 10, they sailed under moderate easterlies; but in lat. 31° 30'N, long. 22° 25'W, W and NW winds suddenly sprang up. They changed continually in strength and direction. Finally, in lat. 27° 50'N, long. 21° 42'W (October 13), they met with the NE trade wind, which, however, blew rather erratically, not infrequently veering to the E and even ESE. There were squalls and conditions were overcast. Near the Equator, on October 30, the trade wind perceptibly veered to the SE.

On November 4, the wind moved gradually away to the E, and by the 6th was blowing from NE. A hundred miles out from Rio de Janeiro, it died away completely, and the transport was becalmed for more than 24 hours. The Baikal finally dropped anchor in the roadstead by Rio de Janeiro on November 15. The preparing of extra spars, the caulking of the outer wales, and other work detained her here until December. On December 1, she finally put to sea with a gentle westerly wind. Next day, she crossed the southern tropic in long. 43°W, and headed for the Horn. Until the 9th, the Baikal made insignificant daily progress under light SE and NE winds. From then on high westerlies blew, not infrequently reaching storm force. On December 13, in lat. 44° 3'S, long. 51° 30'W, they blew with particular strength, and the transport went under reefed main-trysail.

On December 31, the westerly winds changed into a coast wind from the SSE, and this bore the transport up to Valparaiso. The meridian of Cape Horn was passed on January 2, 1849, in lat. 57° 21'S. Right from Rio de Janeiro, the weather had been cloudy and conditions bad. Despite these unfavorable conditions, however, no more than three men were sick in the transport; and Valparaiso was reached on February 2.

After a stay of four days and nights here, they put to sea again on February 6. For the first three days thereafter they had light variable winds. On the 9th they encountered the SE trade wind (lat. 30° 2'S, long. 74° 30'W), which blew moderately. On the 25th the wind began to veer east, and then variable winds again prevailed. These were interspersed with frequent and protracted calm periods. Finally, on March 9 and in lat. 1° 30'S, long. 110° 51'W, the Baikal met with the NE trade wind, which accompanied her to lat. 16° 13'N in long. 142° 28'W. The Equator had been crossed for the second time on March 4, in long. 110° 51'W. On March 22, the trade wind gave way

to light variable winds, chiefly from the eastern side of
the compass. On April 1 they dropped anchor in the harbor
of Honolulu, Oahu.

On April 10, having completed provisioning of victuals
and water, they put to sea once more. Light or moderate
NE winds followed the transport as far as lat. 31° 30'N;
but in that latitude, on April 21, the wind swung first to
the SE, then varied in strength and direction until
Petropavlovsk was reached. The weather remained obscure
throughout. On May 11, within sight of Avacha Bay, heavy
snow fell on the transport. She dropped anchor in that
bay on the 12th, 8 months and 23 days after leaving
Kronshtadt.

When the transport Baikal had been dispatched to
Kamchatka in 1848, the Governor-General of Eastern Siberia
had requested the Naval Ministry to instruct her commander
to examine in more detail, on his reaching the shores of
Siberia, the SE coast of the Sea of Okhotsk from Tugurskii
Bay to the mouth of the River Amur. He had made the
request in connection with the urgent question of trans-
ferring Okhotsk Port to a more convenient place. Prince
Menshikov had accordingly furnished Captain-Lieutenant
Nevel'skoi with the following instructions:

1) To examine the NE and NW coasts of Sakhalin
Island and determine if there was not, along them, a safe
anchorage.

2) To determine the lie of the approach to the
estuary of the Amur from the north, as of the firth itself,
and to discover whether or not there was, in the regions
of Cape Golovachev or Cape Romberg, a site suitable for
an open port, or at least a site from which it might be
possible to protect the estuary entrance from the north.

3) To follow the estuary of the Amur and the river
itself, to the place where it flows within its own fixed
banks, thereby assessing the nature of the entrance into
the river from the firth; also to establish if there was
a spot, on the estuary and near the river-mouth, or on the
river itself, from where the river-entrance could be
defended.

4) To describe the banks of the Amur near its mouth,
as well as the shores of its estuary, from the topographical
and statistical viewpoints.

5) To determine the nature of the estuary-entrance
from the south, and to establish the correctness or other-
wise of data given in the charts of Captains Laperouse and
Broughton and supported by Admiral Kruzenshtern's suppositions,
i.e., to the effect that Sakhalin was an island separated
from the mainland by a strait too shallow for navigation.
If the data proved false, and if the strait had sufficient
depth of water, then the approach and entrance into the

132

estuary of the Amur and the river itself from the Tartar
Strait was to be followed.

6) To sail along the SE shore of the Sea of Okhotsk
and of Grand Duke Constantine Bay, and to chart that coast
with the greatest possible clarity and precision, for the
safe navigation of our ships on the Sea of Okhotsk.

It was further directed that these investigations
were to be made in rowing-boats. The transport herself
was to remain at anchor off Cape Golovachev.

The unloading of the cargo and repairs necessary after
the long voyage detained the Baikal in Petropavlovsk
harbor until May 31. On leaving Avacha Bay, she headed
for the east coast of Sakhalin Island, thence to begin
the exploration. Light winds alternating with calms
slowed her, so that she entered the Sea of Okhotsk, by
way of the fourth Kurile strait, only on June 7. Here,
mists and bad visibility were encountered. On the night
of June 11-12, sailing with a wind from SSW-NW, they
heard a sound of breakers in the west and therefore turned
onto the right tack. The lead showed a depth of 19
sazhens. At dawn, the coast of Sakhalin showed 10 miles
off: the Baikal was in lat. 51° 35'. Approaching the
island to a distance of three miles, they then followed
it northward, sounding and surveying as they went. Having
found and examined by boat the Blagopoluchiia (Prosperity)
skerries, they then rounded the island's northernmost
extremity. On the 14th, they encountered floating ice in
various directions. The extremely light winds and calm
periods hampered the successful prosecution of the survey
work. On July 19, a bay was sighted and, imagining that
this was the strait between Sakhalin and the mainland,
they anchored in it. When rowing-boats made an examination
of its coast, however, it transpired that the transport
had put in at the same Obman (Deceit) Bay which in 1846
had led Second Lt. Gavrilov into error when he had visited
this shore. Part of this bay, which was sheltered from
all winds and lay in lat. 53° 35' and long. 142° 30',
Captain Nevel'skoi called 'Baikal Harbor.' He then proceeded towards the SW but meeting with sandbars by Cape
Golovachev, he anchored 1 1/2 miles from the west coast
of Sakhalin and 2 1/2 miles from Cape Romberg. The boats,
which had been sent off to seek a fairway into the Amur,
again returned having had no success; so the transport
weighed and turned from Cape Golovachev to the NW, following
the sandbars towards the mainland shore. When the mists
cleared, the hilly coast of Manchuria could now be seen.
Going no closer than four miles to this coast, they rounded
a bank and proceeded south. On June 28 they entered the
estuary of the Amur and dropped anchor about five miles to
the south of Cape Golovachev. Boats were put off to examine
the fairway. Midshipman Grote was sent in one of the
launches along the coast of Sakhalin, the senior lieutenant,
Lt. Kozakevich, in the other. The former had orders to
investigate the west coast of Sakhalin as far as lat. 52° 51',

to gather information about the route to the south, and
to see if there was not some direct connection between
Baikal Bay and the Amur's estuary. The latter's instructions
were to examine the shore of the mainland from Cape Romberg
as far as the estuary of the Amur and ten miles along the
north shore of the river. Examining all the bays that he
came upon, Lt. Kozakevich after some little time sighted
a long and extensive bay, in which he noted a fairly
strong current. It was the estuary of the Amur.

Going into the river, and proceeding along its left
bank, Lieutenant Kozakevich pulled in by a Giliak village
called Chadbakh, where he met the inhabitants. He then
continued upstream to the village of Chnyrrakh, whence
he was obliged to return to the transport for want of
provisions. On his return passage, Mr. Kozakevich
climbed to the top of Cape Tabakh (the left-hand cape by
the entrance to the Amur estuary), and from there, at
low tide, he saw the whole visible expanse of the estuary,
filled with shoals and intersected by channels.

Lieutenant Kozakevich returned to the transport on
July 13. Midshipman Grote returned from Sakhalin on the
very same day. The latter reported that south along the
shore of Sakhalin lay solid bars, and no direct connection
existed between Baikal Bay and the firth.

Instructing Lt. Kozakevich to continue the examination of the estuary from the transport, moving southward,
Captain Nevel'skoi himself, with three officers in
three launches, on July 15 made for the estuary, seeking
a fairway as he went.

Going up to the present Konstantin Peninsula, Captain
Nevel'skoi then headed back to the entrance from the River
Amur. Passing over the sandbanks in the estuary, he now
and then came into the deep channel which is the principal
modern fairway into the Amur from the sea. Following the
estuary southward, he approached the spot where the shore
of the mainland draws near to the facing (west) coast of
Sakhalin. There, by the capes that he named Lazarev and
Murav'ev, and instead of the isthmus posited by Laperouse,
Broughton and Kruzenshtern, he discovered a strait in
which the minimal depth of water was found to be five
sazhen. Proceeding south along the same parallel and so
south of that reached in the previous century by Captain
Broughton, he then turned back north from the mainland
cape named Cape Nevel'skoi. Passing through a deep channel
along the coast of Sakhalin, he returned to the transport
on July 30.

Having settled the main question, which was: Is
there communication between the River Amur, the Sea of
Okhotsk, and the Tartar Strait, Captain Nevel'skoi left
further investigation of the estuary until later and on
August 1 went out into the Sea of Okhotsk.

Following its coast, he discovered near the Giliak
village of Iskai a bay which was closed off from the sea
by a low sandy spit. This was examined by the boats
and named Schast'e (Good Fortune) Bay. Continuing the
survey of the coast northward, the Baikal first proceeded
round the continental shore, describing it accurately.
Coming up to Cape Mukhtel', Captain Nevel'skoi noticed
an extension which had opened up to the south. A boat
was put off to investigate. Entering the extension with
the transport - it was Ul'banskii Bay - the captain described it and named it Nikolai Bay. After 48 hours
here, he put to sea again on August 28 and laid a course
for Port Aian. A contrary wind and mists slowed the
transport: only on September 1 did she drop anchor at
Aian, where she found the Governor-General of Eastern
Siberia. His flag flew on the transport Irtysh.

On September 3, the Baikal put to sea. On the 6th,
she arrived in the port of Okhotsk where, once she had
been drawn upriver, her flag was lowered (October 10)
and her mission ended.

The results of Captain Nevel'skoi's investigations
were extremely important. They dispersed the delusions
perpetuated by Laperouse, Broughton and Kruzenshtern,
regarding the existence of a low sandy isthmus joining
Sakhalin and the mainland which, however, none of the
three had seen. Captain Nevel'skoi was the first to prove
that Sakhalin is an island, that the River Amur is
accessible to vessels coming from the sea and, finally,
that there is communication between two seas, the Seas
of Japan and Okhotsk, through the strait that he discovered.

Based on files of the Staff of the Governor-General
of Eastern Siberia and the logbook (note by A. Sgibnev),

APPENDIX I

A LIST OF PARTICIPANTS IN CIRCUMNAVIGATIONS

Names and Rank

1. Ship Nadezhda (1803-06)

Commander, Capt.-Lt. Ivan
   Fedorovich Kruzhenshtern

d. 1846; admiral;
attached to His
Imperial Majesty's
suite.

Lt. Makar Ratmanov — d. 1833; vice-adm.;
duty general.

Lt. Fedor Romberg — Died in the service
as a captain.

Lt. Petr Golovachev — Shot self in 1806
on St. Helena Island.

Lt. Ermolai Levenshtern — d.

Midshipman Faddei Bellingshausen
   (Bellingsgauzen) — d.

Navigator Filipp Kamen'shchikov — d.

Assistant Navigator Vasilii
   Spolokhov — d.

Dr. Karl Espenberg

Sub-physician Ivan Sidgam

Astronomer Horner — Went abroad.

Naturalist Tilesius — Went abroad.

Naturalist Langsdorf — d. 1852.

Naval Cadet Otto Kotzebue — d. in retirement as
Capt. (1st rank).

Naval Cadet Moritz Kotzebue — d.

Envoy to the Court of Japan,
   Actual Counsellor of State,
   Nikolai Petrovich Rezanov — d. 1807 in Krasnoiarsk,
on return journey from
Kamchatka.

Major Ermolai Frideritsi

Guards Lieutenant Count Fedor
   Tolstoi

Court Counsellor Fedor Foss

Artist Stepan Kurliandtsev

Dr. Brinken (Brykin)

R.-Amer. Company Agent Fedor
   Shemelin — d.

Lower ranks: 51

2. Ship Neva (1803-06)

Commander, Capt. Lt. Iurii
   Fedorovich Lisianskii

d. 1837; in retirement
since 1809: Capt.
(1st rank).

Lt. Pavel Arbuzov — d. 1837 in ret.

Lt. Petr Povalishin — d. in the service as
Capt.

Midshipman Fedor Kovediaev

Midshipman Vasilii Berkh — d. 1834; Colonel;
section head in Hydro-
graphy Depot.

Dr. Moritz Laband

Names and Rank

Navigator Danilo Kalinin — Perished in the wreck of the Neva, 1813.

Assistant Navigator Fedor
   Mal'tsov
Assistant Surgeon Aleksei Mutovkin
Hieromonk Gedeon
Clerk Nikolai Korobitsyn
Lower ranks: 42

3. Ship Neva (1806-07)

Commander, Lt. Leontii Vasil'evich Gagemeister (Hagemeister) — d. 1833 as Capt. (1st rank).
Lt. Moritz Berkh — d.
Lt. Aleksandr Kozlianinov
Nav. Ivan Vasil'ev — d. in the service.
Assistant Nav. Efim Klochkov — d. 1832, Captain in charge of the Instruments Bureau, Hydrography Depot.

Surgeon Karl Mordgorst
Company Agent Rodion Zakharov
Lower ranks: 36

4. Naval sloop Diana (1807-09)

Commander, Lt. Vasilii Mikhailovich Golovnin — d. 1831, Vice-Admiral and Commissary-General.
Lt. Petr Rikord — d.
Midshipman Fedor Mur (Moore) — Shot self in Kamchatka, 1812.
Midshipman Il'ia Rudakov — d. in Iakutsk, Head of Iakutsk Region.
Surgeon Bogdan Brandt — d.
Nav. Andrei Khlebnikov — d.
Naval Cadet Dmitrii Kartavtsev
Naval Cadet Vsevolod Iakushkin
Naval Cadet Nikandr Filatov — d. in ret. as a Capt.-Lt.
Assistant Nav. Vasilii Novitskoi — d. 1847; Colonel; commanding St. Petersburg veterans' home.
Apprentice Nav. Vasilii Srednii — d. in service of Russ.-Am. Company.

Lower ranks: 55

5. Ship Suvorov (1813-16)

Commander, Lt. Mikhailo Petrovich Lazarev — d.
Lt. Semen Unkovskii
Lt. Pavel Povalo-Shveikovskii
Navigator Maksim Samsonov — d. in ret. See No. 16.

Names and Rank

Navigator (hired) Aleksei
   Rossiiskii
Navigator (hired) Iosif   Jumped ship in Port
   Desil'e   Jackson.
Dr. Egor Sheffer (Georg Anton   Subsequently Brazilian
   Schaeffer)   Envoy at one of the
                             German Courts.

Supercargo German Molvo
Clerk Fedor Krasil'nikov   See. No. 8.
Lower ranks: 26 Hunters: 7

6. Brig Riurik (1815-18)

Commander, Lt. Otto Evstaf'evich d. 1846 in ret,
   Kotzebue   Capt. (1st rank).
Lt. Gleb Shishmarev   d. 1835, rear-adm.,
                             commanding a Guards
                             equipage.

Lt. Ivan Zakharin
Apprentice Navigator Vasilii   d. 1849, retired Capt.
   Khromchenko   (2nd rank).
Apprentice Navigator Vladimir   d. in the service.
   Petrov
Apprentice Navigator Mikhailo   d. on service in
   Korenev   America.
Dr. Ivan Eschscholts
Naturalist Adalbert Chamisso   Went abroad.
Naturalist Vormskel'd (Wormskiöld) Went abroad.
Artist Choris (to Sitkha)
Lower ranks: 24

7. Ship Kutuzov (1816-19)

Commander, Capt. Lt. Leontii   See above No. 3.
   Vasil'evich Hagemeister
Lt. Aleksandr Selivanov   d. 1849, rear-adm.,
                             member of Gen.
                             Committee of Naval
                             Intend.
Lt. Nil' Kropotov   d. 1827, Capt.-Lt.
Reserve Midshipman Otto de Roberti d. 1817 at Sitkha.
Navig. Efim Klochkov   See above No. 3.
Nav. Ivan Kislakovskii   d.
Hired navig. Prokopii Tumanin   d. in Company service.
   (to Ross)
Staff Surgeon Lavrentii Kerner   See No. 8.
   (to colonies)
Supercargo Kiril Khlebnikov   d. 1830, Commercial
   (to Sitkha)   Counsellor and Company
                             Director.

Clerk Aleksandr Meshchovskii
Lower ranks: 49 Hunters: 4

8. Ship Suvorov (1816-18)

Commander, Lt. Zakhar Ivanovich Ponafidin	d. 1830, Lt.-Col. and Inspector of School of Navigators.
Lt. Semen Ianovskii (to Sitkha)	d. Capt. (1st rank).
Lt. Valeriian Novosil'tsov	in ret.; Lt.
Nav. Dionisii Zarembo	
Navig. Andrei Domashnev	d.
Agent Fedor Krasil'nikov	See No. 5, 10.
Clerk Iona Sukhanov	
Surgeon Vasilii Bervi	
Surgeon Lavrentii Kerner (from colonies)	See No. 7.
Lower ranks: 30	

9. Sloop Kamchatka (1817-19)

Commander, Capt., 2d Rank, Vasilii Mikhailovich Golovnin	See. above No. 4.
Lt. Matvey Murav'ev	d. 1832, Major-Gen., member of Uchetn. Kom.
Lt. Nikandr Filatov	See above No. 4.
Lt. Fedor Kutygin	d.
Midshipman Fedor Litke (Lütke)	Admiral, General-Adjutant.
Midshipman Baron Ferdinand Vrangel' (Wrangell)	
Naval Cadet Ardalion Lutkovskii	d. 1821 in Holland, on Aiaks. See No. 19.
Naval Cadet Stepan Artiukov	d. on service with Black Sea Fleet.
Naval Cadet Feopemt Lutkovskii	See No. 18.
Naval Cadet Vikentii Tabulevich	
Collegiate Secretary Matiushkin	
Navigator Grigorii Nikiforov	d. See No. 18.
Assist. Nav. Prokopii Kozmin	d. See No. 25.
Assist. Nav. Ivan Afanas'ev	
Nav. apprentice Petr Il'in	d. in Okhotsk, Lt.-Col., inspector of navigators.
Staff Surgeon Anton Novitskii	d.
Artist Mikhailo Tikhanov	See No. 26.
Lower ranks: 119	

10. Naval sloop Vostok (1819-21)

Commander, Capt. (2nd R.) Faddei Faddeevich Bellingshausen	See No. 1.
Capt.-Lt. Ivan Zavodovskii	d. retd. rear-adm.
Lt. Ivan Ignat'ev	d. in the service, Capt.-Lt.
Lt. Konstantin Torson	Exiled to Siberia in 1826.
Lt. Arkadii Leskov	See No. 23.

<u>Names and Rank</u>

Midshipman Dmitrii Demidov
Navig. Iakov Poriadin   d. in ret.; Lt.-Col.
Naval Cadet Robert Adams
Astronomer Ivan Simonov
Artist Pavel Mikhailov   See No. 26.
Staff-Surgeon Iakov Berkh   d. as Senior Surgeon
                                         in the School for
                                         Navigators.

Clerk Ivan Rezanov
Lower ranks: 105

10a. Naval sloop <u>Mirnyi</u> (1819-21)

Commander, Lt. Mikhailo Petrovich   See No. 5.
   Lazarev
Lt. Nikolai Obernibesov
Lt. Mikhailo Annenkov   d. 1839 as retd. capt.
                                         2nd rank.
Midshipman Ivan Kupreianov   d. See No. 20, 34.
Midshipman Pavel Novosil'skii
Navig. Nikolai Il'in   d. in the service.
Dr. Nikolai Galkin   d. in the service.
Lower ranks: 65

11. Naval sloop <u>Otkrytie</u> (1819-22)

Commander, Capt.-Lt. Mikhailo   d. 1847; vice-adm.,
   Nikolaevich Vasil'ev   commissary general.
Lt. Aleksandr Avinov   d.
Lt. Pavel Zelenoi   d. 1829 as Capt. 2nd
                                         rank and Ship commander.
Lt. Roman Boil' (Boyle)   d.
Midshipman Ivan Stogov
Midshipman Roman Gall   (Hall)   d. 1822 at Rio de
                                         Janeiro, on the return
                                         voyage.
Naval Cadet Prince Grigorii   d. in service, on ship,
   Pagava   Capt.-Lt.
Nav. Mikhailo Rydalev   d. in Astrakhan, Lt.-
                                         Col., special inspector
                                         of navigators.
Assist. Nav. Aleksei Korguev   d, in the service.
Assist. Nav. Andrei Khudobin   d. aboard the <u>Moller</u>
                                         on voyage from Kamchatka
                                         to Kronshtadt.
Surgeon Ivan Kovalev
Astronomer Pavel Tarkhanov   d. 1839; astronomer
                                         in the St. Petersburg
                                         Observatory.
Artist Emel'ian Korneev
Lower ranks: 63

11a. Naval sloop <u>Blagonamerennyi</u> (1819-21)

Commander, Capt.-Lt. Gleb Semenovich See No. 6.
   Shishmarev
Lt. Ivan Ignat'ev
Lt. Aleksei Lazarev
Midshipman Nikolai Shishmarev   d. 1844, Capt. 2nd
                                      Rank, See No. 24.
Midshipman Karl Gellesem   retd.
   (Gilsen or Hillsen)
Navig. Vladimir Petrov   See No. 6.
Assist. Navig. Vedeneev   d. in ret.
Staff-Surgeon Grigorii Zaozerskii   d. in the service.
Father Mikhail Ivanov
Lower ranks: 71

12. Ship <u>Borodino</u> (1819-21)

Commander, Lt. Zakhar' Ivanovich   See. No. 8.
   Ponafidin
Lt. Vsevolod Ponafidin   d. in ret.
Lt. Petr Chistiakov   d.
Lt. Dmitrii Nikol'skii   d. 1833, Capt. 2nd Rank.
Navigator Dionisii Zarembo   See No. 8.
Navigator Mikhailo Prokof'ev   d. 1833, Lt., in
   (to Sitkha)   Company service.
Navigator Aleksandr Kil'khen
   (to Sitkha)
Hired Navigator Petr Resukhin
Surgeon Karl Shpigel'berg   d. during the voyage.
Supercargo Fedor Krasil'nikov   See. No. 5, 8.
Lower ranks: 80 Hunters: 27

13. Ship <u>Kutuzov</u> (1820-22)

Commander, Lt. Pavel Afanas'evich   d. 1847 in ret., Actual
   Dokhturov   Counsellor of State.
Lt. Valeriian Novosil'tsov   See. No. 8.
   (to Sitkha)
Lt. Vladimir Romanov
Lt. Pavel Naumov   d.
Navigator Ivan Lazarev   drowned in 1834, at
                                        Lovisa, as Lt.
Navigator Dmitrii Iakovlev   d. in the service,
                                        as Capt.
Dr. Vasilii Bervi (to Sitkha)
Dr. Vasilii Volkov (on return
   voyage)
Agent Sergei Chernyshev
Clerk Stepan Kitaev
Lower ranks: 45 Hunters: 26

14. Brig Riurik (1821)

Commander, Navigator 12th Class, Efim Alekseevich Klochkov	See No. 3,7.
Assist. Navig. Maksim Samsonov	See No. 5.
Assist. Navig. Vasilii Nabokov	d. in the service, Capt.
Assist. Nav. Ivan Vasil'ev	d. in the service, Lt.
Lower ranks: 22 Hunters: 6	

14a. Ship Elisaveta (1821)

Commander, Navigator 14th Class, Ivan Mikhailovich Kislakovskii	See No. 7.
Assist. Navig. Mikhailo Nozikov	d. 1833, Lt., at Okhotsk.
Assist. Navig. Nikolai Antonov	d. in the service.
Assist. Navig. Mikhailo Pashinnikov	
Lower ranks: 17 Hunters: 14	

15. Naval sloop Apollon (1821-24)

Commander, Capt. 1st Rank, Irinarkh Stepanovich Tulub'ev	d. on the sloop in 1822 between Rio de Janeiro and Port Jackson (Sydney).
Lt. Stepan Khrushchov	
Lt. Pavel Baranov	
Lt. Pavel Kutygin	See. No. 9.
Lt. Mikhailo Kiukhel'beker	d. in exile.
Midshipman Aleksandr Tulub'ev	d. at San Francisco, during the voyage, in 1823.
Midshipman Feopemt Lutkovskii	See No. 9.
Midshipman Karl von Nolken	drowned on Oesel Island, 1846; retd. Capt.-Lt.
Navigator Grigorii Nikiforov	See No. 9.
Assist. Navig. Varlam Sergeev	
Assist. Navig. Semen Pakhtusov	d. in ret.
Staff-Surgeon Anton Novitskii	See. No. 9.
Interpreter Akhilles Shabel'skii	
Lower ranks: 119	

16. Naval brig Aiaks (1821)

Commander, Lt. Nikandr Ivanovich Filatov	See No. 4, 9.
Lt. Fedor Filatov	
Midshipman Ardalion Lutkovskii	See No. 9.
Midshipman Aleksandr Moller	
Navigator Fedor Khalezov	
Assist. Navig. Il'ia Atrep'ev	d. 1845 in Astrakhan, as a Lt.
Navigator's apprentice Dmitrii Orlov	d.
Surgeon Nikolai Brailov	
Lower ranks: ?	

17. Frigate Kreiser (1822-25)

Commander, Capt. 2nd Rank Mikhailo Petrovich Lazarev	See No. 5, 7.
Lt. Ivan Kad'ian	
Lt. Mikhailo Annenkov	See No. 12.
Lt. Ivan Kupreianov	See No. 12, 34.
Lt. Fedor Vishnevskii	dismissed in 1826.
Lt. Dmitrii Nikol'skii (to Sitkha)	See No. 21.
Midshipman Pavel Nakhimov	(later admiral)
Midshipman Dmitrii Zavalishin	(exiled to Siberia)
Midshipman Ivan Butenev	d. 1826, fligel'-ad'iutant, Capt. 2nd r.
Midshipman Pavel Murav'ev	d. 1848, State Counsellor and Director of the Mercantile Marine School.
Midshipman Efim Putiatin	Adjutant-General, Count.
Midshipman Aleksandr Domashenko	drowned off Sicily, Sept. 1827.
Dr. Petr Aleman	d. 1847, Actual State Counsellor and senior surgeon with the Black Sea Fleet.
Navigator Pantelei Kononov	d. in ret.
Navigator Vasilii Klopotov	d. 1849 as Capt. See No. 31.
Assist. Nav. Trifanov	d. Staff-Capt., Keeper of Magazines.
Lower ranks: 162	

17a. Naval Sloop Ladoga (1822-24)

Commander, Capt. Lt. Andrei Petrovich Lazarev	d. 1849, Vice-Adm., Divisional Chief.
Lt. Matvei Berens	
Lt. Anton Bartashevich	
Lt. Dmitrii Nikol'skoi (to Sitkha)	See No. 20.
Lt. Ivan Kad'ian (from Sitkha)	See No. 20.
Midshipman Ivan Fofanov	drowned at Okhotsk, 1827, as Capt.-Lt.
Midshipman Nikolai Lomen	
Midshipman Fedor Bodisko	
Midshipman Mikhailo Baranov	
Nav. Mikhailo Kharlov	d. 1850, Lt.-Col.
Staff-Physician Petr Ogievskii	
Lower ranks: 67	

18. Naval Sloop Predpriiatie (1823-26)

Commander, Capt.-Lt. Otto Evstaf'evich Kotzebue	See No. 1, 6.
Lt. Timofei Kordiukov	d. 1838, rear-adm. commanding a brigade.

143

Names and Rank

Lt. Nikolai Rimskii-Korsakov	d. 1846, Vice-Adm., Director of the Naval Cadet Corps, member of Admiralty Council.
Lt. Petr Bartashevich	
Lt. Nikolai Pfeifer	d. Capt.-Lt.
Midshipman Egor Ekimov	
Midshipman Pavel Chekin	d. 1835, Capt. 2nd r.
Midshipman Aleksandr Moller	See No. 19.
Midshipman Vladimir Golovnin	
Midshipman Count Loggin Geiden (Heiden)	
Midshipman Petr Murav'ev	
Midshipman Stepan Vukotich	d. 1832, Capt.-Lt. at the Naval Cadet Corps.
Midshipman Pavel Moller	
Assist. Nav. Fedor Grigor'ev	d. in the service as Capt.
Assist. Nav. Nikolai Ekimov	
Assist. Nav. Vasilii Simakov	
Dr. Ivan Eschscholts	See No. 6.
Dr. Geinrikh Zival'd (Heinrich Seewald)	
Hieromonk Viktor	
Naturalist Emilii Lents (Lenz)	
Naturalist Ernest Gofman (Hoffman)	
Astronomer Vil'gel'm Preis (Price)	d. in Dorpat
Lower ranks: 99	

19. Ship Elena (1824-26)

Commander, Lt. Petr Egorovich Chistiakov (to Sitkha)	See No. 10
Captain 2nd Rank Matvei Ivanovich Murav'ev (on ret. voyage)	See No. 9
Lt. Zakhar' Balk	
Lt. Nikolai Shishmarev	See No. 14.
Lt. Aleksandr Stadol'skii	
Navigator Nikolai Rodionov	d. in the service
Assist. Navig. Dmitrii Iakovlev	See No. 15.
Seaman Adol'f Kristiern	
Surgeon Ivan Sakharov	
Agent Ivan Severin	
Lower ranks: 41	

20. Naval sloop Smirnyi (1824)

Commander, Capt.-Lt. Pavel Afanas'evich Dokhturov	See No. 15.
Lt. Ivan Podchertkov	d. in ret.
Lt. Pavel Naumov	See No. 15.
Lt. Boris Bodisko	exiled in 1826
Lt. Prince Martyn Miroslavich	
Lt. Aleksandr de-Livron	
Midshipman Andrei Bakhtin	d. Col. transport corps.

Names and Rank

Midshipman Aleksandr Ogil'vi
  (Ogilvy)
Midshipman Aleksei Naumov
Midshipman Ivan Engel'gardt
Midshipman Grigorii Engel'gardt
Midshipman Vladimir Kornilov   d.
Midshipman Samuil Mofet (Samuel   See No. 26.
  Moffet)
Midshipman Konstantin Istomin
Navigator Vasilii Semenov
Assist. Navig. Dmitrii Orlov   See No. 19.
Staff-Surgeon Nikolai Brailov   See No. 19.
Surgeon Karl Izembek   See No. 26.
Naturalist Tem'ianskii
Company Agent Gavrilo Kulaev
Hieromonk Varrava
Passenger Lt. Arkadii Leskov   See No. 11.
Lower ranks: ?

21. Naval sloop Krotkii (1825-27)

Commander, Capt.-Lt. Ferdinand   See No. 9.
  Petrovich Wrangell
Lt. Mikhailo Lavrov
Lt. Fedor Matiushkin   See No. 15.
Midshipman Karl Nol'ken   See No. 18.
Midshipman Adol'f Deibner   killed in 1826 at
                              Port Chichagov, Nuku
                              Hiva.
Dr. Avgust Kiber
Navigator Prokopii Kozmin   See No. 9.
Pilot Mikhail Pashinnikov   See No. 9.
Lower ranks: 42

22. Naval transport Moller (1826-29)

Commander, Capt.-Lt. Mikhail
  Nikolaevich Staniukovich
Lt. Arkadii Leskov   See No. 11.
Lt. Aleksandr Leontovich
Midshipman Leontii Bodisko (to
  Kamchatka)
Midshipman Samuil Mofet   See No. 23.
Midshipman Aleksandr Voronikhin   d. in ret. at Capt.-Lt.
  (to Kamchatka)
Midshipman Vladimir Glazenap
Assist. Navig. Andrei Khudobin   See No. 13.
Pilot Alekseii Rydalev
Pilot Filipp Larionov   d. in the service
Surgeon Karl Izembek   See No. 23.
Naturalist Ivan Kastal'skii
Artist Pavel Mikhailov   See No. 11.
Lower ranks: 75

23. Naval sloop Seniavin (1826-29)

Commander, Capt.-Lt. Fedor   See No. 9.
    Petrovich Lütke
Lt. Nikolai Zavalishin (to Kamchatka)d. 1847, retd. Lt.
Lt. Nil Aboleshev   d. 1842, Capt. 2nd
                                     Rank, commanding a
                                     frigate.
Midshipman Ivan Ratmanov   d. 1842, Capt.-Lt.,
                                     commanding a frigate.
Midshipman Fedor Maiet
Midshipman Nikolai Butakov
Midshipman Gotlib Glazenap
Cadet Pavel Kruzenshtern
Staff-Captain Vasilii Semenov   d.
Pilot Gavrilo Nozikov   d.
Pilot Dmitrii Orlov   See No. 19, 23.
Naturalist Karl Mertens   d. 1830.
Mineralogist Aleksandr Postel's
Volunteer Baron Kitlits (Kittlitz)   Went abroad.
Lower ranks: 48

24. Elena (1828-30)

Commander, Capt.-Lt. Vasilii   See No. 6.
    Stepanovich Khromchenko
Lt. Baron Lavrentii Levendal'
    (Loewendal)
Lt. Petr Dmitriev
Company Navigator Aleksandr   d.
    Kashevarov
Pilot Otto Greil
Dr. Vebel'
Company Agent Arakelov
Clerk Vasilii Kashevarov
Passenger, Captain 1st Rank Pavel   d. 1850 as Rear-Adm.,
    Kuzmishchev   Port Captain at
                                     Arkhangel'sk.
Passenger, Titular Counsellor Til'
Lower ranks: 38

25. Naval transport Krotkii (1829-30)

Commander, Capt.-Lt. Leontii   See No. 3, 7.
    Vasil'evich Hagemeister
Lt. Nikolai Sinitsyn   d. as State Counsellor
                                     and Director of the
                                     Rishel'evskii Lycee
                                     (Richelieu Lyceum)
                                     in Odessa.
Lt. Pavel Sarychev
Midshipman Aleksei Naumov   See No. 23.
Midshipman Petr Okonishnikov
Midshipman Evgenii Berens   Vice-Admiral.
Midshipman Nikolai Tokmachev   d.

Sub-Lt. Navigator's School Dmitrii   See No. 15.
   Iakovlev
Staff Surgeon Nikolai Peters   d. 1846.
Lower ranks: 49

26. Naval transport Amerika (1831-33)

Commander, Capt.-Lt. Vasilii   See No. 6, 28.
   Stepanovich Khromchenko
Lt. Egor' Tsebrikov
Lt. Fedor Bodisko   See No. 21.
Cadet Andrei Freigang
Sub-Lt., Navigator's School   See No. 28.
   Aleksandr Kashevarov
Sub-Lt., Navigator's School
   Kristian Klet
Sub-Lt., Navigator's School
   Vasilii Zhivodarov
Pilot Aleksandr Khalezov   Lt.-Col.
Botanist Lushnat (to Rio and back)   Went abroad.
Staff-Surgeon Averkii Skrypchinskii
Lower ranks: 54

27. Naval transport Amerika (1834-36)

Commander, Capt.-Lt. Ivan   Admiral
   Ivanovich fon-Shants (von Schants)
Lt. Evgenii Berens   See No. 29.
Lt. Vasilii Zavoiko   Vice-Adm.
Midshipman Prince Pavel Gagarin   d. 1848.
Midshipman Prince Aleksandr
   Shtakelberg
Company Navig. Vasilii Klopotov   See No. 20.
Pilot Stepan Moiseev
Pilot Vasilii Eremeev
Dr. Tremer
Lower ranks: 57

28. Ship Elena (1835)

Commander, Lt. Mikhailo Dmitrievich
   Teben'kov
Lt. Rostislav Mashin
Company Pilot Aleksandr Khalezov   See No. 30.
Pilot Mikhailo Murashev
Cadet Konstantin Timkovskii
Surgeon Nikolai Volynskii
Agent Aleksandr Rotchev
Lower ranks: 26

29. Ship Nikolai (1837-39)

Commander, Capt.-Lt.   Evgenii   See No. 29.
   Andreevich Berens
Lt. Vasilii Zavoiko   See No. 31.

Lt. Mikhailo Diugamel'
Lt. Vasilii Illiashevich (from   d. 1849 as ret.
    Sitkha)   Capt.-Lt.
Cadet Aleksei Timkovskii
Pilot Aleksandr Gavrilov   See No. 35, 37.
Hired Navigator Iogann Konradi
Dr. Fridrig Fisher
Supercargo Baron Al'fred Geiking
Lower ranks: 52

30. Ship Nikolai (1839-41)

Commander, on the voyage to Sitkha,
    Capt. 2nd Rank and Governor
    designate of the Company colonies
    Adol'f Karlovich Etolin (Etholen)
Commander of the vessel, Lt.   drowned in the Company's
    Nikolai Kondrat'evich Kadnikov   service in 1842.
Lt. Ivan Bartram
Company Navigator, Staff-Capt.   See No. 18.
    Varlaam Sergeev
Physician Aleksandr Romanovskii
    (on return voyage from Sitkha)
Commander on the voyage from Sitkha   See No. 12 and 20.
    Capt. 1st Rank and former
    Governor of the colonies
    I. A. Kupreianov
Commander of the vessel, Capt.-Lt.   Vice-Adm.
    Stepan Vasil'evich Voevodskii
Lt. Rostislav Mashin   See No. 32.
Navigator's School Ensign   See No. 30, 32.
    Aleksandr Khalezov
Staff-Surgeon Eduard Blashke
    (Blaschke)
Company official Kostromitinov
Lower ranks: 40

31. Ship Naslednik Aleksandr (1840)

Commander, Capt.-Lt. Dionisii   See No. 8, 10.
    Fedorovich Zarembo
Lt. Arkadii Voevodskii   Vice-Adm.
Lt. Egor Ogil'vi
Navigators School Sub-Lt.   See No. 33, 37.
    Aleksandr Gavrilov
Dr. Aleksandr Frankengeizer
    (Frankenheiser)
Agent Valerian Bazhenov
Lower ranks: 30

32. Naval transport Abo (1840-42)

Commander, Capt.-Lt. Andrei Loginovich Iunker	d. 1849 as Collegiate Counsellor.
Lt. Aleksei Butakov	
Lt. Petr Bessarabskii	
Lt. Pavel Shkot	Rear-Adm.
Midshipman Baron Nikolai Frederiks	
Midshipman Prince Evgenii Golitsyn	
Navigators School Sub-Lt. Khristian Klet	See No. 30.
Staff Physician Ivan Isaev	
Cadet Aleksandr Teriaev	
Pilot Aleksandr Kostin	Captain
Pilot Egor Iunkman	
Pilot Gustav Blok	
Lower ranks: 73	

33. Naval transport Irtysh (1843-45)

Commander, Captain 1st Rank Ivan Vasil'evich Vonliarliarskii	
Lt. Aleksandr Zelenoi	
Lt. Aleksandr Vasil'ev	
Lt. Vasilii Poplonskii	
Lt. Leonid Murav'ev	
Midshipman Apollon Grigor'ev	drowned
Sub-Lt., Engineer's Corps, Molinari	drowned in service at Okhotsk.
Sub-Lt., Navigator's School Aleksandr Gavrilov	See No. 33, 35.
Pilot Sharypov	
Staff-Physician Petrashevskii	
Lower ranks: 53	

34. Naval transport Baikal (1848-49)

Commander, Capt.-Lt. Genadii Ivanovich Nevel'skoi	Vice-Adm.
Lt. Petr Kozakevich	Vice-Adm.
Lt. Aleksandr Grevens	
Lt. Baron Aleksei Geismar	
Midshipman Eduard Grote	
Cadet Prince Konstantin Ukhtomskoi	
Sub-Lt. Navigator's School Aleksandr Khalezov	See No. 30, 32, 34.
Sub-Lt. Navigator's School Lev Popov	
Physician Vladimir Berg	
Lower ranks: 42	

APPENDIX II

LATER RUSSIAN CIRCUMNAVIGATIONS AND LONG VOYAGES
(Partial List)

On 10 November 1846, the ship Sitkha, Capt. Conradi, left Kronshtadt, and sailing via Cape Horn, arrived at Sitka (Novo-Arkhangel'sk) on 15 April 1847. On 5 October she left Sitka and via Cape Horn arrived at Kronshtadt 2 May 1848.

On 17 August 1847, the ship Atkha, Capt. Ridell, left Kronshtadt and via Cape Horn arrived at Sitka 16 April 1848. On 30 October   she left Sitka and via Cape Horn arrived at Kronshtadt 21 June 1849.

On 26 June 1848, the Sitkha, Capt. Conradi, left Kronshtadt and via Cape Horn arrived at Sitka 22 March 1849. On 17 October   she left Sitka, and via Cape Horn arrived at Kronshtadt 11 June 1850.

On 21 August 1848, the transport Baikal, Capt. Lt. G.I. Nevel'skoi, left Kronshtadt and via Cape Horn arrived at Petropavlovsk, Kamchatka, December 5 1849. In 1850 she aided the Russian exploration and occupation of the mouth of the Amur.

On 17 July 1849, the Atkha, Ridell, left Kronshtadt and via Cape Horn arrived at Sitka 28 March 1850. She then made a voyage to Aian and Kamchatka and back. At Petropavlovsk she delivered a pre-fabricated house, built in Sitka, as a residence for the Kamchatka commissioner of the Russian-American Company. On 22 November 1850, she left Sitka, and via Cape Horn arrived at Kronshtadt 18 May 1851. She carried a cargo of furs, 63 lbs. of California gold, and 489 boxes of tea. Passengers included former Chief Manager Capt. 1st Rank Teben'kov and his family, Staff Physician Ivanitskii, and 22 Company employees.

Built in New York for the Company, the ship Imperator Nikolai I arrived in Kronshtadt 22 June 1850. On 18 July 1850, under Conradi, she left Kronshtadt, and via Cape Horn arrived at Sitka 23 April 1851. On 21 May, she left under skipper Lindenberg for Shanghai, returning on 29 September. On 5 December, under Conradi, she left Sitka and via the Sandwich and Society Islands arrived at Kronshtadt 18 May 1852. She carried furs and 2,052 boxes of tea. She brought back from colonial service Dr. Tiling, skippers Garder and Klinkovstrem and their families, the priest Omaforovskii, pharmacist Tranchuk, 30 workers, including several with families, and nine other passengers.

On 23 September 1850, the corvette Olivutsa, Capt.
Lt. I.N. Sushchov, left Kronshtadt and via Cape Horn
arrived at Petropavlovsk 29 June 1851. She remained in
the Far East for several years and on 3 October 1856,
under Capt. 2nd Rank N.A. Rimskii-Korsakov, left Imperatorskaia Gavan and via Sunda Strait and the Cape of Good
Hope arrived at Kronshtadt 16 September 1857.

On 2 October 1850, the Sitkha, skipper Vekman, left
Abo, Finland, with a cargo of rye flour and other food-
stuffs, and via Cape Horn arrived at Sitka 28 April 1851.
She returned to Kronshtadt and was decommissioned.

On 22 July 1851, the ship Suomi, the first of several
vessels to be sent out by the newly-formed Russia-Finland
Whaling Company, left Abo and via Bremen reached Petropavlovsk 8 May 1852, and 18 May left for the Okhotsk Sea for
whaling. She returned to Bremen three years later, on
25 March 1854.

On 4 October 1851, the Atkha, Ridell, left Abo and
via Cape Horn arrived at Petropavlovsk 20 May 1851, and
at Sitka 27 July 1852. On 28 November 1852, she left
Sitka and via the Cape of Good Hope arrived at Kronshtadt
on 15 July 1853.

Purchased in Hamburg for the colonial flotilla, the
ship Kad'iak, 500 tons, arrived in Kronshtadt 26 July
1851. On 9 August, under skipper Ber, she left Kronshtadt
and via Cape Horn arrived at Sitka on 7 May 1852. She
brought Assistant Chief Manager Fleet Capt. 2nd Rank
Rudakov and his family, Dr. Malyshevskii, Hieromonk
Bonifatii Korsunskii, 4 hired navigators, 3 assistant
navigators, 1 medical assistant, and 25 workmen. She
remained in service in the colonies until 30 March 1860,
when, under skipper Arkhimandritov, with a cargo of ice,
she hit an uncharted rock off Spruce (Elovoi) Island and
sank. It was said that her skipper had failed to keep a
promise to hold a service in the chapel on Spruce Island
to honor the memory of the revered Father German (Herman).

In 1852, two foreign freighters, the MARY RAY and
the LAURENSON, were sent to the colonies. Dates of
departure, arrival and return unknown.

On 20 August 1852 the Imperator Nikolai I, M. Klinkov-
strem, left Kronshtadt and via Cape Horn arrived at
Sitka 25 April 1853. From there she sailed to San Fran-
cisco, where she remained for the duration of the war.
On 17 July 1856 she arrived at Sitka under 1st Mate
Aleksandrov, with a hired crew of 28. On 10 November,
under Iuzelius, she left Sitka and via Honolulu and Cape
Horn arrived at Kronshtadt 23 June 1857.

Purchased in Lübeck, on 11 October 1852 the brig Shelekhov, Iuzelius, left Hamburg and via Cape Horn arrived at Sitka 8 July 1853, and remained for service in the colonies.

Purchased in Hamburg, the ship Tsesarevich, 650 tons, arrived in Kronshtadt 26 July 1852. On 15 September, under skipper Iorgan, she left Kronshtadt and via Hamburg and Cape Horn arrived at Petropavlovsk 17 May 1853, and from there proceeded to Sitka, arriving 7 September. On 8 December she left Sitka, and via Honolulu and Shanghai (where she picked up a cargo of tea), arrived at Hamburg 22 June 1854, there to remain for the duration of the war.

On 20 September 1852 the naval transport Dvina, Capt. Lt. P.N. Bessarabskii, left Kronshtadt and via the Cape of Good Hope and Port Jackson (Sydney) arrived at Petropavlovsk 8 August 1853. On the way, 16 atolls were discovered in the Ralik group of the Marshall Islands, and named in honor of the Grand Duke Constantine, the last discovery made by Russian sailing vessels in the Pacific. On 13 October 1856, under Capt. Lt. I.I. Butakov, she left the Amur region and via Cape Horn arrived at Kronshtadt 15 September 1857.

On 7 October 1852, the naval frigate Pallada, Capt. 2nd Rank I.S. Unkovskii, left Kronshtadt, and via the Cape of Good Hope and the Sunda Strait arrived at Imperatorskaia Gavan' 22 May 1854. At Portsmouth, England, she picked up Rear Admiral E.V. Putiatin, enroute to the Far East on a diplomatic mission. As a midshipman Putiatin had sailed around the world in 1822-25 on the frigate Kreiser. In England, Putiatin purchased the iron steam schooner Vostok, 210 tons, which was placed under Capt. Lt. V.A. Rimskii-Korsakov and also proceeded to the Far East. In 1855, in need of a major overhaul, which could not be performed because of the war, the Pallada was disarmed and scuttled. Putiatin's secretary, I.A. Goncharov, made the voyage famous in his literary classic, Fregat Pallada.

On 21 August 1853 the naval frigate Avrora, Capt. Lt. I.N. Izyl'met'ev, left Kronshtadt and via Cape Horn and Callao arrived at Petropavlovsk 19 June 1854. On 17 October 1856, under Capt. 2nd Rank M.P. Tirol', she left DeCastries Bay and via Sunda Strait and the Cape of Good Hope arrived at Kronshtadt 11 June 1857.

On 26 September 1853 the Russia-Finland Whaling Company ship Aian left Abo and via Cape Horn arrived at Sitka 27 April 1854, bearing new employees. On 21 May she left Sitka, and proceeded to the Okhotsk Sea for whaling. The Aian wintered in Petropavlovsk and in 1855 was caught by the Anglo-French squadron and burned.

Purchased in Hamburg in 1853, a new, 3-masted vessel of 900 tons, named the Kamchatka, left Hamburg on 28

November and via Cape Horn arrived in Petropavlovsk on 20 June 1854. She later proceeded to Sitka, and sat out the war in San Francisco. In 1856, under A. Ridell, she left San Francisco and on 24 June 1856 arrived in Sitka. About 10 November   she left Sitka and via Shanghai and the Cape of Good Hope arrived at Kronshtadt in 1857.

Built in Hamburg for the Russian-American Company, in 1 November 1853 the ship Sitkha, 1200 tons, under Conradi, left Hamburg and via Cape Horn arrived at Sitka 17 April 1854. She bore the new Chief Manager, Capt. 1st Rank Voevodskii and his family, Lieutenants Verman and Koskull, the mining engineer E.H. Furuhjelm, with an assistant and two miners, Dr. Schneider, a medical assistant, and three naval seamen. From Sitka she sailed to Aian and Petropavlovsk, where she was captured by the Anglo-French squadron 27 August 1854. She was taken, via San Francisco and Cape Horn, to France, where she was sold as a prize.

Built in Europe in 1853, but laid up during the war, on 21 July 1856 the iron screw sailing vessel Velikii Kniaz' Konstantin, skipper Ofterdinger, left Kronshtadt. On 10 September she left Hamburg and via Cape Horn arrived at Sitka 20 February 1857. On 25 May she left Sitka for Aian and the Amur region, and further service in North Pacific waters.

On 19 September 1856, the ship Tsesarevich, Ior'ian, left Hamburg, where she had sat out the war, and via Cape Horn arrived at Sitka 2 May 1857. On 24 October she left Sitka for Shanghai, where she picked up a cargo of tea, left there 6 February, and via the Cape of Good Hope arrived at Kronshtadt on 3 July 1858.

On 27 September 1857 the Kamchatka, Iuzelius, left Kronshtadt and via Cape Horn arrived at Sitka on 8 July 1858. On 19 July   she left for DeCastries Bay, returning on 16 November. On 27 November she left Sitka with a cargo of furs and with employees who had completed their service, and via Honolulu and Cape Horn arrived at Kronshtadt on 29 June 1859.

On 9 October 1857 the Imperator Nikolai I, Krogius, on temporary service with the Navy, left Kronshtadt and via the Cape of Good Hope arrived at Hong Kong 9 June 1858. In July she arrived at the mouth of the Amur. On 3 October she arrived at Shanghai to pick up a cargo of tea. On 13 December she left Shanghai, and via the Cape of Good Hope arrived at Kronshtadt on 26 April 1859.

On 6 September 1858 the ship Tsaritsa (former American clipper Coeur de Lion, 1,900 tons, of oak with copper reinforcing, purchased by the Russian-American Company in Hamburg for 70,000 silver rubles), under Capt. Ridell, left Kronshtadt. On 12 November she left Hamburg, but suffered storm damage and had to stop at Plymouth for repairs. To save time, her cargo was sent on in the hired foreign vessel Johann Kepler, Capt. Jansen, which arrived at Sitka about 16 September 1859. On 26 May 1859, the Tsaritsa left Plymouth and via the Cape of Good Hope and Sunda Strait sailed to the China Sea in the remarkable time of only 2½ months. On 22 September she arrived at DeCastries Bay, and on 5 December arrived at Sitka. She made voyages in the colonies and, probably at the end of 1860, sailed for Kronshtadt.

On 24 August 1859 the Tsesarevich, Ior'ian, left Kronshtadt and via Cape Horn arrived at Sitka 20 April 1860. She made a voyage to Unalashka and the Pribylovs with supplies and timber, and on 3 November   left Sitka and after a stop at Honolulu for repairs proceeded to Shanghai, arriving 9 January 1861. Picking up a cargo of tea, on 29 January 1861 she left Shanghai and via the Cape of Good Hope arrived in Kronshtadt 22 June 1861.

On 26 September 1859 the Imperator Nikolai I, Krogius, left Kronshtadt and via Cape Horn arrived at Sitka 16 April 1860. She made a voyage to Aian and back, and on 8 December left Sitka for Honolulu, arriving 29 December. After selling a cargo of 862 barrels of salted fish, she left Honolulu in early January 1861, and via Cape Horn arrived at Kronshtadt on 11 June 1861. Among her passengers were the creole youths Klim Terent'ev, son of machinist Koz'ma Terent'ev, and Filipp Kashevarov, son of assistant controller of the Sitka office Gavriil Kashevarov, both going to St. Petersburg for education. The crew included a Sitka Tlingit, Andrei Tenkhentin, taken at his request to visit the Russian capital. There he aided the philologist, Radlov, with first hand information about the languages of southern Russian America, and was to return in the fall on another Company ship.

In the spring of 1860 ? the Tsaritsa, Ridell, left Kronshtadt and via Cape Horn and San Francisco arrived at Sitka 23 November 1860. On 17 October 1861 she left Sitka and via Honolulu, with a cargo of fish, and China, where she picked up a cargo of tea, and the Cape of Good Hope, she arrived at Kronshtadt on 30 September 1862.

On 5 July 1860, the Kamchatka, Iuzelius, left Kronshtadt, stopped at Finland for cargo, and via Cape Horn, arrived at Sitka 8 May 1861. Under Capt. Lt. Gavrishev she made a voyage to DeCastries Bay, returning 21 October. On 19 December, under Assistant Chief Manager Prince Maksutov, she sailed to San Francisco with a cargo of sealskins, returning on 23 February 1862 with foodstuffs. After two voyages from Kad'iak to San Francisco with cargoes of ice, she left Sitka on 17 November 1862 for Honolulu, and from there sailed to China, where she picked up a cargo of tea. Sailing via the Cape of Good Hope, she arrived at Kronshtadt 8 August 1863.

On 30 September 1861, the Imperator Nikolai I, Krogius, left Kronshtadt. She arrived at Hamburg on 13 October, stopped 4-5 November at Portsmouth to wait out a storm, and via Cape Horn arrived at Sitka 26 April 1862. In 1863 she made two voyages from Sitka to Aian and back. Date of return to Russia not known.

On 18 December 1861 the naval transport Giliak, Capt. Lt. A. I. Enkvist, left Hamburg and via the Cape of Good Hope and Sunda Strait arrived at DeCastries Bay on 31 August 1862. On 26 October 1862 she left Imperatorskaia Gavan' and via the Strait of Malacca and the Cape of Good Hope arrived at Kronshtadt 3 August 1863.

On 28 August 1862 the Tsesarevich, Aleksandrov, left Kronshtadt and arrived at Hamburg on 3 October. Laid up for repair of a leak, her cargo and passengers were transferred to the hired freight ship Costa Rica, which left Hamburg on 19 October and arrived at Sitka in March 1863. On 30 October 1863, the Tsesarevich left Hamburg and sailed for Aian, arriving 13 July 1863, and at Sitka on 20 November. On 26 November she left Sitka and made a voyage to Honolulu and from there to San Francisco to deliver a cargo of sealskins, and from there back to Sitka. On 16 April 1864 she left Sitka for Kad'iak to pick up a cargo of ice for San Francisco, and was occupied with the ice ice trade thereafter. On 9 October 1867, as part of the liquidation of Company property, she was sold at Sitka to a private individual for $12,000.

In 1863, the hired freighter Sofia-Elena, Capt. Stover, was sent from Hamburg ? to the colonies with goods and personnel, arriving at Sitka 16 June 1864. Among the arriving passengers were Dr. Tilling, to replace Dr. Berendt, a navigator, a machinist, and a shipbuilder.

Also in 1863, simultaneously with passage of a naval flotilla under Admiral Lessovskii from Kronshtadt to New York, another flotilla under Admiral Popov left Nagasaki and going via Sitka (4-8 October) arrived in San Francisco, where it remained until 1 August 1864.

On 26 July 1864, the naval transport Giliak, Capt. Lt. A.I. Enkvist, left Kronshtadt and via Cape Horn arrived at DeCastries Bay on 5 June 1865. On 28 August 1865 she left DeCastries Bay and via the Strait of Malacca and the Cape of Good Hope returned to Kronshtadt on 7 August 1866, completing the last round-the-world voyage by a Russian naval sailing vessel.

In 1864, the naval corvette Variag, R.A. Lund, which had made the voyage to New York with Admiral Lessovskii's squadron, went to the Pacific via the Strait of Magellan, the first Russian vessel to traverse the entire strait. In 1865-66 the Variag sailed the Pacific, aiding the Western Union Telegraph Company project. In 1867 she is said to have left Sitka (date unknown) and via the Cape of Good Hope to have returned to Kronshtadt.

In 1865, the hired freighter Susanna, Liut, left Hamburg, and going via Cape Horn ? arrived at Sitka 12 June 1865. On 17 November 1865, she left Sitka and returned to Europe.

In 1866, the ship Kamchatka, Eberg, left Kronshtadt, and sailing via Cape Horn arrived at Sitka 28 May 1866. She made a voyage to San Francisco for foodstuffs, and 18 November 1866 left Sitka and via Honolulu arrived at Kronshtadt, date unknown.

In 1866, the Tsaritsa, Capt. ? , left Kronshtadt and via Cape Horn, arrived at Sitka about June 1867. Further movements uncertain. On 14 December she left Sitka for Russia via London, with 168 passengers.

MATERIALS FOR THE STUDY OF ALASKA HISTORY

1. R.A. Pierce. ALASKAN SHIPPING, 1867-1878. ARRIVALS AND DEPARTURES AT THE PORT OF SITKA. 1972. 72 pp.

2. F.W. Howay. A LIST OF TRADING VESSELS IN THE MARITIME FUR TRADE, 1785-1825. 1973. 209 pp., bibliog., index. Ships and fur traders on the Northwest Coast.

3. K.T. Khlebnikov. BARANOV, CHIEF MANAGER OF THE RUSSIAN COLONIES IN AMERICA. 1973. 140 pp. Transl. from the Russian edition of 1835. (OUT OF PRINT)

4. S.G. Fedorova. THE RUSSIAN POPULATION IN ALASKA AND CALIFORNIA (LATE 18TH CENTURY TO 1867). 1974. 367 pp. Transl. from the Russian edition of 1972. (OUT OF PRINT)

5. V.N. Berkh. A CHRONOLOGICAL HISTORY OF THE DISCOVERY OF THE ALEUTIAN ISLANDS. 1974. 121 pp. Transl. from the Russian edition of 1823.

6. R.V. Makarova. RUSSIANS ON THE PACIFIC, 1743-1799. 1974. 301 pp. Transl. from the Russian edition of 1968.

7. DOCUMENTS ON THE HISTORY OF THE RUSSIAN-AMERICAN COMPANY. 1976. 220 pp. Trade practices, conditions of life, and leading figures of early Alaska. Transl. from the Russian edition of 1957.

8. R.A. Pierce. RUSSIA'S HAWAIIAN ADVENTURE, 1815-1817. 1976. 245 pp. Documents concerning the Alaska-based attempt to take over the Hawaiian Islands for Russia. Reprint of the 1965 edition, with maps and illustrations.

9. H.W. Elliott. THE SEAL ISLANDS OF ALASKA. 1976. 176 pp., with many of Elliott's sketches. Reprint of the 1881 edition, prepared for the Tenth Census of the United States. A fundamental work on the Pribilof Islands and the sealing industry soon after the Alaska purchase.

10. G.I. Davydov. TWO VOYAGES TO RUSSIAN AMERICA, 1802-1807. 1977. 257 pp. Transl. from the Russian edition of 1810-1812. Travel, history and ethnography in Siberia and Alaska.

11. THE RUSSIAN ORTHODOX RELIGIOUS MISSION IN AMERICA, 1794-1837. 1978. 186 pp. Transl. from the Russian edition of 1894. Materials concerning the life and works of the monk German (St. Herman) and ethnographic notes by the hieromonk Gedeon.

12. H.M.S. SULPHUR ON THE NORTHWEST AND CALIFORNIA COASTS, 1837 AND 1839. THE ACCOUNTS OF CAPTAIN EDWARD BELCHER AND MIDSHIPMAN FRANCIS GUILLEMARD SIMPKINSON. 1979. 144 pp.

13. P.A. Tikhmenev. A HISTORY OF THE RUSSIAN-AMERICAN COMPANY. Vol. 2: DOCUMENTS. 1979. 257 pp. Transl. from the Russian edition of 1861-1863. Materials on the period 1783-1807.